B1
STUDENT'S BOOK
BEYOND

**Robert Campbell
Rob Metcalf
Rebecca Robb Benne**

		IN THE PICTURE	READING	GRAMMAR (1)
UNIT 1	**LIFE STAGES** pages 6–15	Special days *Talk about special days in your life* Vocabulary (1): Special days PRONOUNCE the /e/ and /ɜː/ sounds ▶ Special days	Coming of age *Find specific information*	Present tenses review *Talk about present actions*
		UNIT REVIEW page 15		
UNIT 2	**PACK YOUR BAGS** pages 16–25	Travel *Talk about travel items* Vocabulary (1): Travel items PRONOUNCE the /p/ and /b/ sounds ▶ Travel	Be a voluntourist *Identify the purpose of a text*	Present perfect *Talk about how long something has happened*
		UNIT REVIEW page 25		

PROGRESS CHECK 1&2   pages 26–27

		IN THE PICTURE	READING	GRAMMAR (1)
UNIT 3	**MY MUSIC** pages 28–37	Live music *Talk about music and music events* Vocabulary (1): Music words PRONOUNCE the /ɔː/ and /ɒ/ sounds ▶ Live music	A dream concert *Understand new words*	Verbs followed by -ing form or to + infinitive *Talk about things you enjoy doing*
		UNIT REVIEW page 37		
UNIT 4	**VERY IMPORTANT PEOPLE** pages 38–47	Relationships *Talk about people you know* Vocabulary (1): People and relationships ▶ Relationships	Close friends *Recognise examples*	First conditional with if/unless *Talk about possible situations in the future*
		UNIT REVIEW page 47		

PROGRESS CHECK 3&4   pages 48–49

		IN THE PICTURE	READING	GRAMMAR (1)
UNIT 5	**FIVE SENSES** pages 50–59	Can you feel it? *Talk about how we use our senses* Vocabulary (1): The senses and sense verbs PRONOUNCE Consonant combinations ▶ Can you feel it?	Fragrance fact file *Use pictures to help you understand*	Passives (past, present and future) *Use the past, present and future passives to talk about senses*
		UNIT REVIEW page 59		

LISTENING & VOCABULARY	GRAMMAR (2)	LANGUAGE & BEYOND	SPEAKING	WRITING
Leaving home **Recognise informal speech** **Vocabulary (2):** Adjectives for describing objects	Past tenses review **Talk about past actions**	Get organised **Collaborate to organise a group activity**	Invitations **Make and react to invitations** ▶ I'd love to	A special object (description) **Make a writing plan**
Around the world **Listen for the information you need** **Vocabulary (2):** Travel	The future **Talk about events in the future**	Respect others **Respect other people's personal space**	At the airport **Check in at the airport** ▶ I'd like to check in	Wish you were here (postcard) **Use correct verb tenses**
Talking music **Transfer spoken information to a table** **Vocabulary (2):** Adverbs of degree	Comparison of adverbs **Compare how people do things**	Get organised **Stay on task and avoid distractions**	My sister thinks … **Present other people's opinions** ▶ What's your opinion?	My music profile (profile) **Link contrasting ideas**
Back from the future **Use stress and intonation to help you understand** **Vocabulary (2):** Extreme adjectives	Second conditional **Talk about imaginary situations in the present and future** PRONOUNCE stressed words and phrases	Know yourself **Decide what's important to you**	Do you mind? **Make and react to requests** ▶ Go ahead	A poem about true friends (poem) **Use a dictionary**
The power of colour **Follow a conversation** **Vocabulary (2):** Colour idioms	(In order) to … , so (that) … **Talk about the purpose of doing things**	Communicate & cooperate **Recognise non-verbal communication**	At the chemist's **Ask for help with words** ▶ What's the difference?	A place I really like (description) **Link similar ideas**

	IN THE PICTURE	READING	GRAMMAR (1)
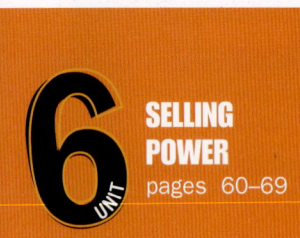 **UNIT 6 SELLING POWER** pages 60–69	In a shop *Talk about shopping* Vocabulary (1): Shopping PRONOUNCE the /æ/ and /ɑː/ sounds ▶ In a shop	What's it for? *Identify the tone of written comments*	Possibility and impossibility *Make logical guesses*
UNIT REVIEW page 69			

PROGRESS CHECK 5&6 pages 70–71

	IN THE PICTURE	READING	GRAMMAR (1)
 **UNIT 7 TRADITION AND CHANGE** pages 72–81	Traditional ways *Talk about traditional and modern ways of living* Vocabulary (1): Traditional activities ▶ Traditional ways	Living in the past *Make notes*	*Used to* *Talk about habits and situations in the past* PRONOUNCE the /s/, /ʒ/ and /z/ sounds
UNIT REVIEW page 81			

	IN THE PICTURE	READING	GRAMMAR (1)
 **UNIT 8 SHE SAID, HE SAID** pages 82–91	In the news *Talk about people working in the media* Vocabulary (1): Print and digital media jobs PRONOUNCE stressed syllables and the /ə/ sound ▶ In the news	Media culture *Recognise formal and informal writing*	Reported speech *Report what people say*
UNIT REVIEW page 91			

PROGRESS CHECK 7&8 pages 92–93

	IN THE PICTURE	READING	GRAMMAR (1)
 **UNIT 9 LEARNING JOURNEYS** pages 94–103	At school *Talk about different types of school* Vocabulary (1): Types of school PRONOUNCE sentence stress and meaning ▶ At school	School journeys *Understand referring words*	Reported requests and commands *Say what people ask and tell you to do* PRONOUNCE word stress
UNIT REVIEW page 103			

	IN THE PICTURE	READING	GRAMMAR (1)
 **UNIT 10 CHANGING FASHIONS** pages 104–113	In fashion *Talk about changing fashions* Vocabulary (1): Fashion PRONOUNCE the /t/ and /d/ sounds ▶ In fashion	Fashion statements *Understand paraphrase*	*So* and *such … that* *Emphasise somebody's or something's qualities*
UNIT REVIEW page 113			

PROGRESS CHECK 9&10 pages 114–115

EXTRA READING pages 116–119 **GRAMMAR DATABASE** pages 120–129 **WORDS & BEYOND** pages 130–139

LISTENING & VOCABULARY	GRAMMAR (2)	LANGUAGE & BEYOND	SPEAKING	WRITING
Smart shopping **Understand the speaker's intention** **Vocabulary (2):** Things and people in a shop	Indirect questions **Ask polite questions**	Communicate & cooperate **Be assertive**	At the cash desk **Return goods and make a complaint** ▶ It doesn't fit	We look forward to hearing from you (letter and survey) **Use polite phrases in formal emails and letters**
The Pretty Colored Snake **Understand the situation** **Vocabulary (2):** Feelings	Past perfect simple **Talk about things that happened before another time in the past**	Respect others **Value your elders**	At the library **Join and use a library** ▶ Can I borrow a DVD?	Telling tales (story) **Say how and when things happen in a story**
Picture stories **Infer meaning** **Vocabulary (2):** Reporting verbs	Reported questions **Report what people ask**	Get thinking **Compare and evaluate information that you read or hear**	Excuse me … **Interrupt someone** ▶ Can I say something?	School news (news story) **Use correct punctuation**
Circus school **Understand spoken instructions** **Vocabulary (2):** Words with *self-*	Reflexive pronouns; *each other* **Use reflexive pronouns and each other**	Know yourself **Learn to be more self-confident**	Go on! **Persuade people to do things** ▶ Don't be boring	Our school (website section) **Express reasons and results**
Materials and more **Recognise formal and informal speech** **Vocabulary (2):** Adjectives with *-able*	Ability **Talk about ability in the past, present and future**	Get thinking **Consider all the options**	You look great! **Give and react to compliments** ▶ Thanks!	For sale (online advert) **Refer to two options**

IRREGULAR VERBS page 140   **EXTRAS** pages 141–142   **PROJECTS** page 143

UNIT 1

LIFE STAGES

IN THE PICTURE Special days

>>> Talk about special days in your life

WORK WITH WORDS

1 **RECALL** Work in pairs. Do the tasks. You have three minutes.

   a Match the stages of life to the photos (1–10). Some photos match more than one word/phrase.

   ...... baby   ...... child   ...... teenager   ...... university student
   ...... young adult   ...... adult   ...... parent

   b Complete the sentences with the words/phrases in the box. Then match them to the photos.

   > middle-aged person   pensioner

   1 A .... is old enough to stop working and receive money from the government. Photo ......
   2 A .... is about 40 to 60 years old. Photo ......

2 Match the photos (1–10) to the actions in the box.

   Go on a first date – 4

   > get a driving licence   get a job   get married
   > go on a first date   go to university   have children
   > leave home   retire   start school   vote

3 ▶1.01 Listen and check your answers.

4 Write the events in Exercise 2 in the order people usually do them in your country.

5 a ▶1.02 **PRONOUNCE** Listen and repeat the /e/ and /ɜː/ sounds.

   /e/ get   /ɜː/ first

   b ▶1.03 Listen to these words. Which words have the /e/ sound and which have the /ɜː/ sound?

   > fri**e**nd   p**e**rson   w**o**rk   N**e**t   univ**e**rsity

   c ▶1.03 Listen again and repeat the words.

6 a Complete sentences 1–6 with verbs from Exercise 2. Then guess the ends of the sentences.

   b ▶1.04 Listen and check your answers.

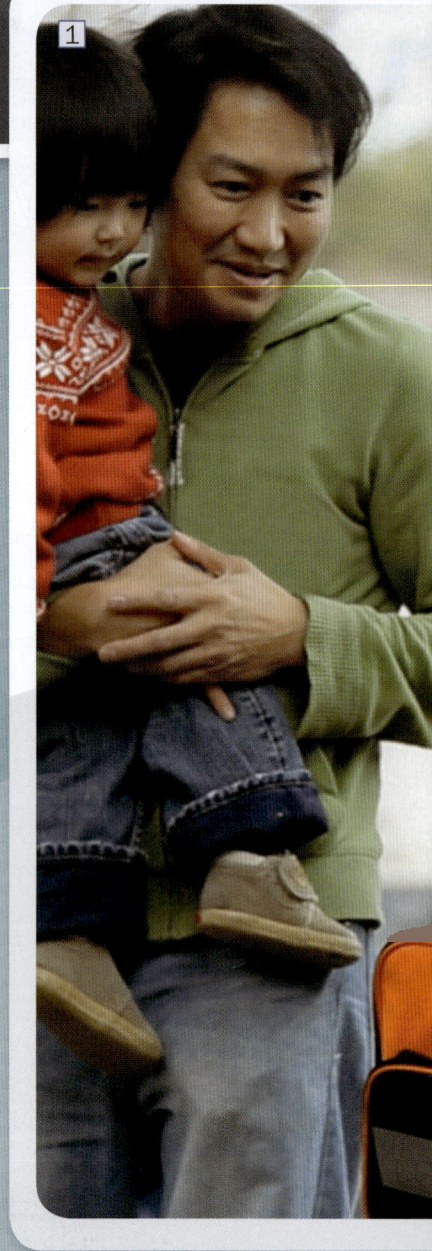

1. In some parts of the USA, you can .... married at **13 / 14 / 20**.
2. Children in Finland don't .... school until they're **7 / 8 / 9**.
3. In Brazil and Austria, you can .... in an election when you're **14 / 16 / 17**.
4. In Niger, you can't .... a driving licence until you're **19 / 21 / 23**.
5. People in Saudi Arabia can't .... on a date before they get *a job / married / a driving licence*.
6. Most people can only .... one child in *China / Korea / Japan*.

SPECIAL DAYS
because *every day* is special

Upload your video   Upload your photo

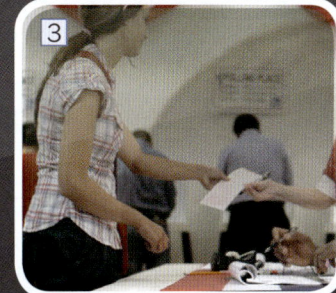

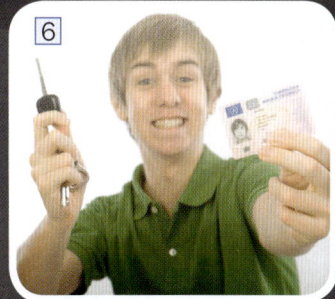

7 THE MOVING PICTURE ▶ Watch the video. Describe the people. What are they doing?

SPEAK

8 Work in pairs. Ask and answer the questions.

This week's survey:
AGE AND EXPERIENCE

1 In your country, when can you …
- start and finish school?
- get a driving licence?
- vote?

2 When do people in your country usually …
- go on a first date?
- leave home?
- get married?
- have children?

PHRASE BYTES

You can … at … / when you're …
You can't … until …
People usually … in their twenties/thirties/forties.

GO BEYOND

Do the Words & Beyond exercises on page 130.

Workbook, page 4

READING Coming of age

>>> Find specific information

SPEAK AND READ

1 **Work in pairs. Answer the questions about *coming of age* – the age when a person becomes an adult.**
   1 At what age do people come of age in your country? Is it the same for boys and girls?
   2 What do people do to celebrate their coming of age where you live?
   3 What other coming-of-age traditions do you know about? Where are they celebrated?

2 ▶1.05 **Read the texts and answer the questions.**
   1 Who wrote the texts?
   2 Do they mention your country, or a country you talked about in Exercise 1?

3 a **Read the tips in the HOW TO box.**

   HOW TO
   find specific information
   ☐ Don't read all the text.
   ☐ Are there headings? Use them to find the information you need.
   ☐ Read the start of each paragraph. Does it have the information you need? If not, read the next paragraph.
   ☐ Look for words connected to the information you need.

   b **Complete the table with information about all three texts. If a text doesn't include the information, write *doesn't say*.**

COMING-OF-AGE TRADITIONS AROUND THE WORLD

We did some research into traditional coming-of-age celebrations and rituals around the world. This is what we discovered. We hope you enjoy reading about them. *Class 3B*

Seijin no Hi
In Japan, the second Monday of January is Seijin no Hi – 'Coming-of-Age Day'. It's a celebration for girls and boys who have turned 20 in the last year. A 20-year-old is considered an adult and can therefore vote. First, there's a ceremony at the local city offices called Seijin-Shiki, then a party with friends and family. Girls wear a special kimono and boys often wear suits. In the photo above the girls are wearing traditional kimonos.

Satere-Mawé
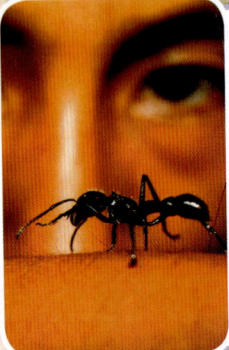
The Satere-Mawé tribe in Brazil use the bullet ant in their coming-of-age ritual. If this ant bites you, it hurts more than any other insect bite in the world, and it continues to hurt for 24 hours. During the ritual, boys have to wear gloves with hundreds of ants in them for ten minutes, and they mustn't scream. They have to do this 20 times over the coming months or years. Some boys start the ritual when they're just 12.

Quinceañera

A Quinceañera is a coming-of-age party for girls on their 15th birthday in many Latin American countries. The girls usually wear a pink dress and crown. The celebration starts with a church ceremony. Then there's a big party. The birthday girl gets a present called la última muñeca – 'the last doll'. She dances with it, then gives it to a younger girl. She's now an adult and can go on her first date.

COMING-OF-AGE CELEBRATIONS AND RITUALS AROUND THE WORLD

Name	Type Party? Ritual?	Boys/Girls	When	Age	Clothes	Activities
Seijin no Hi	Special day		Second Monday of January			

4 **Which tips in the HOW TO box did you use for help with Exercise 3b? Tick (✓) them.**

REACT

5 **Work in pairs. Discuss these questions.**
   1 Are you familiar with any of the traditions above? If so, is the description a true reflection of what happens? If not, what else would you like to know about them?
   2 What do you think of each tradition? Why?

GO BEYOND
Test your memory. Choose a ritual and write down what you remember about it. Then read the text again to check your notes.

>>> Workbook, page 5

GRAMMAR Present tenses review

>>> Talk about present actions

READ AND LISTEN >>> Grammar in context

1 ▶1.06 Read and listen to the conversation. Where are the girls? What are they doing?

Miyu: What are these girls doing?
Tina: They're probably at a Sweet 16. It's a typical coming-of-age party here in the US.
Miyu: What do people usually do at a Sweet 16?
Tina: They do different things. This girl's celebrating with friends and she isn't wearing special clothes. My sister wants a big formal party. She's preparing for it at the moment and she talks about it every day. The problem is, I don't think we can afford a big party.

STUDY

2 a Underline eight examples of the present simple in the conversation in Exercise 1 and circle four examples of the present continuous.

   b Complete the explanations with examples from the conversation.

Present tenses review
Present simple
Use: For habits, routines, things that are generally true.
Time expressions: never, _____ , from time to time, _____ , etc
Present continuous
Use: For things in progress now or around now.
Time expressions: now, right now, _____ , etc
State verbs: Don't use these verbs in the present continuous: like, need, _____ (for preferences) know, _____ (for thoughts, opinions)

See GRAMMAR DATABASE, page 120.

PRACTISE

3 ▶1.07 Choose the correct options to complete the conversation. Then listen and check.

Miyu: Why (1) **do they paint** / (**are they painting**) this girl's face?
Tina: I (2) **don't know** / **'m not knowing** a lot about Native American traditions, but I think she (3) **'s preparing** / **prepares** for the Sunrise Dance. It's a coming-of-age ceremony for Apache girls.
Miyu: So (4) **do the girls dance** / **are the girls dancing** when the sun comes up?
Tina: I'm not sure, but I know that the ceremony (5) **lasts** / **'s lasting** for four days and that the girls (6) **dance** / **are dancing** for hours each day. So it's a very difficult physical test.

4 Complete the questions with the present simple or present continuous form of the verbs.

1 What _are you studying_ (you / study) at school these days?
2 _____ (you / think) that your classes prepare you well for adult life?
3 What clothes _____ (most teenagers / wear) at the moment?
4 _____ (adults / usually / wear) these kinds of clothes?
5 At what age _____ (a person / really / become) an adult?
6 Think of an adult you know well. What _____ (they / do) right now?

SPEAK

5 Work in pairs. Ask and answer the questions in Exercise 4. Ask each other for examples, details and reasons.

> In maths, we're studying … and in …

>>> Workbook, pages 6–7

LISTENING AND VOCABULARY Leaving home

>>> Recognise informal speech

SPEAK AND LISTEN

1 Work in pairs. Answer the questions.
   1 Describe the things in the photos.
   2 Do you own any similar things? Describe them.
   3 What do you do with things when you stop using them?

2 ▶1.08 Aidan is leaving home. Listen to the conversation with his sister, Katie. Put the photos in order.

3 ▶1.08 Listen to the conversation again and decide if each sentence is correct or incorrect. If it's correct, write *C*. If it's incorrect, write *I*.
   1 Aidan's father gave him the phone.
   2 The football shirt is big.
   3 Uncle Harry gave him the shirt on his eighth birthday.
   4 Katie thinks the action figure is worth a lot of money.
   5 Katie wants to keep Aidan's CDs.
   6 She says she likes Aidan's music.

4 a Read the tips in the **HOW TO** box.

   b ▶1.09 Listen to the extracts from the conversation and complete them with words from the **HOW TO** box. Then find six contractions.

REACT

5 Work in pairs. Answer the questions.
   1 Do you think Katie is going to miss Aidan? Why?/Why not?
   2 Which thing might Aidan decide to keep? Why?

WORK WITH WORDS

6 ▶1.10 When you use more than one adjective before a noun, the adjectives go in the order of the table. Complete the table with the adjectives in the box. Then listen and repeat.

| antique colourful cotton enormous old-fashioned |
| square tiny unusual useful valuable |

HOW TO
recognise informal speech

- Listen for contractions (*don't = do not*).
- Listen for informal forms (*dunno = don't know*, *kinda = kind of*, *stuff = things*, *ya = you*, *yeah = yes*).
- Listen for fillers (*um, you know, hey*).

Katie:	Look at this. It's enormous.
Aidan:	(1) _____, don't laugh. That was my first mobile phone.
Aidan:	It's (2) _____ …
	(3) _____ …
Katie:	Colourful?
Katie:	So if it's special, why are you throwing it out?
Aidan:	I (4) _____. I've got too much (5) _____. I can't keep everything.
Katie:	(6) _____ … see (7) _____.
Aidan:	(8) _____. See ya.

Opinion	Size	Shape	Age	Colour	Material	
		round	old	red	plastic	+ noun
special						

SPEAK

7 a Think of an interesting present you gave and one you received. Write a few sentences describing each present. Use more than one adjective.

   For my fourth birthday, my mother made an amazing chocolate cake. It was enormous.

   b Work in pairs. Talk about your presents.

GO BEYOND

Do the Words & Beyond exercise on page 130.

Workbook, pages 8–9

GRAMMAR Past tenses review

>>> Talk about past actions

READ AND LISTEN >>> Grammar in context

1 ▶1.11 **Read and listen to the conversation. What type of object are they talking about?**

Jordi: Where did you get this?
Megan: My dad bought it for me while we were staying in New York.
Jordi: What were you doing there?
Megan: My dad was working there for a few months. We were walking down the street one day when I saw it in a shop window. I didn't know how to play it, but I found some videos on the internet. Mum and Dad weren't very happy.
Jordi: Why not?
Megan: Because I played it all the time, and it sounded terrible.

STUDY

2 **Complete the explanations. Use the conversation in Exercise 1 to help you.**

Past tenses review
Past simple
Use: For completed actions in the past.
Form: Regular: verb + ed: *played*, _____ Irregular: *be > was/were, buy >* _____ , etc
Past continuous
Use: For actions in progress in the past.
Form: *was/* _____ + verb + *-ing*
Past simple and past continuous
Use: To say something happened while another action was in progress.
Form: *when* + past _____ *while* + past _____
See GRAMMAR DATABASE, page 120.

PRACTISE

3 **Choose the correct options to complete the description.**

Megan (1) *met / was meeting* Jordi while she (2) *visited / was visiting* Barcelona. They soon (3) *became / were becoming* good friends, and Jordi (4) *occasionally came / was occasionally coming* to the UK to see Megan. One day Jordi and Megan (5) *sat / were sitting* in her room when he (6) *saw / was seeing* the harmonica.

4 ▶1.12 **Complete the conversation with the past simple or past continuous form of the verbs. Then listen to check your answers.**

Megan: Hi Mum. I can't find my harmonica.
Mum: When (1) _____ (you / see) it last?
Megan: I (2) _____ (see) it last week while Jordi (3) _____ (stay). We (4) _____ (talk) when he (5) _____ (notice) it on the table.
Mum: Maybe Jordi (6) _____ (take) it while you (7) _____ (not look).
Megan: I don't think so. Wait … I remember now. I (8) _____ (see) it later the same day while I (9) _____ (do) my homework. I (10) _____ (put) it in a drawer so I wouldn't lose it.

5 **Write the questions using the past simple, past continuous or both, if necessary.**
1 What / you / lose? *What did you lose?*
2 When and where / you / lose / it?
3 What / you / do / when / you / lose / it?
4 How long / you / look / for it?
5 While / you / look / for it, / other people / help / you?
6 you / ever / find / it?

6 **Think of something you lost in the past. Write answers to the questions in Exercise 5.**
I lost my …

SPEAK

7 **Work in pairs. Talk about things you lost. Use your answers in Exercise 6 to help you. Ask questions for more information and make notes.**

Can you describe it? What did it look like?

What happened next? And then what happened?

Do you still have … ?

Workbook, page 10

LANGUAGE & BEYOND

What do you think about group work? To find out, decide which option you think is better, A or B.

1. A An activity is more fun if everybody helps to organise it.
   B It's not important who does the work. The important thing is the result.
2. A Some people have ideas, and other people are workers.
   B It's good to hear other people's ideas and add to them.
3. A It's best if one person makes the decisions for everybody.
   B Voting is the best way to make decisions if people don't agree.
4. A Giving people specific jobs makes it easier to organise an activity.
   B Groups work best if people are free to do what they want.

>>> **Collaborate to organise a group activity**

SPEAK AND READ

1. Work in pairs. Answer the questions about the last time you worked with others to organise an activity.
   1. What did you organise?
   2. Who did you work with?
   3. Who had the most ideas? Who did the most work?
   4. What part of the organising went well? What was difficult?

2. Do the survey above about organising activities.

3. Compare your answers in groups. Which options did most people choose?

4. Make a list of tips for organising a group activity. Then compare your list with the tips on page 141. What differences are there?

DO

5. 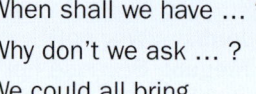 Work in groups. You're organising a sale of second-hand things to make money for an end-of-term trip. Work together to do the following things:
   - choose a day for the sale
   - find a place for the sale
   - decide how to collect the things to sell
   - think about how to advertise the sale
   - calculate how many people need to work at the sale
   - decide who is going to do the different jobs

6. Tell the class about your decisions.

PHRASE BYTES

When shall we have … ?
Why don't we ask … ?
We could all bring …
How about making … ?
Does everyone agree?
Let's vote on it.

REFLECT

7. Discuss the questions with your class. Do you agree with the **REFLECTION POINT**?
   1. Which tips from Exercise 4 did you use when you planned your sale?
   2. Which tips were easy to follow? Which were more difficult?
   3. Do you think you worked well as a group? Why?/Why not?

REFLECTION POINT

Group activities are more successful when everybody contributes ideas, has a specific job to do and does an equal share of the work.

EXTEND

8. Work in groups. Plan your end-of-term trip. Decide where to go and what needs to be done. Then give everybody a job to do.

GET ORGANISED

Workbook, page 13

SPEAKING Invitations

>>> Make and react to invitations

SPEAK

1 Work in pairs. Answer the questions.
   1 When was the last time you received a party invitation?
   2 Did you go to the party? If so, was it good?
   3 Look at the invitation on the right. Would you like to go to Ethan's party? Why?/Why not?

WATCH OR LISTEN

2 ▶ 1.13 Watch or listen to the scenes. Who can't come to the party? Why not?

Ethan:	Hi Alice. (1) _____ come to my birthday party?
Alice:	When is it?
Ethan:	It's next Saturday, the 6th. I'm having a barbecue.
Alice:	Sure. That sounds great. Thanks for inviting me.
Ethan:	Great. See you there!
Ethan:	Hey, Leo. I'm having a birthday party next Saturday. (2) _____ free?
Leo:	Sorry. I'd love to come, but I can't. I'm visiting my grandparents that day.
Ethan:	That's too bad.
Leo:	Yeah. But thanks for the invitation!
Ethan:	Max, (3) _____ like to come to my birthday party?
Max:	Yes, I'd love to. When is it?
Ethan:	It's next Saturday.
Max:	I'm sorry, but I can't. I'm going to a barbecue in Wilson Park.
Ethan:	A barbecue in Wilson Park?
Max:	Yeah. Alice is going, and she invited me.
Ethan:	Max, that's my party!
Max:	Really? Well, I guess I'll see you there!

3 ▶ 1.13 Complete the questions in the conversation. Then watch or listen again and check.

4 ▶ 1.14 Listen and repeat the invitations.

5 a Underline the following sentences in the conversation. Write the sentences below.

Two ways to accept an invitation:
1 _____ 2 _____
Two ways to refuse an invitation:
3 _____ 4 _____
Two ways to say thank you for an invitation:
5 _____ 6 _____

b ▶ 1.15 Listen and check. Then listen and repeat.

ACT

6 ✎ Write an invitation to a party that you're organising. Use Ethan's invitation to help you.
   – Student A: Think of a party and invite Student B.
   – Student B: Find out the day of the party. Accept or refuse the invitation.

7 Work in pairs. Write your own conversation. Then present it to another pair.

>>>> Workbook, page 11

PHRASEBOOK ▶ 1.16

Make an invitation

Can you come to … ?
Would you like to come to … ?
I'm having a … on …
Are you free?

Accept an invitation

Sure. That sounds great.
Yes, I'd love to.
Thanks for inviting me.

Refuse an invitation

Sorry. I'd love to come, but I can't. I'm visiting / going to …

I'm sorry, but I can't come. I have/need to …

13

WRITING A special object

>>> Make a writing plan

SPEAK AND READ

1. Work in pairs. Describe and compare the elephants in the photos. Which do you like best? Why?

2. Read Jessica's description. Which elephant is she describing? What does Lucy's elephant look like?

My special object

I'm looking at my special object now. It's a small, black, wooden model elephant. It's standing on a shelf in my room with some books and photos.

I got the elephant while I was staying with my friend Lucy in Wales. We were walking through an antique market one day when she saw two elephants. She said they were best friends like us. They weren't expensive, so we bought both of them. I kept one elephant, and Lucy kept the other.

People say that elephants never forget. When I see my elephant, it reminds me of that summer and my friend. It's a nice feeling to know that Lucy has an identical elephant.

 SEND TO TEACHER

Get it right

Remember = have the memory of something
Remind = help/make someone remember something

3. a Read the tips in the HOW TO box.

HOW TO

make a writing plan

- Write a heading for each paragraph summarising its content.
- Write short questions for each paragraph.
- Make notes of the answers to your questions.

b Look at Jessica's writing plan. Did she follow all of the steps and answer all of the questions? Underline the answers to the questions in Jessica's description.

A description of a special object

Paragraph 1 – Describe the special object
What is the object? Is it new or old?
What is it made of? Where do you keep it?

Paragraph 2 – Explain the object's history
How and when did you get it?
Is the object connected to a place or person?

Paragraph 3 – Say why it is special
What do you think of when you see the object?
How does it make you feel?

PRACTISE

4. Make a writing plan for another description called 'A special day'.
   Paragraph 1
   Paragraph 2
   Paragraph 3

PLAN

5. You're going to write a description. Follow these steps.

WRITING PLAN

1. Choose one of the topics: 'A special object' or 'A special day'.
2. Look at each step in the writing plan in Exercise 3b or Exercise 4 and note down answers to the questions.
3. When you finish writing, check the plan.

WRITE AND CHECK

6. Use your plan and your notes to write your description. Then check it. Tick (✓) the things in the plan.

SHARE

7. Swap your description with other students. Discuss the similarities and differences.

14   Workbook, pages 12–13

UNIT REVIEW

VOCABULARY Special days

1 Tony's four years old. Complete his life plan with the words/phrases in the box.

| children | driving licence | first date | home |
| job | married | retire | school | university | vote |

MY LIFE PLAN

▶ Start (1) _____ next year. Be the best student ever!
▶ Get my (2) _____ as soon as I'm 16, buy a car, then go on my (3) _____ .
▶ Leave (4) _____ when I'm 18 and go to (5) _____ to get a first-class degree.
▶ Get a really well-paid (6) _____ when I finish studying.
▶ Get (7) _____ on a beach in Hawaii and have five (8) _____ .
▶ Stand for president. Persuade everybody to (9) _____ for me!
▶ (10) _____ when I'm 50 and spend all day playing golf.

___/10

Adjectives for describing objects

2 Tony's 16 now. Complete the adjectives in the message to his friends.

Hi guys!

I need some money to buy an old car, so I'm selling some of my things. Here's a description of what's for sale. Offers welcome!

1 An (1) a_____e watch that my great-grandfather gave me. It's broken, so not very (2) u_____l, and it's too (3) old-f_____d to wear, but I think it's made of gold, so it could be (4) v_____e.
2 An (5) e_____s, brightly-(6) c_____d (7) c_____n carpet. It's (8) s_____e in shape, and it was on the floor in my room till recently, but it still looks quite new.
3 An MP3 player. It's really (9) t_____y so you can put it in your pocket. But it's got a lot of memory, and it's full of really (10) u_____l music – the type of songs you never hear on the radio.

___/10

GRAMMAR Present tenses

3 Tony's 30. Choose the correct options to complete the conversation.

Stan: Hello? Tony? Is that you?
Tony: Hi Stan. It's been a long time.
Stan: It has. So what (1) *do you do / are you doing* these days?
Tony: Not much. I (2) *don't work / 'm not working* at the moment, so I (3) *usually spend / 'm usually spending* all day at home. I (4) *look / 'm looking* for a job, but with my poor qualifications, it isn't easy.
Stan: What about Sally? (5) *Do you ever see / Are you ever seeing* her?
Tony: No, we're not in touch. I (6) *don't know / 'm not knowing* where she lives, to be honest.
Stan: That's a shame. She was your first date! But listen, Tony, I (7) *make / 'm making* dinner right now.
Tony: Oh, OK. I'll call you back later.

___/14

Past tenses

4 Tony's 70. Complete his email with the past simple or past continuous form of the verbs.

Hey Stan!
How are things? I (1) _____ (look) for old friends from high school on the net, and I (2) _____ (find) your page. The last time we (3) _____ (speak) was over 40 years ago. I (4) _____ (phone) you, but you (5) _____ (do) something, and you couldn't talk for long. I remember that you asked me about Sally. Well, I (6) _____ (see) her a few months ago while I (7) _____ (shop) at the mall. She was there with her husband and three adult kids. She (8) _____ (get) married when she was 30. I had no idea! Anyway, get back to me if you have a moment.
All the best,
Tony

___/16

Your score: ___/50

SKILLS CHECK

✓✓✓ Yes, I can. No problem!
✓✓   Yes, I can. But I need a bit of help.
✓   Yes, I can. But I need a lot of help.

I can find specific information when I read. _____
I can recognise informal speech. _____
I can collaborate to organise a group activity. _____
I can make and react to invitations. _____
I can make a writing plan. _____

Workbook, pages 14–15

UNIT 2 PACK YOUR BAGS

IN THE PICTURE Travel

>>> Talk about travel items

WORK WITH WORDS

1 **RECALL** Work in pairs. Do the tasks. You have two minutes.

   a Make a list of methods of transport under the headings.

Air	Rail	Road	Sea
plane	train	bike	boat

   b Choose the correct preposition to complete the phrase.
   travel with / by / to plane/train/bike, etc

   c Match the verbs in the box to the correct methods of transport.

   drive   fly   ride   sail

   You can drive a bus, a …

2 a ▶1.17 Look at the pictures. Put items a–l in the correct groups. Then listen and check.

   b Which item or items in the backpack can't you take on a plane in your hand luggage? Why not?

suitcase

luggage/ baggage

personal items

money and documents

> ✓ **Get it right**
>
> *Luggage/Baggage* is uncountable. With uncountable nouns we don't use *a* or the plural form (*a luggage/luggages*).

3 a ▶1.18 **PRONOUNCE** Listen to the words and repeat. Pay attention to the /p/ and /b/ sounds.
   backpack   **b**rush   **b**ag   **p**assport   shampoo   toothpaste

   b ▶1.19 Listen to these words and circle the one you hear. Then listen and repeat both words.
   1 (back) / pack   2 beach / peach   3 Ben / pen   4 bear / pear   5 big / pig

16

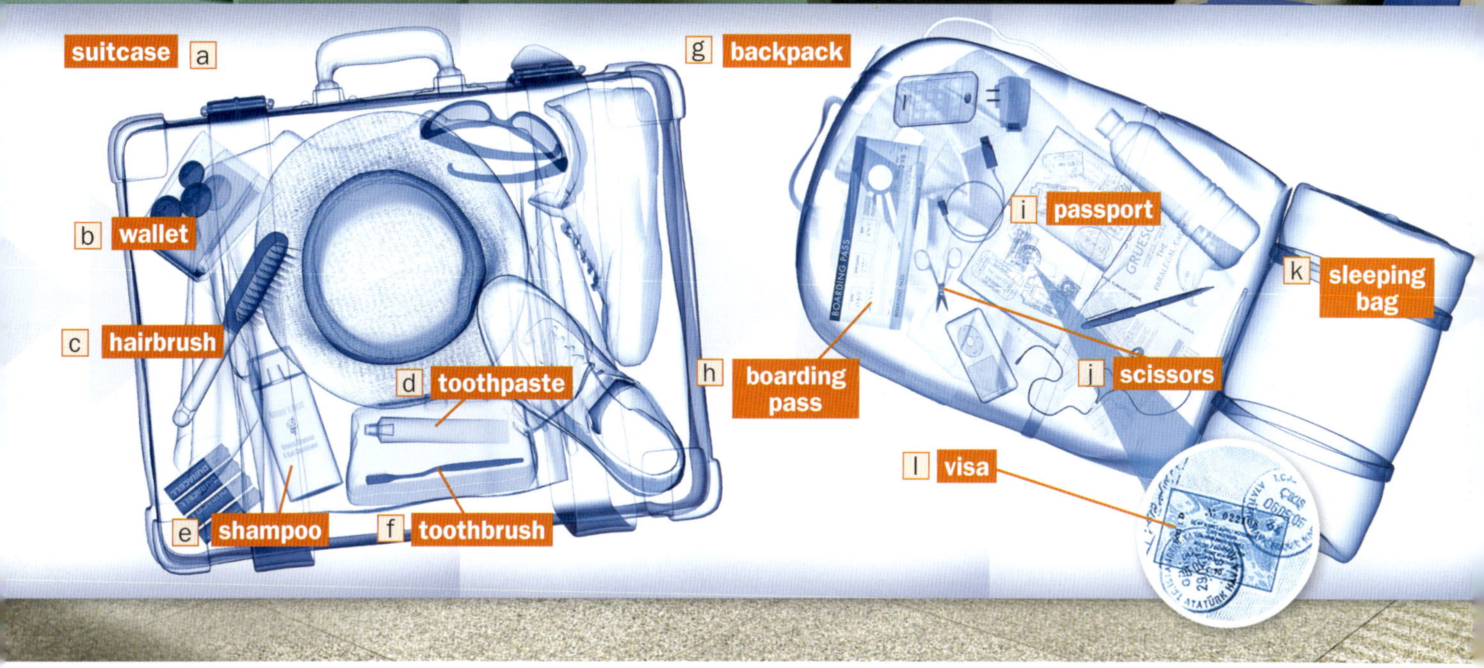

a	suitcase
b	wallet
c	hairbrush
d	toothpaste
e	shampoo
f	toothbrush
g	backpack
h	boarding pass
i	passport
j	scissors
k	sleeping bag
l	visa

4 Work in pairs. Describe and guess the objects in Exercise 2a.

You use it to keep your hair tidy.   *Brush.*

5 Work in pairs. Look at the pictures again. What other objects are in the backpack and suitcase? Make a list.

6 THE MOVING PICTURE Watch the video of an airport scanner. Shout the names of the items that you see.

SPEAK

7 Work in pairs. You're going on a school camping trip in your area.
  – With your partner, decide on the five most important things to pack. Look at the pictures for ideas and think of other items.
  – Compare your ideas with another pair.

PHRASE BYTES

What about taking/packing … ?

Let's take … / Why don't we take … ?

We definitely need …

I don't think / I'm not sure … is necessary/particularly useful …

GO BEYOND

Do the Words & Beyond exercises on page 131.

Workbook, page 16

17

READING Be a voluntourist

>>> Identify the purpose of a text

SPEAK AND READ

1 Work in pairs. Talk about your best holiday. Answer these questions.
   1 Where did you go and who were you with?
   2 What sort of holiday was it?
   3 Why was it so good?

2 a Read the tips in the **HOW TO** box.
   b ▶1.20 Read the first part of the text and identify its purpose.

3 Which tips in the **HOW TO** box did you use for help with Exercise 2b? Tick (✓) them.

HOW TO
identify the purpose of a text
☐ Use the headings, layout, pictures and weblinks to identify the **type of text**.
☐ Read the beginning of the text to find **who it's for** – everybody, or particular readers.
☐ Identify the **writer** and the **writer's aim** – is it to give information?, to entertain you?, etc.

HOLIDAY HELP: see the world and change it!

What's a voluntourist?
You know what a tourist is. And you've probably heard of volunteers (people who help others for free). Voluntourists are people who travel to a different place in their holidays to provide aid after a natural disaster or help a local community.

What's Holiday Help?
Since 2001, *Holiday Help* has offered voluntourist programmes for 14- to 18-year-old students at home and abroad. For 2–4 weeks, you can live with a host family and do a programme of social or environmental work. All you need is a backpack, your toothbrush and a positive attitude! We have programmes in North and South America, Africa, Asia, Europe and Australia.

Interested? Click here and read what some of our students have said.

4 ▶1.20 Read the students' stories. Complete the report form for Molly and Alex.

```
        Programme report
Area: _____
Project: _____
Project length: _____
How the programme has helped you:
_____
```

Molly, 15 (New Zealand)
I've just spent four weeks in Mtubatuba, South Africa. I've been home for a week now and I haven't got used to it yet. I miss everything about South Africa, but especially the people. They were always cheerful and ready to share food or tell stories. I miss the children in the activity centre where I worked too. The programme gave me the opportunity to experience the world in a new way. I've learned that you don't need a lot of money or material goods to enjoy life.

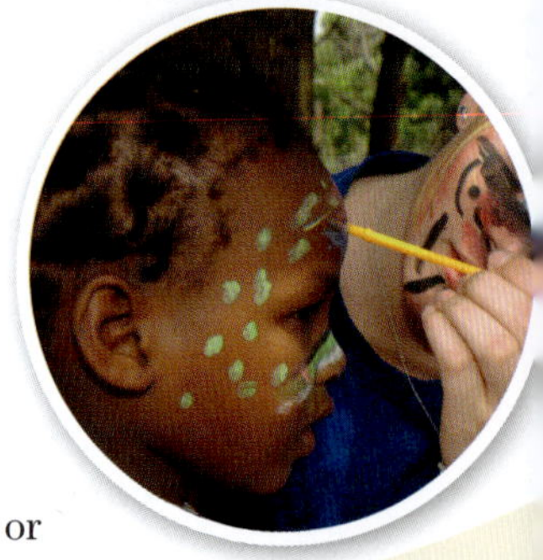

Alex, 16 (USA)
I've never been abroad and I was a bit nervous about travelling outside the USA, so I chose a two-week project in Boston. My team helped elderly people with housework and shopping. It was my first time away from home alone, but I wasn't homesick because I made so many new friends. I can really recommend programmes like this. Since the trip I've felt much more confident. Making a difference as a voluntourist is definitely better than sitting at home!

REACT

5 Work in pairs. Discuss the questions.
   1 What helps communities in need more: volunteers or donations of money?
   2 As a voluntourist, what kind of programme would you choose?
   3 Which place, country or continent would you most like to visit?

GO BEYOND
Underline the names of six continents in the text. Which continent is missing?

Workbook, page 17

GRAMMAR Present perfect

>>> Talk about how long something has happened

READ >>> Grammar in context

1 Read the article. What volunteer activities are the Rawlins family doing and why?

Since 2006, thousands of voluntourists have travelled to New Orleans, USA to rebuild the city. Hurricane Katrina destroyed 300,000 homes in 2005, and the city hasn't completed rebuilding work yet. The Rawlins family have been in New Orleans for one week.

'We've already finished a playground and we've just started on a park project,' explains Amy Rawlins. 'I've never been on a trip like this before,' says 16-year-old Elena. 'Have you ever worked on vacation? Since we've arrived we've worked for eight hours every day. The weird thing is – I've had a fantastic time!'

STUDY

2 Read the explanations. Then underline examples of the three different uses of the present perfect in Exercise 1.

Present perfect (1)

Use:
For past actions when we don't know the exact time.
With *ever/never* for experiences in your life.
With *just/yet/already* for recent events.

Form:
have(n't)/has(n't) + past participle
Irregular past participles: See page 140.

3 Underline *for* and *since* in Exercise 1. Then complete the explanations.

Present perfect (2): with *for* and *since*

Use:
To answer the question *How long ... ?* about actions that started in the past and continue to now.
Use _____ with dates, points in time.
Use _____ with periods of time.

See GRAMMAR DATABASE, page 121.

PRACTISE

4 a Ben wants to be a voluntourist. Complete the interview with the present perfect form of the verbs and the adverbs.

I: (1) _____ (you / ever / be) to the USA?
Ben: Yes, I (2) _____ (already / visit) Boston on a sight-seeing trip.
I: (3) _____ (you / ever / stay) in a tent with 10 people?
Ben: Er … no, I (4) _____ (never / be) camping. But I (5) _____ (sleep) in a sleeping bag at my friend's house.
I: (6) _____ (you / ever / work) eight hours in a day?
Ben: No, (7) I _____ (not do / that / yet). Erm, I think I (8) _____ (just / change) my mind …

b Write your answers to the three questions in Exercise 4a. Use *already*, *not yet* and *never*.

5 Complete the visitor's form. Write the questions and complete the answers with *for* or *since*.

1 How many years _____ ?
We've spent our holidays in Westbourne ___since___ I can remember.
2 How many years _____ ?
We've stayed at the Beach Campsite _____ 10 years.
3 How long _____ ?
We've been here _____ Saturday.
4 How many days _____ ?
We've had good weather _____ we came here.
5 How long _____ ?
I've looked forward to this holiday _____ a long time!

WRITE AND SPEAK

6 a Work in pairs. First write five activities you do regularly. Give your list to your partner.
I eat toast for breakfast. I do gymnastics. I annoy my brother. …

b Ask your partner how long he/she has done the activities on their list. Answer your partner's questions.

How long have you eaten toast for breakfast?

For 10 years. / Since I was three.

c Tell the class one interesting thing about your partner.

LISTENING AND VOCABULARY Around the world

>>> Listen for the information you need

SPEAK AND LISTEN

1 Work in pairs. Answer the questions.
   1 What are your favourite ways to travel? Why?
   2 What are the positive and negative aspects of travelling by sea?

2 Read the start of Oscar's blog. Why is he writing a blog?

3 a Read the tips in the HOW TO box.

   b ▶1.21 Listen to Oscar's video blog. First listen for the main ideas only and answer the questions. Then listen again and add some details to your answers.
   1 What are the family doing now?
   2 How does Oscar feel about the trip?
   3 At sea, what does he do in the morning?
   4 What does he do in the afternoon?
   5 Who's Oscar meeting in Brisbane?
   6 What are they going to do?

4 Which tips in the HOW TO box did you use for help with Exercise 3b? Tick (✓) them.

REACT

5 Work in pairs. What do you think? Tell your partner.
   1 What are the good things about living on a boat?
   2 What problems are there living in a small space on a boat?
   3 Would you like to have homeschooling? Why?/Why not?
   4 Would you like to do a voyage around the world? Why?/Why not?

Hi, I'm Oscar. My family and I are sailing around the world on a two-year voyage in our boat, Dolphin. Check out myself and the rest of the crew (that's my mum and dad and my sister Poppy) and follow our voyage on this blog. I'll probably post some videos too. Enjoy!

HOW TO
listen for the information you need

First listen for the main ideas.
☐ Don't worry if you can't understand everything.
☐ Listen for words you know. They can help you understand important ideas.

Then listen for specific information.
☐ Decide what you want to know.
☐ Think about the words you might hear.

WORK WITH WORDS

6 ▶1.22 Complete the map and online ticket with the travel words in the box. Listen and check.

| arrival | connection | delay | departure | destination | fare | passenger | reservation | ~~route~~ | seat |

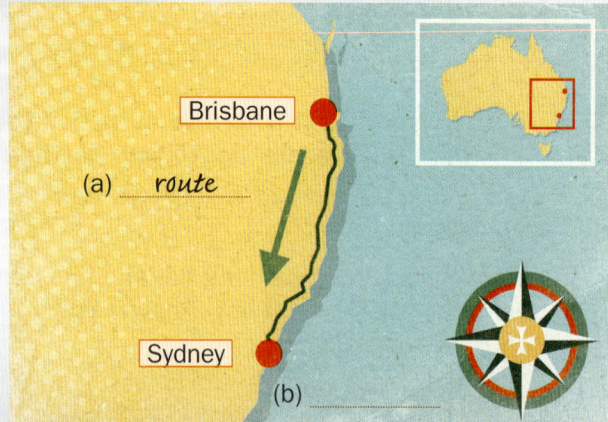

(c) _____ : Brisbane, October 5, 07:30
(d) _____ : Sydney, October 5, 21:06
(e) _____ s: none (direct train)
Please note that there may be a possible
(f) _____ because of work at Sydney Central Station.
(g) 4 _____ s (2 adults, 2 children under 16)
(h) 4 _____ s, (i) _____ s: 21, 22, 23, 24 in coach G
Total (j) _____ : $289.52

7 a Make an online ticket like the one in Exercise 6. Change the journey details (destination, arrival and departure times, the connections, etc). Don't show anybody.

   b Work in pairs. Ask your partner questions to find out the details of his/her journey and make notes.

GO BEYOND
Do the Words & Beyond exercise on page 131.

>>> Workbook, pages 20–21

GRAMMAR The future

>>> Talk about events in the future

READ >>> Grammar in context

1 Read the chat message. What's an InterRail trip?

DAN: My big sister's starting her InterRail trip on Saturday. Her train to Paris leaves at 12 o'clock, and then she's going to travel around Europe by train for a month.

JUAN: Wow, that'll be amazing. Will she be OK?

DAN: Well, she isn't travelling alone and my parents will definitely phone her every day. So she isn't likely to have any problems.

JUAN: What countries are they going to visit?

DAN: They don't know their final route yet – but it's likely to be a lot! You can travel to 30 countries on an InterRail ticket. They probably won't remember which countries they went to!

STUDY

2 Read the explanations. Then underline an example of each form in Exercise 1.

The future

Form	Use
present continuous	future arrangements
present simple	events on a timetable
be + *going to* + infinitive	future plans/intentions
will/won't + infinitive + *definitely* = 100% sure + *probably* = 75% sure	predictions
be + *likely to* + infinitive	probable events

Word order:
will + definitely/probably + infinitive
definitely/probably + *won't* + infinitive

See GRAMMAR DATABASE, page 121.

PRACTISE

3 ▶1.23 Sam and his parents are going on their dream trip on the Trans-Siberian Railway. Choose the correct options to complete the conversation. Then listen and check.

Sam: We (1) *'ll go* / *'re going* on holiday tomorrow.
Fariq: What time (2) *does your train leave* / *is your train likely to leave*?
Sam: At 15:30 tomorrow. It (3) *'s arriving* / *arrives* in Moscow three days later, so I'll sleep on the train. Then it's seven days to Vladivostok.
Fariq: (4) *Are other people going to sleep* / *Do other people sleep* in your train compartment?
Sam: No, we have a reservation for just us three.
Fariq: It sounds exciting. Is it (5) *likely to be* / *being* cold?
Sam: No, it's quite warm in the summer.

4 Read quotes by students about their plans and dreams. Write the correct future forms.

1 Tomorrow, I *'m doing* (do) an audition for a theatre school.
2 My judo course _____ (start) next week.
3 Next year, I _____ (learn) Japanese.
4 In 10 years, I _____ (*definitely* / *be*) a pilot.
5 My dream is to be a famous singer. But it _____ (*not* / *likely* / *come*) true.
6 I _____ (*probably* / *get*) my driving licence and a car when I'm 17.

WRITE AND SPEAK

5 a Work in pairs. Write three sentences about your plans and dreams using these time phrases. (Don't show your partner.)
1 Next week …   3 Next year …
2 In 10 years …

b Try and predict your partner's future. Write three sentences, using your own ideas.

Next week you'll definitely get good marks in your English test.
In 10 years you'll probably be a musician.
You're not likely to be a teacher.

c Tell your partner your ideas. Then look at your partner's sentences from Exercise 5a. Were any of your predictions correct?

This year you'll get on the football team.

Yes, I'm definitely going to do that. / Perhaps I'll do that. / I'm not sure.

No, I'm not going to do that. / I'm not likely to do that. / No, I probably won't do that.

Workbook, page 22

LANGUAGE & BEYOND

Imagine you're in an invisible bubble. This bubble is your personal space – your ideal distance from other people.

The area of the brain which builds this 'bubble' is the same area that controls being scared. So when you know somebody well, you allow them to come closer to you. If you don't know people well, you put more space between you. Two girls usually get closer together when they talk than two boys.

Sometimes it's hard to keep a normal distance from people. This often happens when travelling – for example, when you're a passenger on a busy bus or underground train, or in a queue at a ticket office or bus stop. It can also happen at crowded concerts or in a lift.

Interestingly, personal space is different for different cultures and in different countries. People who live in countries with a large population, like China or India, usually have a smaller personal space. People in North America and northern Europe often need more space than people in South America or southern Europe.

>>> Respect other people's personal space

READ

1 Look at the picture on the right. What do you think it shows? Read the article and check.

2 Choose the correct options for you. Compare your answers with the class.
1. I *don't mind* / *like* being in a crowd.
2. I *don't mind* / *like* standing close to somebody in a queue.
3. I *don't mind* / *like* closed spaces like lifts.

DO

3 Work in groups of three. Do the following task.
1. Two people stand opposite each other but quite far away.
2. Talk about something: free time, your favourite music …
3. Walk slowly towards your partner until you both feel uncomfortable and can't concentrate on your conversation.
4. The third person measures the space between you.
5. Compare your distance with other people in the class.

PHRASE BYTES

I allow my friend/mother/sister
… to come closer.

I feel annoyed/embarrassed/nervous …

I look at them / move back / say something / shout …

REFLECT

4 Discuss the questions with your class. Do you agree with the **REFLECTION POINT**?
1. Which people do you allow to come closer to you than other people?
2. How do you feel if somebody comes too close? Think of an example.
3. What do you do if people come too close? Do you say anything?

EXTEND

5 a ▶1.24 Listen to the sentences about areas of personal space. Write *agree*, *disagree* or *not sure* for each sentence.

b Work in pairs. Compare your answers and explain any differences.

REFLECTION POINT

Different people have different ideas about personal space. Protect your own space and respect other people's space.

RESPECT OTHERS

Workbook, page 25

SPEAKING At the airport

>>> Check in at the airport

SPEAK

1 Answer these questions.
1 Where's the nearest airport to your town or area?
2 What's the best way to get to the airport from your home?
3 How many times have you been to an airport? Did you go there to meet people or fly?

2 Match the airport signs (a–f) to the correct activities (1–6).
1 Planes land at this part of the airport. _e_
2 Planes take off from this part of the airport. ....
3 You board the plane here. ....
4 You get your boarding pass here and/or give in your luggage. ....
5 Somebody checks your passport before you enter a country here. ....
6 Somebody sometimes checks your luggage after your flight here. ....

WATCH OR LISTEN

3 ▶ 1.25 Watch or listen to the scene. Where's Bella? What other airport places are mentioned?

Bella:	Hello, I'd like to check in for the flight to Rome.
Assistant:	Can I have your passport, please?
Bella:	Yes. Here you are.
Assistant:	How many bags are you checking in?
Bella:	One suitcase.
Assistant:	Do you have any hand luggage?
Bella:	I have a backpack.
Assistant:	OK, that's fine. Do you have any sharp objects in there?
Bella:	Sorry, I don't understand. Could you repeat that, please?
Assistant:	Do you have any sharp objects in your hand luggage? Scissors, knives, anything like that?
Bella:	Er, yes, I have some scissors.
Assistant:	I'm sorry, you'll have to put those in your suitcase. ... Here's your boarding pass. Departures is upstairs.
Bella:	Which gate number is it?
Assistant:	You board from Gate 30.
Bella:	Sorry, I didn't hear that. Can you say that again, please?
Assistant:	Gate 30. ... Have a good flight.

4 ▶ 1.26 Underline sentences in the conversation for 1–4 below. Listen and check. Then listen and repeat.
1 you want to check in
2 you give something to somebody
3 you talk about hand luggage
4 you ask about the gate

5 a Read the tips in the HOW TO box.

b ▶ 1.27 Complete the phrases from the conversation. Listen and check. Then listen and repeat.
1 Sorry, I don't ...
2 Sorry, I didn't ...
3 Could you ... ?
4 Can you say ... ?

ACT

6 Work in pairs. One student is at the check-in desk, the other student wants to check in. Decide where you are flying to, how much luggage you have and if you have sharp objects. Prepare and act a scene.

HOW TO

check you understand

- Say you didn't hear or don't understand.
- Ask the other person to repeat the information.
- Be polite: use *sorry* and *please*.

PHRASEBOOK ▶ 1.28

Check in at the airport
I'd like to check in (for) ...
Here you are.
I have a backpack/suitcase ...
Where's Departures?
Which gate number is it?

Check you understand
Sorry, I didn't hear that. Can you say that again, please?
Sorry, I don't understand. Could you repeat that, please?

Workbook, page 23

23

WRITING Wish you were here

>>> Use correct verb tenses

SPEAK AND READ

1 Work in groups. Answer the questions.
   1 Why do people usually write postcards?
   2 Who do you receive postcards from?
   3 Who do you send postcards to?

2 Read Vik's postcard. Tick (✓) the correct pictures on the front.

Dear Marco,
We've been in Spain for three days now, and I'm having a fantastic time! The journey was terrible – our flight had a three-hour delay. I was getting really tired of waiting in the airport. Then we missed our connection, of course, because of the late departure. But our campsite is brilliant! There's a huge swimming pool, a games room and lots of sports like mini golf and table tennis. The weather isn't bad, but it's a bit cloudy. Yesterday we hired bikes and rode along the coast. Then we went to an excellent restaurant. The food here is so delicious! Tomorrow we're taking the train into Barcelona, and we're going to do some sightseeing. I think it'll be exciting.
Wish you were here!
Vik

PRACTISE

4 Write the sentences in another postcard in the correct tense. Use the **HOW TO** box to help you.
   1 We _____ (get) here five days ago.
   2 I _____ (play) tennis here every day.
   3 I _____ (not play) computer games since we got here.
   4 We _____ (watch) a show later this evening.
   5 It _____ (rain) today.
   6 I hope it _____ (stop) later.

PLAN

5 You're going to write a holiday postcard. Think of your ideal holiday and make a plan.

WRITING PLAN

1 **Say hello from your holiday place.**
   Where are you? What was the journey like?

2 **Describe the place.**
   Where are you staying? What's it like there?

3 **Describe your activities and plans.**
   What did you do yesterday?
   What are you going to do tomorrow?
   (Use the correct verb tenses for each part.)

4 **Finish your postcard.**

✓ Get it right

Journey: travel from one place to another, usually with a long distance between places
Trip: travel to a place and back again
Voyage: a long journey by sea or in space
Flight: a journey by air

3 a Read the tips in the **HOW TO** box.

HOW TO
use correct verb tenses

- Decide if the action is past, present or future.
- Look at the rules for past, present and future tenses in Units 1 and 2.
- Use the correct tense with the correct time words (*yesterday*, *tomorrow*, etc).

b Underline examples of seven different tenses in the postcard.

WRITE AND CHECK

6 Use your plan and write your postcard. Then check it. Tick (✓) the things in the plan.

SHARE

7 Swap your postcard with a partner. Whose trip sounds most interesting? Why?

UNIT REVIEW

VOCABULARY Travel items

1 Complete the conversation with the correct words.

Teacher: How much luggage do you have, Luke?
Luke: Er, just two big (1) s_____ with my clothes and shoes …
Teacher: That's a bit much for five days in Berlin! Your (2) b_____ looks heavy too.
Luke: I have my (3) s_____ b_____ so I can sleep on the plane. And my (4) t_____ and (5) t_____ so I can clean my teeth after lunch, my (6) h_____, of course, for my hair. Oh, and (7) s_____, to wash my hair later. I like to be prepared!
Teacher: Right … OK, everybody, did you all check in online? Good, get your (8) b_____ p_____ ready. Ping, do you have your (9) v_____ for Germany? Right, let's take our luggage to the desk. Remember, no sharp items like (10) s_____ in your hand luggage. Yes, Luke?
Luke: Erm … I think I've forgotten my (11) p_____ and my (12) w_____ with all my money in it …

___ /12

Travel

2 Choose the correct options to complete the travel plan.

Tuesday
Our flight is at 14:25. Hopefully there will be no (1) *delays* / *fares*. Please check in online with your (2) *connection* / *reservation* number and choose a (3) *seat* / *destination*. We will meet at the airport an hour before (4) *arrival* / *departure*. Please remember not to disturb other (5) *seats* / *passengers* during the flight. After our (6) *arrival* / *departure* in Berlin, we will get our (7) *passenger* / *connection* to Zoo Station which is our final (8) *delay* / *destination*. We will take the tram, which is the quickest and cheapest (9) *passenger* / *route*. The (10) *reservation* / *fare* for the tram is included in the price of the trip.

Wednesday
Visit to the famous Pergamon Museum.

___ /10

GRAMMAR
Present perfect

3 Write the verbs in the present perfect and choose *for* or *since*.

Guide: This vase is the museum's most expensive item. It (1) _____ (be) in the museum (2) *for* / *since* I started work here. I (3) _____ (work) here (4) *for* / *since* 30 years. (5) *For* / *Since* the last two years a rich collector (6) _____ (want) to buy the vase. We (7) _____ (just / decide) to sell it, but the collector (8) _____ (not take) it away yet. … Don't touch it, young man!
Luke: Oh, er … sorry.

___ /16

The future

4 Choose the teacher's next sentence (A or B).

1 It's our last day today.
   A We're flying back home.
   B We're likely to fly back home.
2 We need to be at the airport at 17:00.
   A The plane leaves at 18:00.
   B The plane is leaving at 18:00.
3 You have a free afternoon.
   A You're enjoying it.   B I hope you'll enjoy it.
4 I've checked the weather for later today.
   A It doesn't rain.   B It isn't likely to rain.
5 Let's meet at Zoo Station at 16:00.
   A We're going to travel to the airport by tram.
   B We travel to the airport by tram.
6 Luke, please make sure you're on time.
   A We aren't waiting for you.
   B We won't wait for you.

___ /12

Your score: ___ /50

SKILLS CHECK

✓✓✓	Yes, I can. No problem!
✓✓	Yes, I can. But I need a bit of help.
✓	Yes, I can. But I need a lot of help.

I can identify the purpose of a text. _____
I can listen for the information I need. _____
I can respect other people's personal space. _____
I can check in at the airport. _____
I can use correct verb tenses. _____

Workbook, pages 26–27

PROGRESS CHECK

READ

1 Read the article and decide if each sentence is correct (write *A*) or incorrect (write *B*).

1. Woolton was part of Liverpool in 1957.
2. Paul McCartney met John Lennon after a concert.
3. There was more interest in the Beatles in the past.
4. Lennon lived in 'Mendips' when he was an art student.
5. Lennon lived in 'Mendips' for a short time with his first wife.
6. People have had the opportunity to visit 'Mendips' since 2003.
7. McCartney met Lennon before he moved to Forthlin Road.
8. Lennon and McCartney met at Paul's house to practise their first songs.
9. The tour guides for the two houses live in the houses.
10. You can only go into the houses if you're on a National Trust tour.

EXAM TIPS

do a true/false activity
- Read the sentences carefully before you read.
- Look at any pictures which can help you to understand the text.
- Read the text carefully and choose the correct answers.
- Check details: if any part of the sentence is false, then it is incorrect.

find specific information
See page 8

identify the purpose of a text
See page 18

LIVERPOOL HIGHLIGHTS:
The Beatles' childhood homes

On a summer's afternoon in 1957 a group called The Quarrymen gave a concert in a field behind a church in Woolton. Now a suburb of Liverpool, Woolton was a separate village at that time. The same evening, The Quarrymen played again, this time in the church hall. A boy called Paul was in the audience for both performances. While they were setting up for the evening concert a friend of his introduced him to John, the group's singer. It was the moment when John Lennon and Paul McCartney met for the first time.

Over half a century has passed since that first meeting, but interest in the Beatles, the group they formed together, has not decreased. People from all over the world still come to Liverpool to see where the Beatles lived and played. Two of the most popular destinations are the houses where John and Paul grew up. 'Mendips' is the house in Menlove Avenue where John lived from the age of five until he left home to study at Liverpool Art College in the late 1950s. He briefly moved back into the house in the early 1960s, with his first wife. Lennon's second wife, Yoko Ono, bought the house in 2003. It was restored and opened to the public the same year. The highlight for Beatles fans is a trip upstairs to the tiny bedroom at the front where Lennon slept. Paul McCartney's childhood home in Forthlin Road is smaller and simpler. The McCartney family moved into the house in 1955, when Paul was at secondary school. It's often referred to as 'the birthplace of the Beatles' because this is where Lennon and McCartney practised their earliest songs. Like 'Mendips', the house has been restored. Visitors can stand in the McCartney sitting room, with its colourful curtains, antique television and old-fashioned wallpaper, and imagine how the teenage McCartney lived.

Today, 'custodians' live in both houses. Their job is to look after the houses and to show groups of visitors around when they arrive four times a day, five days a week.

If you want to see inside the houses, you have to go on a minibus tour organised by the National Trust. It's important to book a place online in advance, because visits are limited to 15 people at a time. It's also important to be punctual. Passengers need to arrive 15 minutes before the minibus departs, and the tour does not wait for people who arrive late.

Reading: _____ /10

PROGRESS CHECK

LISTEN

2 ▶1.29 You will hear an adventure camp organiser talking to a group of teenagers. Listen and write the missing information in the spaces.

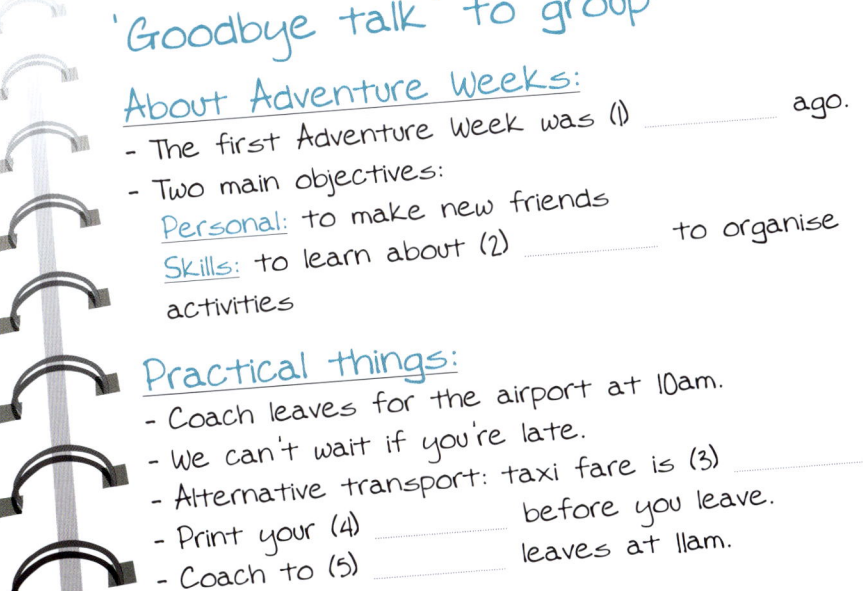

'Goodbye talk' to group

About Adventure Weeks:
- The first Adventure Week was (1) _____ ago.
- Two main objectives:
  Personal: to make new friends
  Skills: to learn about (2) _____ to organise activities

Practical things:
- Coach leaves for the airport at 10am.
- We can't wait if you're late.
- Alternative transport: taxi fare is (3) _____ .
- Print your (4) _____ before you leave.
- Coach to (5) _____ leaves at 11am.

Listening: _____ /10

EXAM TIPS

listen and complete notes
- Read the information carefully before you listen.
- Decide what sort of information is missing.
- Listen for the words before the missing information.
- Write the exact words that you hear.

recognise informal speech
See page 10

listen for the information you need
See page 20

WRITE

3 For each question, complete the second sentence so that it means the same as the first. Use no more than three words.

1. We met when we were maths students at university.
   We met while we _____ maths at university.
2. Can you come to our housewarming party?
   Would _____ to come to our housewarming party?
3. We moved into our new house two weeks ago.
   We've lived in our new house _____ .
4. We're still waiting for John to answer our email.
   John _____ our email yet.

_____ /4

4 You decide to send a short message to an Australian friend called Neil. Write your message (35–45 words).
- Say if you are having a good week and say why or why not.
- Say what you have done.
- Tell him what you plan to do at the weekend or next week.

_____ /6

Writing: _____ /10

Progress check score _____ /30

EXAM TIPS

do sentence transformations
- Read the instructions. How many words can you use?
- Read both sentences carefully.
- Decide if the missing words are nouns, verbs, etc.
- Check that the meaning is the same and your spelling is correct.

EXAM TIPS

write a short message or blog post
- Read the task carefully.
- Include the three things in the task.
- Use the correct tense(s): past, present or future.
- Use the correct number of words – count them.

use correct verb tenses
See page 24

Download extra speaking activities from www.macmillanbeyond.com

27

UNIT 3 MY MUSIC

IN THE PICTURE Live music

>>> Talk about music and music events

WORK WITH WORDS

1 **RECALL** Work in pairs. Do the tasks. You have three minutes.

   a Make lists of words. Use the photos to help you.

Types of music	Instruments	People	Types of group	Places & events
rock	guitar	singer	band	concert

   b Match the verbs *listen* and *play* to the correct categories.
   You can listen to rock music/a guitar …

2 Match two words to each photo. Add them to the table above.

   | audience | ~~band~~ | brass band | conductor | flute | folk |
   | jazz | opera | orchestra | performance | trumpet | ~~venue~~ |

   a – band, venue

3 ▶1.30 Listen and match the speakers (1–6) to the photos (a–f).

4 a ▶1.31 Use the words in Exercise 2 to complete the sentences. Then listen and check.

   1 The _____ is amazing. I've never been to a concert in a place like this with all these hills and rocks. And the _____ is performing really well.
   2 Thank you for coming to the Newtown _____ Festival. Now please welcome one of the greatest _____ players of all time.
   3 I usually perform _____ songs … a mix of old traditional songs and more modern stuff like Ed Sheeran. If I give a good _____ , then people give money.
   4 We started playing together a year ago, but I've played the _____ since I was 12. I also play the trumpet in the school _____ .
   5 I don't like _____ very much, but a friend gave me tickets, and I'm really enjoying it. I think the rest of the _____ is having a good time too.
   6 The sound of the _____ in the concert hall is fantastic. I've seen the _____ before, but I've never seen him conduct Beethoven.

   b ▶1.32 Listen and repeat the words in Exercise 2.

5 a ▶1.33 **PRONOUNCE** Listen to the sounds at the beginning of these words. Listen again and repeat.
   /ɔː/ orchestra   /ɒ/ opera

b ▶1.34 **Listen to the blue part of these words and repeat them. Which words have the /ɔː/ sound? Which words have the /ɒ/ sound?**

st**o**p   **au**dience   perf**o**rmance   s**o**ng   sc**o**re   l**o**st

6 **THE MOVING PICTURE** ▶ **Watch the video. Work in pairs. Describe what you see. What type of performance is it?**

7 Work in pairs. Complete the task. Student A looks at page 141. Student B looks at the survey on the right. Answer the questions in your music survey.

SPEAK

8 Work in pairs. Ask and answer the music survey in Exercise 7, comparing your answers. Make notes of your partner's answers and tell the class one interesting thing about your partner.

Music survey

1 Which music genres do you like/dislike?
2 When and where do you sing?
3 Have you ever been to a rock concert or music festival?
4 What music venues are there where you live?
5 In your opinion, which is better, going to a live concert or listening to recorded music?

GO BEYOND

Do the Words & Beyond exercise on page 132.

Workbook, page 28

READING A dream concert

>>> Understand new words

SPEAK AND READ

1 Work in pairs. Look at the poster and answer the questions.
   1 What type of concert is the poster advertising?
   2 Who would perform at your 'dream concert'?

2 ▶1.35 Read the concert programme and answer the questions.
   1 Why did José Angel Salazar become famous?
   2 Who is the most important person in an orchestra?
   3 What does José Angel want to do in the future?

3 a Read the tips in the **HOW TO** box.
   b Read the text again and try to understand the underlined words.

4 Match the dictionary definitions to the underlined words in the text.
   1 (adj) knowing about a situation or a fact
   2 (v) communicate ideas or feelings
   3 (v) criticise someone for doing something wrong
   4 (n) the ability to understand something
   5 (v) give a short performance in which you sing, dance or act, hoping to perform in a play, concert, etc
   6 (n) movements that communicate a feeling or instruction

5 Which tips in the **HOW TO** box did you use for help with Exercises 3b and 4? Tick (✓) them.

REACT

6 Work in pairs. What do you think? Tell your partner.
   1 Why is José Angel Salazar's story unusual?
   2 What characteristics does a conductor need?
   3 Would you be a good conductor? Why?/Why not?

PHRASE BYTES

I think his story is unusual because …
A conductor needs to be/have / be able to …
I would be a … conductor because …

GO BEYOND

Read about José Angel Salazar again and write different questions about the text. Then ask another student.

A season of **dream concerts**

The Youth Orchestra of Nueva Esparta, Venezuela

performs Schubert's 5th Symphony

with *José Angel Salazar* as conductor

HOW TO
understand new words

☐ Identify the type of word (verb, noun, adjective, adverb).

☐ Is there a similar word in your language? Does its meaning help you?

☐ Look at the words and sentences before and after the new word.

☐ Think what the new word might mean and check your idea in the sentence.

When José Angel Salazar was 14 years old, he became 'the youngest conductor in the world'. Born in Nueva Esparta, Venezuela, José Angel didn't listen to much classical music during his childhood. But when he was eight years old, his father and grandfather took him to a brass band concert, and his life changed forever. He stopped going to karate lessons and learned to play the flute. Soon afterwards, he decided to learn the violin.

In 2011 José Angel <u>auditioned</u> to join the Symphony Orchestra of Nueva Esparta, where he continued studying violin and music theory. The following year he was asked to become the orchestra's conductor. Although conductors usually have their backs to the audience, they are the most important person in an orchestra. Apart from indicating the beat of the music, the conductor interprets how the music is played. He uses different movements, <u>gestures</u> and expressions to communicate with every individual musician.

There are between 70 and 80 musicians in the Youth Orchestra of Nueva Esparta, and more than half of them are older than José Angel.
'It's hard because I have to find the way to communicate, or sometimes <u>tell off</u> kids who are much older than me,' he said in an interview with *The Guardian* newspaper. 'Conducting is a wordless language. I have to <u>convey</u> confidence to the musicians in order to get a confident performance back from them … I have to co-ordinate my body's movements with the music.' José Angel is also <u>aware</u> of the importance of words for a conductor. 'I'd like to study languages. I don't want to go on tour and have to use a translator. Or if I am interpreting Mahler, there are certain criteria, or feelings, that I'd have a better <u>grasp</u> of if I spoke German.'

GRAMMAR Verbs followed by -ing form or to + infinitive

>>> Talk about things you enjoy doing

READ >>> Grammar in context

1 Read the advertisement. Would you like to go to The Rock School? Why?/Why not?

Do you enjoy singing? Are you learning to play the guitar, drums, keyboard or bass? Do you want to become a rock star? If your answer is 'yes' and you'd like to turn your dream into reality, come to The Rock School. At The Rock School you can practise playing music with other young people like you. We love helping talented young people achieve their ambitions. The official school motto is 'To inspire kids to rock on stage and in life'. If you live in the US or Mexico, are between eight and 18, and hope to be a rock star, call us now!

STUDY

2 Complete the explanations with verbs from the advertisement in Exercise 1.

Verbs followed by -ing form or to + infinitive

first verb	+ second verb
_____ , _____ , don't mind, imagine	-ing form (doing)
learn, _____ , would(n't) like, _____ , hope, plan, decide	to + infinitive (to do)

Some verbs can be followed by -ing or to with little or no difference in meaning. Examples are: *like*, *hate*, *love* and *prefer*.

See GRAMMAR DATABASE, page 122.

PRACTISE

3 Read Marta's interview. For each sentence, choose the correct option or both options.

Jeff: Why would you like (1) *coming / to come* to The Rock School?
Marta: I've always imagined (2) *being / to be* famous.
Jeff: Are you learning (3) *playing / to play* any instruments or do you want (4) *being / to be* a singer?
Marta: I don't mind (5) *singing / to sing*, but I prefer (6) *playing / to play* the guitar and piano.
Jeff: So what else do you enjoy (7) *doing / to do* in your free time?
Marta: I love (8) *swimming / to swim*.

4 Complete the text with the correct form of the verbs in the box.

| become | give | ~~go~~ | learn | make | perform |

When he was a teenager, Paul Green planned (1) _to go_ to college, but he didn't have enough money. A lot of young people in his neighbourhood wanted (2) _____ the guitar, so he decided (3) _____ guitar lessons at his home. His classes were popular, and two years later he opened the Paul Green School of Rock Music. It was a place where teenagers could enjoy (4) _____ music and learn (5) _____ in front of an audience. Today there are more than 90 schools in the United States and Mexico. Paul Green hopes he can inspire more young people (6) _____ better musicians.

5 Write the questions. Use the infinitive with *to* or the *-ing* form of the words in blue.

1 Which instruments / you / learn / *play* / at the moment ?
2 Which other instruments / you / would like / *learn* ?
3 you / enjoy / *sing* ?
4 you / like / *perform* / in front of people ?
5 What / you / hope / *do* / in the future ?
6 What other things / like / *do* / in your free time ?

SPEAK

6 Work in pairs. Take it in turns to ask and answer the questions in Exercise 5.

Workbook, pages 30–31

31

LISTENING AND VOCABULARY Talking music

>>> Transfer spoken information to a table

SPEAK AND LISTEN

1 Work in pairs. Answer the questions.
1. Which type of music do you listen to while you're relaxing?
2. Which music, if any, do you listen to while you're doing these other activities?

> doing homework   preparing for an exam   running (or other exercise)

2 a Read the tips in the **HOW TO** box.

b ▶1.36 You will hear different people talking about the music they listen to. For each person, complete the missing information in the table.

HOW TO
transfer spoken information to a table
- [ ] Read all the information in the table.
- [ ] Decide what information you need.
- [ ] Listen for the information you need and write notes in the table.

Name	Marty	Jeannine	Salva	Sheera
Activity	(1) _____	(2) _____	preparing for exam	(5) _____
Type of music	rock music	heavy metal	(4) _____	pop songs
How music helps	helps him think creatively	(3) _____	helps him get focused	(6) _____

3 Which tips in the **HOW TO** box did you use for help with Exercise 2b? Tick (✓) them.

REACT

4 Work in pairs. Answer the questions.
1. Which of the people in the interviews in Exercise 2b is most similar to you? Why?
2. Do you think listening to music could help you study? If so, what would be the best type of music?

WORK WITH WORDS

5 ▶1.37 Write the adverbs of degree in the correct column. Listen and check. Then listen and repeat.

> a bit   a lot   extremely   incredibly   pretty   quite   really
> terribly   totally   very

1 ▁	2 ▃	3 ▅
a bit	a lot	extremely

6 ▶1.38 Listen to extracts from the interviews and complete sentences 1–10 with the adverbs from Exercise 5.

WRITE AND SPEAK

7 Work in pairs. Write an answer to the question below. Include at least three adverbs of degree. Then discuss with a partner.

Does music help you do things better?

1. It's _____ good for your brain.
2. It has a _____ steady rhythm of 60 beats a minute.
3. That sounds _____ boring.
4. It's _____ extreme.
5. It helps me get into the rhythm _____ quickly.
6. They're _____ good to listen to before an exam.
7. They help me get _____ focused.
8. They're _____ powerful.
9. It doesn't help me work _____ better.
10. I find it _____ distracting.

GO BEYOND

Do the Words & Beyond exercise on page 132.

>>> Workbook, pages 32–33

GRAMMAR Comparison of adverbs

>>> Compare how people do things

READ AND LISTEN >>> Grammar in context

1 ▶1.39 Read and listen to the athlete. Does he believe that practice is positive?

'**Our trainer's a cool guy.** He knows a lot. He always says practice makes perfect. He says that if an athlete practises harder than another, then he or she will improve more quickly. In a race, he or she will probably run the fastest and perform the most confidently. But if you practise as hard as other people, you won't always perform as well as them. A lot of people practise the things that they can already do. To do things better, it's important to practise the things that you can't do well.'

STUDY

2 Complete the explanations with the words in the box. Use Exercise 1 to help you.

better   -er   -est   more   the most

Comparative and superlative adverbs

Use:
To compare how people or things do something.

Form: comparative adverbs
short adverb (*hard*) + _____ (+ *than*)
_____ + long adverb (*quickly*) (+ *than*)

Form: superlative adverbs
the + short adverb + _____
_____ + long adjective

Irregular adverbs:
well > _____ > the best
badly > worse > the worst

3 Complete the example from Exercise 1.

(Not) as + adverb + as

Use:
To say two people or things do or don't do something the same.
If you practise _____ other people, you won't always perform _____ them.

See GRAMMAR DATABASE, page 122.

PRACTISE

4 Choose the correct options.
 1 There were eight top runners in the semi-final, but the American ran *the fastest / the most fast*.
 2 The Chinese team is performing *well / better* than last year.
 3 The German isn't swimming *as fast as / faster* the Australian.
 4 The British team is playing *more carefully / most carefully* than the French team.
 5 The Mexican has jumped *higher / the highest* of all the competitors.
 6 He's cycling *the best / as well as* the US champion.

5 ▶1.40 Complete the talent show conversation using comparative and superlative adverbs. Then listen and check.

Simon: Which of the three singers do you think has performed (1) *the best* (well)?
Millie: Amanda can sing (2) _____ (loudly) than anyone I know.
Simon: That's true. But she doesn't sing (3) _____ (well) as Katy.
Millie: I think Amy sings (4) _____ (beautifully) than the others.
Simon: I disagree. Amy can't sing (5) _____ (high) as Amanda or Katy.
Millie: But she's a star. She's worked (6) _____ (hard) of the three.
Simon: She practises (7) _____ (long) than the others because she needs to.
Millie: But which of them is going to become famous (8) _____ (fast)?

6 Complete the sentences with names to give your opinion.

IN MY OPINION ...

❶ _____ sings better than _____ .
❷ _____ doesn't play (the guitar, football, etc) as well as _____ .
❸ _____ acts as well as _____ .
❹ _____ is the most hard-working student in the class.
❺ _____

DO YOU AGREE?

SPEAK

7 Work in pairs. Complete the tasks.
 – Read out one of your opinions from Exercise 6.
 – Your partner gives his/her opinion and explains why.

In my opinion, X sings better than Y.

I don't agree. Y sings better than X. X's last album was terrible.

Workbook, page 34

LANGUAGE & BEYOND

Stay on task and avoid distractions

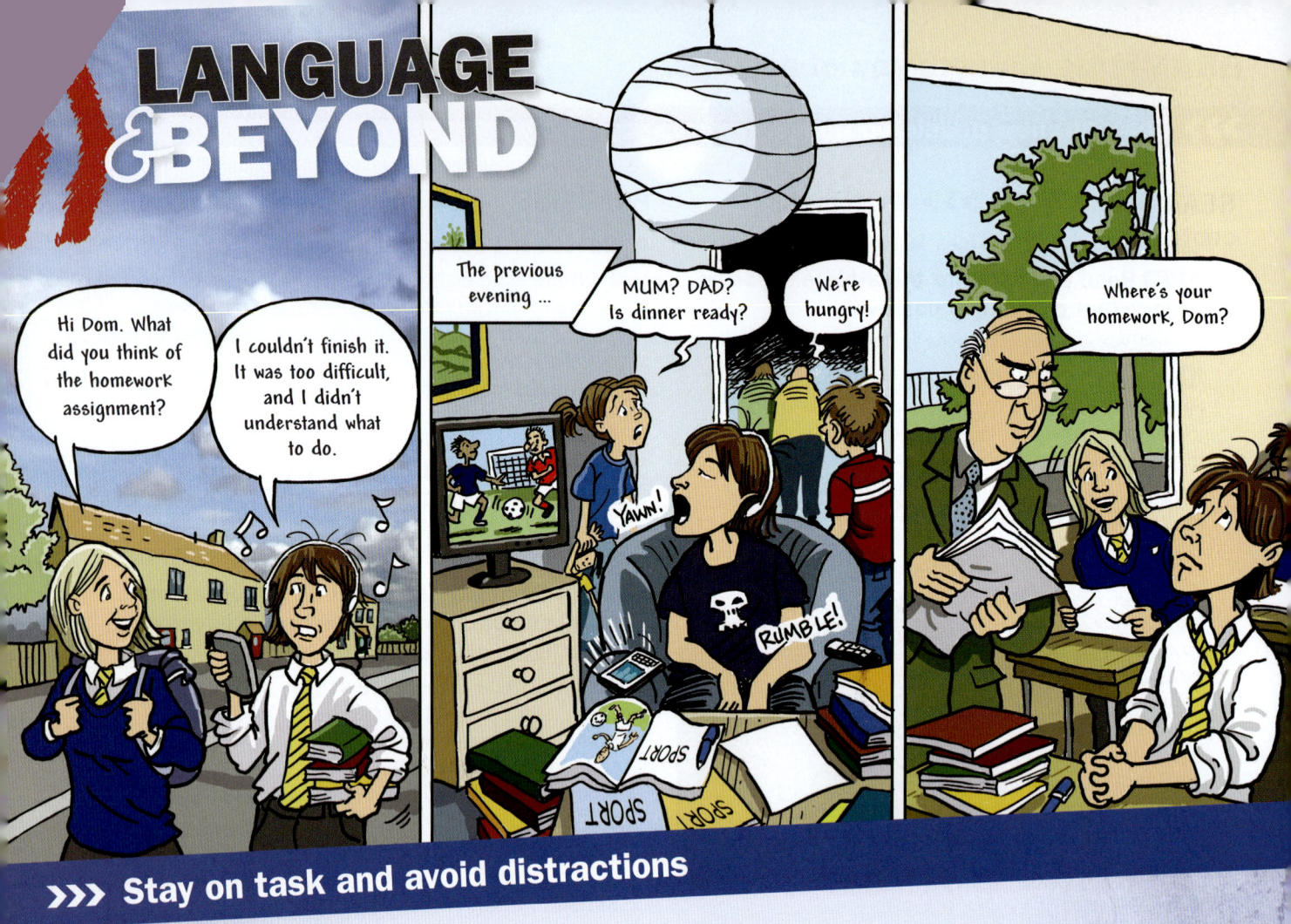

SPEAK AND READ

1 Work in pairs. Read the comic strip. What reasons does Dom give for not finishing his homework?

2 Work in pairs. Think of more possible reasons for Dom not finishing his homework.

PHRASE BYTES

I think he couldn't finish because …
He was distracted by …
He was feeling …

DO

3 Work in groups. Look at the tips for staying on task. Which of the tips should Dom follow?
   1 If you don't understand the task – ask.
   2 Find a quiet place to work.
   3 Work with another person.
   4 Make sure you have everything you need to complete the task.
   5 Set a time limit for the task.
   6 If it's a long task, plan a break after completing part of it.
   7 Do some exercise if you're sitting for a long time or feeling bored.
   8 Have a snack if you feel hungry.

4 What other things should Dom do to stay on task?

REFLECT

5 Discuss the questions with your class. Do you agree with the REFLECTION POINT?
   1 How often do you find it difficult to stay on task? Which tasks are the most difficult?
   2 What's similar or different about Dom's homework situation compared to yours?
   3 Which of the tips in Exercise 3 do you regularly follow? Which other tips do you think you should follow?

REFLECTION POINT

Learning to stay on task helps you work better at school, at home and in other areas of life.

EXTEND

6 Work in groups. Look at the jobs below. When is it important for these people to stay on task? Add other jobs to the list.

pilot   teacher   surgeon   electrician

34

Workbook, page 37

SPEAKING My sister thinks …

>>> Present other people's opinions

SPEAK

1 Work in pairs. Complete the tasks.
1. Individually, write down the names of your top five favourite singers or groups.
2. Compare each other's lists. How many names appear on both lists?
3. What do you think of the other singers or groups on your partner's list?

WATCH OR LISTEN

2 ▶1.41 Watch or listen to the scene. What does Veena want to ask Finn's sister?

Veena:	What do you think?
Finn:	My sister thinks they're great. She's got all their (1) _____ .
Veena:	You're lucky. My sister really hates them.
Finn:	Why?
Veena:	She says they can't sing. She says they're rubbish.
Finn:	Oh, right. A lot of people didn't like their last (2) _____ .
Veena:	People are always saying bad things about them.
Finn:	Maybe they're right. My brother says they don't play their (3) _____ .
Veena:	I don't care what other people think. I think they're totally amazing.
Finn:	Good.
Veena:	So what's your opinion?
Finn:	Sorry?
Veena:	You've told me what everyone else thinks. What about you? What do you think?
Finn:	Honestly? I don't have an opinion.
Veena:	Liar. I'll have to ask your (4) _____ .

3 ▶1.41 Can you remember the missing words? Watch or listen again to check or complete your answers.

4 ▶1.42 Listen and repeat. Pay attention to which words are stressed.
1. My sister thinks they're great.
2. My sister really hates them.
3. She says they can't sing.
4. She says they're rubbish.
5. People are always saying …
6. My brother says …

5 Work in pairs. Answer the questions.
1. What do you think Finn really thinks of the music?
2. Why doesn't he tell Veena?
3. What do you think Finn's sister will say?

ACT

6 Work in groups of three or four. Complete the tasks.
– Talk about things you like (music, films, sport, etc). Find something you have different opinions about.
– Prepare a scene similar to the one in Exercise 2. Talk about your different opinions and include other people's opinions (classmates, friends, family …).
– Present your scene to another group.

PHRASEBOOK ▶1.43

Asking for and giving opinions

What do you think (of …)?
What's your opinion?
I think they're great/amazing.
I don't care what other people think.
I don't have an opinion.

Presenting other people's opinions

My sister/brother thinks/says …
My sister really likes/hates …
She says they …
A lot of people …
People are always saying …

Workbook, page 35

WRITING My music profile

Link contrasting ideas

SPEAK AND READ

1. Work in pairs. Look at the man in the photo. What kind of music do you think he plays?

PHRASE BYTES
He looks like a …
I think he plays pop/jazz …

2. Read the music profile to check your answer to Exercise 1.

I LOVE ROCK MUSIC. However, my music hero is Lang Lang, the Chinese pianist. He grew up in a poor area of Beijing and started playing when he was three years old. His parents thought he would become a famous pianist, but his piano teacher told him he had no talent and should stop playing.

Although his family didn't have much money, they continued to support Lang Lang. He practised night and day and by the age of 17, he was a star. Since then he has performed at concerts around the world.

Even though he's a successful classical pianist, some people don't like his playing. Everyone has different ideas about music, of course. In my opinion, however, he's a great player. He also encourages young people to make music.

3. a Read the tips in the HOW TO box.

HOW TO
link contrasting ideas

- Use *but* to join two parts of a sentence.
- Use *although* and *even though* at the beginning of a two-part sentence.
- Use *however* at the beginning, the middle or the end of a contrasting sentence.

b Underline five examples of contrasting ideas in the profile. Which linking word appears twice?

PRACTISE

4. Link the sentences using the words in brackets.
   1. Lang Lang's teacher said he had no talent. He managed to become successful. (although)
   2. He grew up in China. When he was 15, he moved to the United States. (however)
   3. He normally records classical music. He has also recorded music for video games. (but)
   4. He lives a rock star's life. He finds time to help young people play music. (even though)

PLAN

5. You're going to write a profile of your music hero. Make a plan for your profile.

WRITING PLAN

1. **Write about the musician's life.**
   Where and when was the person born?
   How did they become interested in music?
   When did they become famous?

2. **Give your own opinion.**
   When did you first hear the musician?
   Why do you think the musician is special?

3. **Include the opinion of others.**
   What do other people think of your hero?
   Use phrases from the HOW TO box.

WRITE AND CHECK

6. Use your plan and write your profile. Then check it. Tick (✓) the things in the plan.

SHARE

7. Swap your profile with other students. Say how they are different.

Workbook, pages 36–37

UNIT REVIEW 3

VOCABULARY Music words

1 Complete the poster with the words in the box.

audience   bands   brass band   conductor   flute   folk
jazz   opera   orchestra   performance   trumpet   venue

TONIGHT! Be part of the (1) _____ at the world's most exciting music (2) _____ and enjoy tonight's concert by international superstar – Justin!

January 9
For one night only! A (3) _____ of *Cosi Fan Tutte*, possibly Wolfgang Amadeus Mozart's most famous (4) _____. With the Chicago Symphony (5) _____ and guest (6) _____, José Angel Salazar.

March 5
A night of (7) _____ music, celebrating the music of one of the world's greatest (8) _____ players, Miles Davis.

May 8
Traditional (9) _____ music from England, Scotland and Wales. Sing along to the old songs and listen to Mary Martyn play the (10) _____.

June 23 & 24
The annual International (11) _____ competition is back! Come and listen to (12) _____ from 12 different countries compete to win this year's prize.

___ /12

Adverbs of degree

2 Complete the quotes by members of the audience after Justin's concert.

'It was a (1) r_____ great concert.'
'It was a (2) b_____ boring at the beginning, but it got a (3) l_____ better.'
'His band was (4) t_____ amazing! And they all look (5) p_____ cool.'
'I'm (6) e_____ happy that I came.'
'It wasn't (7) v_____ good. I thought Justin gave a (8) t_____ bad performance.'
'I was (9) i_____ lucky to get a ticket. I still can't (10) q_____ believe it.'

___ /10

GRAMMAR Verbs followed by -ing form or to + infinitive

3 Complete the interview with the -ing form or the infinitive with to form of the verbs.

Interviewer: Are you feeling nervous about the concert?
Justin: No. I love (1) _____ (come) to your country. I always enjoy (2) _____ (play) here.
Interviewer: Can you tell us about your new album? Is it finished?
Justin: Not yet. We hope (3) _____ (finish) the album this summer.
Interviewer: Do you prefer (4) _____ (work) in the studio or (5) _____ (play) live?
Justin: I really love (6) _____ (perform). I like (7) _____ (be) with the fans. I'd like (8) _____ (spend) my whole life on stage.

___ /16

Comparison of adverbs

4 Complete the news story about Justin's concert with the correct form of the adverbs. Add *as* where necessary.

What has happened to superstar Justin? Two years ago his records sold (1) _____ (fast) than any other pop star. He was the star who worked (2) _____ (hard). But at last night's concert he didn't play (3) _____ (well) as he did in the past. In fact, he wanted to get off stage (4) _____ (quickly) as possible. His fans have waited (5) _____ (long) than two years for a new album. If you can hear me, Justin – try (6) _____ (hard) next time!

___ /12

Your score: ___ /50

SKILLS CHECK

✓✓✓	Yes, I can. No problem!
✓✓	Yes, I can. But I need a bit of help.
✓	Yes, I can. But I need a lot of help.

I can understand new words when I read. _____
I can transfer spoken information to a table. _____
I can stay on task and avoid distractions. _____
I can present other people's opinions. _____
I can link contrasting ideas when I write. _____

Workbook, pages 38–39

UNIT 4 VERY IMPORTANT PEOPLE

IN THE PICTURE Relationships

>>> Talk about people you know

WORK WITH WORDS

1 **RECALL** Work in pairs. Do the tasks. You have three minutes.

   a Complete the answers with the words in the box.

   | a small nose   bad-tempered   patient   shy   tall   wavy hair |

   What's she like?
   She's _____ / _____ / _____ .

   What does she look like?
   She's _____ . And she's got _____ / _____ .

   b Make a list of four other ways to complete each answer.

2 Work in pairs. Take it in turns to describe a person in the photos on the relationship tree. Can your partner identify the person?

3 ▶1.44 Listen and match the relationship words to the twelve definitions that you hear.
   ___ acquaintance   ___ boyfriend/girlfriend   ___ classmate   _1_ close friend
   ___ enemy   ___ friend of a friend   ___ guest   ___ neighbour   ___ old friend
   ___ online friend   ___ relative   ___ teammate

4 ▶1.45 Listen and check. Then listen again and repeat the words.

5 ▶1.46 Louise is talking about people on her relationship tree. Listen and write a relationship from Exercise 3 next to the names. Note their personality too if you hear it.

Name	Relationship	Personality	Photo
Mel			
Nicola			
Jack			
Matt			
Donna			

6 ▶1.46 Listen again and match the people to some of the photos in the relationship tree.

7 **THE MOVING PICTURE** ▶ Watch the video of Veena making a relationship tree. Make a note of the names of the people and their relationship with her.

38

SPEAK

8 a Draw your own relationship tree and write the names of at least six people on the leaves. Include people you know very well but also acquaintances or relatives you don't know well.

b 🗨 Work in pairs. Ask and answer questions about the people on your relationship tree.

GO BEYOND

Do the Words & Beyond exercise on page 133.

PHRASE BYTES

Who's this boy/girl with the green eyes / in the blue T-shirt?

His/Her name's … He/She's a classmate / an online friend …

We met … years ago in/at …

We've known each other since/for …

We keep in touch online / by email …

Workbook, page 40

39

READING Close friends

>>> Recognise examples

SPEAK AND READ

1 Work in pairs. Answer the questions.
   1 What's your definition of a close friend?
   2 How many close friends do you think people generally have?

2 ▶1.47 Read the article. Match the qualities of a close friendship in the box to the headings (1–5). Also find out how many close friends we have.

| Good company   Honesty   Respect   Support   Trust |

Best of friends?

How many friends have you got?

The answer, of course, depends on how you define 'friend'. For instance, if you count everybody you know – relatives, classmates, neighbours and other acquaintances – the answer could easily be 20, 30, 40 or more. And if you include people you don't usually meet, like online friends, you might have hundreds or even thousands of friends. But what about *close* friends? According to a recent survey, we have fewer close friends than you might think. (Read to the end to find out how many.)

So how can you know who your close friends are?
As a general rule, a close friendship should have all of these qualities.

1 _____ A close friendship won't survive unless this quality is present. It means that you accept your close friends the way they are and don't want them to change.

2 _____ We all want to hear nice things about ourselves. But if it's necessary, a really good friend will also tell you things you *don't* want to hear, such as pointing out your mistakes.

3 _____ Close friends are generous with their time. They will listen patiently if you need to talk and will help if you have a problem. They will also defend you if other people are giving you a hard time.

4 _____ A close friend is somebody you can share your ideas with. You may not have things like hobbies and interests in common, but your friend will always take an interest in what you do.

5 _____ This is perhaps the most important quality of all. If you tell your friend private information, they won't tell anybody else about it. And they won't talk about you behind your back.

(Oh, and the survey says we have just two close friends.)

3 a Read the tips in the **HOW TO** box.

   b Underline four words or phrases in the article that come before examples.

   c Under two of the headings, the first sentence is an example. Which sections?

4 Which tips in the **HOW TO** box did you use for help with Exercises 3b and 3c? Tick (✓) them.

REACT

5 Work in pairs. What do you think? Tell your partner.
   1 Are you surprised that we generally have only two close friends? Why?/Why not?
   2 Which two qualities in the article are the most important in a close friendship? Why?

HOW TO
recognise examples

☐ Look at the words after *like* and *such as* in the middle of sentences.

☐ Look at the words after *For example* and *For instance* at the start of sentences.

☐ Look under headings. The first sentence is sometimes an example.

GO BEYOND

Think of one more quality of a close friendship. Then write two sentences to explain what the quality is and why it's important.

40

>>> Workbook, page 41

GRAMMAR First conditional with *if/unless*

>>> Talk about possible situations in the future

READ AND LISTEN >>> Grammar in context

1 ▶1.48 Read and listen to the conversation. Who does Olga want at her birthday barbecue?

Jay: Are you going to invite Tim to your birthday barbecue?
Olga: I don't know. If I invite Tim, he'll probably argue with Bren. But Bea won't come unless I invite Tim. And what will Tim say if I don't invite him? He's one of my oldest friends.
Jay: If you talk to Tim and Bren, they might stop arguing for one day.
Olga: You're right. I'd really like all three to be there.

STUDY

2 Complete the explanations with examples from the conversation in Exercise 1.

First conditional with *if/unless*

Use:
To talk about possible situations in the future and their results.

Form:
If + *I/you*, etc + present simple ... (= the action)
_____ to Tim and Bren,
... *I/you*, etc + *will/may/might* + infinitive (= the result)
_____ for one day.

unless
unless + positive verb means *if ... not*:
Bea won't come unless I _____ Tim.
= Bea won't come if I don't invite Tim.

See GRAMMAR DATABASE, page 123.

PRACTISE

3 Complete the second sentence so that it means the same as the first. Use no more than three words. (Contractions count as one word.)

1. I won't enjoy the barbecue if Sabrina doesn't come.
   Unless Sabrina comes, I won't enjoy the barbecue.
2. Unless you send invitations, people won't remember when it is.
   If _____ invitations, people won't remember when it is.
3. Vasily won't come unless he can bring his girlfriend.
   Vasily won't come _____ bring his girlfriend.
4. If you don't invite the neighbours, they may complain about the noise.
   _____ the neighbours, they may complain about the noise.
5. My parents won't let me have another barbecue if we don't clean up afterwards.
   My parents won't let me have another barbecue _____ up afterwards.
6. I might not have time to tidy up unless people help me.
   I might not have time to tidy up _____ help me.

4 ▶1.49 Choose the correct options to complete the conversation. Then listen and check.

Olga: I'm going to invite Bren to my barbecue.
Tim: I (1) *don't / won't* come if he (2) *'s / 'll be* there. He told lies about me.
Olga: If he (3) *says / 'll say* sorry, (4) *do / will* you change your mind?
Tim: But he won't.
Olga: He (5) *says / might say* sorry if he thinks you (6) *stop / 'll stop* being so angry.
Tim: I've got a good reason to be angry.
Olga: Yes, but unless you (7) *'re / 'll be* more friendly, people (8) *stop / will stop* talking to you. And not just Bren.
Tim: OK, you're right. I'll talk to him.

WRITE AND SPEAK

5 Complete the sentences about friends and other relationships with your ideas.

1. If you forget a good friend's birthday, ...
2. You won't have many good friends unless ...
3. Unless you make mistakes ...
4. If you're always honest, ...
5. People will respect you if ...

6 Work in pairs. Compare your sentences in Exercise 5. Do you agree with your partner's sentences? If not, explain why.

Workbook, pages 42–43

41

LISTENING AND VOCABULARY Back from the future

>>> Use stress and intonation to help you understand

SPEAK AND LISTEN

1 **Work in pairs. Look at the picture and answer the questions.**
   1 Describe the situation. What do you notice about the face in the mirror?
   2 The picture represents a story. What do you think happened?

2 a **Read the tips in the HOW TO box.**

   b ▶1.50 **Listen to a podcast. Were your predictions in Exercise 1 correct?**

3 **Which tips in the HOW TO box did you use for help with Exercise 2b? Tick (✓) them.**

4 ▶1.50 **Listen again and choose the correct options.**
   1 The story *is / isn't* true.
   2 Naomi *heard / didn't hear* another person's voice.
   3 She *recognised / didn't recognise* the face in the mirror.
   4 She was suffering from *a common / an unusual* condition.
   5 She *still remembered / didn't remember* that she had a child.
   6 Her memory came back *slowly / quickly*.

HOW TO
use stress and intonation to help you understand

☐ People stress the most important words when they speak. Listen for stressed words.

☐ When people express strong feelings, their voice goes up and down more. Listen for these changes.

WORK WITH WORDS

5 **Match the underlined 'extreme' adjectives in the podcast extracts (1–10) to the definitions.**

   1 … <u>amazing</u> real stories.   very good or surprising
   2 I'd be <u>furious</u>!   very interesting
   3 … she was <u>shocked</u> …   very surprised (in a negative way)
   4 … she looked <u>ancient</u> …   very angry
   5 She looked <u>exhausted</u> …   very old
   6 … with <u>huge</u> black bags under her eyes.   very bad
   7 That's <u>awful</u>.   very frightened
   8 I'd be <u>terrified</u>.   very tired
   9 That's <u>unbelievable</u>!   very big
   10 That really is a <u>fascinating</u> story.   very difficult to believe

   Get it right
   Don't use *very* before extreme adjectives. Use *really* or an extreme adverb of degree: *totally / completely / absolutely amazing*.

6 ▶1.51 **Listen and repeat the adjectives from Exercise 5.**

7 a **Choose three adjectives from Exercise 5 and write a true sentence for each one.**

   b **Work in pairs. Take it in turns to read your sentences to each other. Ask your partner at least one question about each sentence.**

   > I was furious with my little sister on Thursday.

   > Why? What did she do?

   > She broke my games console.

REACT

8 **Imagine that you wake in the morning and you're 34 years old. Work in pairs. Answer the questions.**
   1 Where are you? Describe the room and the house.
   2 How do you feel?
   3 You look in the mirror. What do you look like? How do you feel now?

GO BEYOND
Do the Words & Beyond exercise on page 133.

GRAMMAR Second conditional

>>> Talk about imaginary situations in the present and future

READ AND LISTEN >>> Grammar in context

1 ▶1.52 Read and listen to the conversation. What type of parents do Raj and Kim think they might be?

Raj: It's a shame you couldn't come to the film. It was terrifying!
Kim: You know my parents. If I **had** kids, I **wouldn't be** so strict. **I'd be** much more easy-going.
Raj: I'm not so sure.
Kim: So what about you? What **would** you **be** like if you **were** a parent?
Raj: If I **was** a dad, **I'd be** quite strict, I think. It's a big responsibility!

STUDY

2 Complete the explanations. Use the words in orange in Exercise 1 to help you.

Second conditional

Use:
To talk about unlikely or imaginary situations in the present or future and their results.

Form:
If + past simple, ... would/_____ + infinitive
The contracted form of *would* is _____.

Questions and short answers
_____ + I/you, etc + infinitive + if + past simple
Yes, I would. / No, she wouldn't.

See GRAMMAR DATABASE, page 123.

PRACTISE

3 Match the two parts of the sentences.
1. If I was a parent, *d*
2. My kids would have to do housework
3. I wouldn't let my kids have a house party
4. If their friends invited them to go on holiday,
5. They couldn't go out at night
6. If we went shopping,

a. I wouldn't let them choose their clothes.
b. if they wanted pocket money.
c. unless they came home before 10pm.
d. I'd be very strict.
e. unless I was there.
f. I'd tell them they couldn't go.

4 Are the sentences in Exercise 3 true for you? If not, change them to make them true.

5 Complete the sentences with the correct form of the verbs.
1. If I _____ (wake) up with superpowers, I'd fly round the world.
2. I _____ (live) in Japan if I could study in another country.
3. If I _____ (have) a special talent, I'd want to be an amazing singer.
4. I _____ (spend) the extra day relaxing if there _____ (be) eight days in a week.
5. If I _____ (can) travel back in time for a day, I _____ (go) back to the time of the dinosaurs.
6. My family _____ (give) the money to charity if we _____ (win) the lottery.

6 Write questions for the sentences in Exercise 5.
1. If you ... , what / do? *If you woke up with superpowers, what would you do?*
2. Where / live if ... ?
3. If you ... , what / want to be?
4. What / do on the extra day if ... ?
5. If you ... , where / go?
6. What / your family / do if ... ?

7 a ▶1.53 **PRONOUNCE** Second conditional sentences often have two stressed words or phrases in each part. Listen and underline the stressed words or phrases.

A: If you woke up with superpowers, what would you do?
B: I'd fly round the world.
C: I wouldn't do anything. I'd go back to sleep.

b ▶1.54 Listen again and repeat the sentences, paying attention to their rhythm.

SPEAK

8 Work in pairs. Ask and answer the questions in Exercise 6. Give reasons for your answers.

Workbook, page 46

43

LANGUAGE & BEYOND

What's really important?

Do the activities to find out what's really important to you.
Name and age: *Claire Tate, aged 15*

Activity 1
Write two options for each question and a short explanation of your choices.

1 If you won a six-day Caribbean cruise for two, who would you take with you?
   A: *I'd take my best friend Lola. We never stop talking when we're together!*
   B: *I'd take my sister, because she'd be unhappy if I didn't.*

2 If your house was on fire and you could only take one thing, what would you take?
   A: *I'd take my violin, because it's really old and valuable.*
   B: *I'd take my tablet, because it's got all my photos and music on it.*

3 If you could do whatever you wanted with your time tomorrow, what would you do?
   A: *I'd tidy up my room. It's in a real mess, and I can never find anything.*
   B: *I'd do nothing at all, just sit and read. I love reading!*

Activity 2
Quickly choose one of your options. Don't think too much – choose the option that feels better to you.

>>> **Decide what's important to you**

SPEAK AND READ

1 Read Claire's answers on the activity sheet. What do you think she's like? Choose two adjectives and then compare with a partner.

| bad-tempered | clever | creative | friendly | kind | patient | shy | serious |

2 Work in pairs. Talk about Claire's answers. Which options do you think she'll choose in Activity 2? Explain why.

DO

3 Do Activity 1 on the activity sheet.

4 Do Activity 2. Don't take longer than 30 seconds.

5 Work in pairs. Explain your choices to your partner. After speaking, are there any choices you'd like to change?

REFLECT

6 Discuss the questions with your class. Do you agree with the **REFLECTION POINT**?
   1 What area of life is each question in Activity 1 about?
   2 Did you find it difficult to choose just one alternative in Activity 2? Why?/Why not?
   3 Why is it sometimes difficult to make the choices we want?

EXTEND

7 Repeat Exercises 3, 4 and 5 for these questions. What do your answers tell you about you and your plans for the future?
   1 If you had to choose just three school subjects to continue studying, which ones would you choose?
   2 If you could decide now what job you'll do in the future, what job would it be?

KNOW YOURSELF

PHRASE BYTES

I think she'll take … with her because …

I (don't) agree. I reckon she'll take … in the end because …

I think she'll try to save her … from the fire because …

But if she saved her … she'd / she wouldn't …

If she had the choice, I think she'd prefer to …

REFLECTION POINT
It's good to know what's important to you in different areas of your life. It can help you decide what you really want to do and not what you think you should do.

Workbook, page 49

SPEAKING Do you mind?

>>> Make and react to requests

SPEAK

1 Work in pairs. Look at the situations. Who would you talk to? What would they say?
   1 You need somebody to drive you somewhere.
   2 You need to borrow some money.
   3 You need to phone somebody but don't have your mobile.

WATCH OR LISTEN

2 ▶ 1.55 Watch or listen to the scene. Who does Leo talk to in each situation? Who says 'no' to his requests?

Leo:	Dad, can you drive me to the festival?
Dad:	All right. But you'll have to wait 20 minutes.
Leo:	No problem. Can we (1) _____ Jack too?
Dad:	OK.
Leo:	Thanks. And can you come and get me later?
Dad:	Sorry, I can't. Mum needs the car tonight.
Leo:	Jack, could you (2) _____ me some money for a drink?
Jack:	Sure.
Leo:	And do you mind if I (3) _____ your phone to call Kate?
Jack:	No, go ahead.
Leo:	Thanks.
Leo:	Mr Giggs, could I (4) _____ you a favour?
Mr Giggs:	Of course.
Leo:	Would you (5) _____ me home, please? My dad can't come and get me, and I think I've missed the last bus.
Mr Giggs:	I'm sorry, but there's no space in the car.
Leo:	OK. Would you mind if I (6) _____ your phone to call my mother?
Mr Giggs:	No, of course not. Here you are.
Leo:	Thank you.

3 ▶ 1.55 Complete the conversations with the verbs in the box. Then watch or listen again to check.

ask   drive   lend   take   use   used

4 Choose the best option or options for formal situations (with people you don't know very well). Use the conversations to help you.
   1 Use *Could* / *Can* / *Would* you … ?
   2 *Say* / *Don't say* 'please' and 'thank you'.
   3 Use *Do* / *Would* you mind if … ?
   4 Accept a request with *Of course* / *Sure*.
   5 Refuse a request with *Sorry, I can't.* / *I'm afraid …*

5 ▶ 1.56 Watch or listen again and repeat the requests and the reactions.

ACT

6 🔲 Work in pairs. Prepare a conversation for each situation below. Make one formal and the other informal. Then present your conversations to another pair. Can they guess who's talking?
   1 You want to change channels and watch a different TV programme.
   2 You want someone to check your English homework.

>>> Workbook, page 47

PHRASEBOOK ▶ 1.57

Make and react to requests

Can/Could I borrow/use … , please?

Can/Could you lend me / take … , please?

Would you drive/phone … , please?

✓ OK. / All right.
   Sure.
   Of course.

✗ Sorry, I can't.
   I'm afraid …

Do you mind if I use/borrow … ?

Would you mind if I used/borrowed … ?

✓ No, go ahead.
   Not at all.

✗ I'm afraid …

45

WRITING A poem about true friends

>>> Use a dictionary

SPEAK AND READ

1 Work in pairs. Answer the questions.
1. Do you ever read poems? If so, what type of poems do you like? If not, why not?
2. Have you ever written a poem? If so, what was it about?

2 Read the poem about friends and answer the questions.
1. Which lines do you agree with? Tick (✓) them.
2. Do you like the poem? Why?/Why not?

Best Friends

True friends accept you how you are
And don't try to change you
They'll help you through the difficult times
And they'll share the good times with you
If you want to talk, they'll be there
But if you need some space, they'll understand
And even if you had a row
And said 'I never want to see you again!'
You know you'd miss them if they left
They're like your sister or your brother
You'd do anything for each other
And that's because you're best friends

3 a Read the tips in the HOW TO box.

HOW TO
use a dictionary

- Use a bilingual dictionary to translate words. Use a monolingual dictionary to see definitions in English.
- Look for the correct type of word: noun, verb, adjective, etc.
- Make sure you choose the correct translation or definition if there is more than one. Look at the examples.
- Read the phonetic transcription to see how you pronounce the word.

b Read the poem again and answer the questions.
1. Circle words in the poem that are new for you. Are they nouns, verbs, adjectives or another type of word?
2. Two of the lines rhyme. Which ones?

PRACTISE

4 Use the dictionary entry and the tips in the HOW TO box to help you answer the questions about the word *row* in the poem.
1. What type of word is *row* in the poem?
2. Which definition of *row* in the dictionary is the correct one? Tick (✓) it.
3. Does this meaning of *row* rhyme with *now* or with *know*?

☐ **row** /rəʊ/ noun [C]
a series of people or things arranged in a straight line: *The teacher stopped in front of a little boy in the front row.*

☐ **row** /rəʊ/ verb
to move a boat through the water using long poles with flat ends: *We rowed past the harbour.*

☐ **row** /raʊ/ noun [C]
a noisy argument: *Dave left angrily after a row.*

PLAN

5 You are going to write a poem about your friends, like the example in Exercise 2. Start each line of your poem with the phrase in green used in Exercise 2. For example, start line 1 with *True friends*. Make a plan for your poem.

WRITING PLAN

1. **Decide what you want to say.**
   Write your ideas for each line. ☐
2. **Decide if you want your poem to rhyme.**
   Think about which words in your poem are going to rhyme (or not). ☐
3. **Find new words.**
   Use a dictionary to help you find new words. Check the pronunciation of words that need to rhyme. ☐
4. **Complete the lines in the poem.**
   Now try to finish each line (1–12) of your poem. ☐
5. **Give your poem a title.**
   The title could be part of one of your lines. ☐

WRITE AND CHECK

6 Use your plan and write your poem. Then check it. Tick (✓) the things in the plan.

SHARE

7 Swap your poem with a partner. Do you like the poem(s) you read? Why?/Why not?

>>> Workbook, pages 48–49

UNIT REVIEW 4

VOCABULARY People and relationships

1 Match the people and relationships on the notice to the definitions.

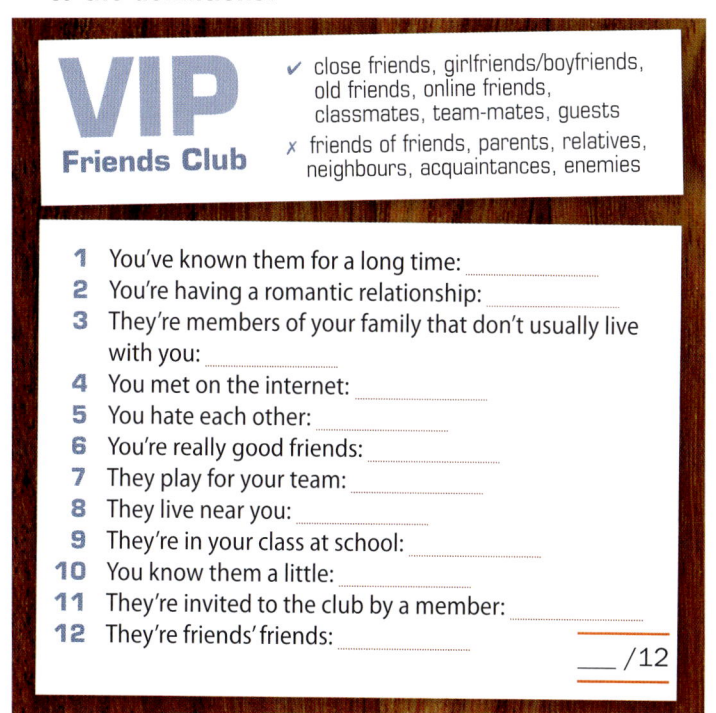

VIP Friends Club
✓ close friends, girlfriends/boyfriends, old friends, online friends, classmates, team-mates, guests
✗ friends of friends, parents, relatives, neighbours, acquaintances, enemies

1 You've known them for a long time: _____
2 You're having a romantic relationship: _____
3 They're members of your family that don't usually live with you: _____
4 You met on the internet: _____
5 You hate each other: _____
6 You're really good friends: _____
7 They play for your team: _____
8 They live near you: _____
9 They're in your class at school: _____
10 You know them a little: _____
11 They're invited to the club by a member: _____
12 They're friends' friends: _____

___ /12

Extreme adjectives

2 Complete the adjectives in the description of the picture.

Harry   Farah   Eric   Amy

Harry's (1) h_____e and although he's only 16, he looks (2) a_____t. He's (3) t_____d of Farah. She gets (4) f_____s, and her face goes bright red when he doesn't show enough interest in her (5) f_____g stories. Eric's always (6) e_____d from laughing so much at his own jokes and is (7) s_____d when we tell him how (8) a_____l they are. (They really are terrible!) And Amy's got (9) a_____g white teeth and she always has the most (10) u_____e hairstyles. They're my best friends, and I love them!

___ /10

GRAMMAR First conditional with *if/unless*

3 Complete the club rules with the first conditional form of the verbs.

RULES VIP Friends Club

1 If I (1) _____ (become) a member, I (2) _____ (not repeat) what I hear in the club.
2 I (3) _____ (not bring) a friend if another member (4) _____ (not want) them in the club.
3 Unless I (5) _____ (break) the club rules, I (6) _____ (be) a club member for the rest of my life.
4 Members always help each other.

___ /12

Second conditional

4 Choose the correct options to complete the interview.

Erin: If someone (1) *asked / would ask* you about the club, what would you say?
Matt: I (2) *said / 'd say* that the club's activities were secret.
Erin: OK. And what (3) *did / would* you do if a friend of yours (4) *wanted / would want* to come to the club?
Matt: I (5) *didn't / wouldn't* bring them unless the other members (6) *gave / would give* me permission first.
Erin: Good. And what if another member needed help?
Matt: I'd help them. And if I (7) *couldn't / wouldn't* help, I (8) *found / 'd find* someone who could.
Erin: Excellent! Welcome to the club!

___ /16

Your score: ___ /50

SKILLS CHECK

✓✓✓ Yes, I can. No problem!
✓✓ Yes, I can. But I need a bit of help.
✓ Yes, I can. But I need a lot of help.

I can recognise examples. _____
I can use stress and intonation to help me understand. _____
I can decide what's important to me. _____
I can make and react to requests. _____
I can use a dictionary. _____

Workbook, pages 50–51

47

PROGRESS CHECK

READ

1 You want to buy a music album as a present for the following people. Read the album reviews and decide which album would be most suitable for each person.

1. Kylie downloads a lot of songs to listen to on the move. She's a big fan of pop music, especially songs and artists currently in the music charts.

2. Danny is Kylie's boyfriend, but they have very different tastes in music. Although he likes some pop music, Danny much prefers American rock or British folk music.

3. Holly doesn't buy much music. She prefers going to The Basement, a local venue for new bands. She enjoys discovering new music, but it has to be rock.

4. Hiro wants to be a conductor. He loves listening to classical music at home. He often plays music loudly and pretends to conduct an orchestra.

5. Max really likes traditional jazz. He mostly listens to jazz music from the 1940s and 50s. He likes jazz singers and isn't fond of contemporary jazz music.

EXAM TIPS

do a matching exercise (people and texts)
- Read all the texts carefully.
- In the people profiles, underline important words or phrases.
- In the reviews, look for ideas that match the important words.
- Make sure <u>all</u> the information about the people matches the review.

understand new words
See page 30

recognise examples
See page 40

This week's album reviews

A Room for More
If you enjoy listening to traditional jazz music, such as Louis Armstrong, then this isn't the album for you. If, however, you like extremely loud and incredibly fast modern jazz music, then you'll love this new CD from trumpeter Lilo Watts. It's not easy to listen to, but it is fascinating.

B Ancient Monsters
If I had to pick the best pop album of the year, this would be my last choice. These pop superstars may have been the greatest thing on the planet in prehistoric times but not anymore. The album title says it all. It's awful!

C The Brass Ring
Although I like classical music, I'm not a huge fan of opera or brass bands. So I didn't expect to enjoy this album. But the brass band's performance of extracts from Wagner's *Ring* is surprisingly good, and I didn't miss the orchestra or the singers.

D Step Back
Surprisingly, the new album from boy band OneStep is even better than last year's debut album. It includes this week's number one hit 'New Acquaintance'. The members of this Liverpool band are performing more confidently all the time. It looks as if they're here to stay.

E Undercover
This week's top choice is a live recording by new British band Classmates. Listen to the audience reaction to the performance! If the band continues producing amazing rock music like this, Classmates will be together for a long, long time.

F Moonrise
I don't normally enjoy classic songs from the big-band era like 'What a Wonderful World', but this collection of rare performances by well-known jazz vocalists is unbelievably good. You'll love it – unless your heart is made of stone (or rock!).

G Double H
If you decide to buy just one album this year, make it this one. In the past I've been pretty rude about traditional English folk music such as last year's *Arthur*. However, Beth Hands has transformed the genre and sings beautifully on this album.

H The Essential Collection V
Even though the composer of the music on this album was born almost 250 years ago, his compositions still sound totally fresh and exciting today. I was exhausted after listening to this collection of greatest hits from his symphonies. Inspiring.

Reading: _____ /10

48

PROGRESS CHECK 3&4

LISTEN

2 ▶1.58 **You will hear a guest on a radio programme talking about her work on a magazine. Tick (✓) the correct box for each question.**

1 Belinda Vine …
   A helps people with their problems.
   B writes letters for a problem page.
   C tells people how to be happy.
2 Belinda thinks we can see problems more clearly …
   A in a magazine.
   B if we write them down.
   C when we talk to our friends.
3 Kate has a problem with her …
   A classmates.
   B parents.
   C best friend.
4 If Belinda answered Kate's message, first she'd …
   A suggest giving her friend space.
   B ask some questions.
   C tell her to do something else.
5 Belinda has given advice to teens …
   A since the magazine first appeared.
   B for more than 10 years.
   C all around the world.

Listening: _____ /10

EXAM TIPS

answer multiple choice questions

- Read the rubric. What are you going to hear?
- Read the questions and choices. Underline important words.
- Listen. Decide which choices are not possible.
- Listen again. Choose the best of the possible options.

use stress and intonation to help you understand
See page 42

WRITE

3 **Read part of a letter from your aunt who lives on the other side of the world.**

> It's been so long since I saw you. Write and tell me about yourself. What do you like doing? Who are your friends? Are you studying hard?

Now write a letter, answering your aunt's questions.
Write 90–100 words.

Writing: _____ /10

Progress check score _____ /30

EXAM TIPS

reply to a letter

- Read the task. Who are you writing to?
- Read the letter and underline the points to include.
- Plan your letter before you write.
- Include phrases to start and end your letter.

link contrasting ideas
See page 36

use a dictionary
See page 46

Download extra speaking activities from www.macmillanbeyond.com

UNIT 5 FIVE SENSES

IN THE PICTURE Can you feel it?

>>> Talk about how we use our senses

WORK WITH WORDS

1 **RECALL** Work in pairs. Do the tasks. You have three minutes.

   a Write down the letters of the alphabet. Write the names of parts of the body for as many letters as you can.
   Use the photos to help you.

   b Which of the words can you match to the five icons in Exercise 2a?

2 a Write the names of the five senses next to the correct icons.

   | hearing | sight | smell | taste | touch |

1	2	3	4	5
eye	ear	hand	nose	mouth

   b ▶2.01 Listen and check. Then listen and repeat.

3 a Match the verbs to the five senses. Write them in the table in Exercise 2a.

   | feel | hear | listen | look | see | sound | touch | watch |

   b Which of the sense words in Exercise 2 can also be verbs?

   c ▶2.02 Listen and check. Then listen and repeat the verbs.

4 ▶2.03 Listen and match sentences 1–10 to the photos a–e.

5 ▶2.04 Complete the sentences with the correct form of the verbs in Exercise 3. Listen and check.

   1 It's so good not wearing shoes. The grass _____ so soft under my feet.
   2 There's so much traffic. Everything _____ so noisy here.
   3 'What do you think of this one?' 'Wow! That _____ fantastic.'
   4 There's so much to _____ in the city. It's huge.
   5 It's so hot here, and that water _____ so cool.
   6 I like Mexican food. This _____ really good.
   7 I can't _____ anything apart from amazing music.
   8 Sometimes I lie on the grass and imagine I can _____ the clouds in the sky.
   9 I love _____ the sea. It's so blue under the sky.
   10 I like _____ to music while I walk. It's relaxing.

6 a ▶2.05 **PRONOUNCE** Listen to the consonants in blue in the words below. Then listen and repeat.
   smell   taste   sound   watch   strong   grass   text message   sky   hand   soft

  b Do you find any of the consonant combinations difficult? Which ones? If so, practise saying the consonants slowly.
   ssssssssmmmmellllll

7 **THE MOVING PICTURE** ▶ Watch the video and imagine you are in each scene. Say something using the sense verbs.

8 Some sense verbs can also be nouns. Choose the correct nouns for these sentences.
   1 I like the *smell / sound* of fresh bread. It reminds me of home.
   2 I hate the *taste / sound* of motorbikes. They're so noisy.
   3 I really like the *look / taste* of honey. It's sweet.
   4 I don't like the *look / smell* of this homework. It's really difficult.

SPEAK

9 Work in pairs. Write the names of things you love or hate. Tell your partner.
   1 I *love / hate* the smell of _____ .
   2 I *love / hate* the taste of _____ .
   3 I *love / hate* the sound of _____ .
   4 I *love / hate* the look of _____ .

GO BEYOND
Do the Words & Beyond exercise on page 134.

Workbook, page 52

READING Fragrance fact file

>>> Use pictures to help you understand

SPEAK AND READ

1 **Work in pairs. Answer the questions.**
  1 Which perfumes and fragrances can you name?
  2 What different types of products use fragrances?

2 a **Read the tips in the HOW TO box.**

  b **Before you read, look at the text and pictures, and answer the questions.**
  1 Where do you think the text comes from – an encyclopaedia, a magazine or a history book?
  2 What is it about?
  3 What information do you think it includes?

HOW TO
use pictures to help you understand

- <u>Before</u> you read, look at any pictures or other visuals.
- Think about the connection between the pictures, the title, the topic and the style of text (news story, manual ...).
- Look at the visuals <u>when</u> you read. They can help you understand new words.

9 things you should know about FRAGRANCES

1. The world's first chemist was a woman called Tapputi, who made perfumes in Mesopotamia in the 2nd millennium BC.

2. The word 'perfume' comes from the Latin *per fumum* which means 'through smoke'. The first form of perfume was incense. It was produced from burning wood or plants and was used in religious ceremonies.

3. Ancient Egyptians and Romans created the first liquid perfumes using water and oils. In Rome, perfume was used by both women and men on their bodies and in their houses.

4. Today, perfumes are often called fragrances. A new fragrance appears almost every day, and many of them are promoted by celebrities.

5. When you buy a fragrance, the cheapest thing you are buying is the actual fragrance. The bottle and the box cost more to produce.

6. It is almost impossible to tell the difference between fragrances that have been created for women and for men. The first popular unisex fragrance for both women and men was first sold in 1994.

7. Companies that create perfume for fragrances also make the fragrances that are used for cleaning products, air fresheners and crisps.

8. More than 4,000 ingredients are used in the fragrance industry. The formula of each perfume is kept secret, and the ingredients aren't listed on the bottle.

9. Some fragrances can cause headaches or allergic skin reactions in some people. Many people don't like the smell of fragrances and hope they will be banned in public spaces.

3 ▶2.06 **Read the text and decide if each sentence is correct or incorrect. If it's correct, write *C*. If it's incorrect, write *I*.**
  1 The very first perfumes were oils and water.
  2 New fragrances appear every day.
  3 The world's first perfume maker was called Mesopotamia.
  4 The first fragrance for men appeared in 1994.
  5 Each fragrance has more than 5,000 ingredients.
  6 The fragrance bottle is often more expensive to produce than the fragrance.

4 **Which tips in the HOW TO box did you use for help with Exercises 2b and 3? Tick (✓) them.**

REACT

5 **Work in pairs. What do you think? Tell your partner.**
  1 Which facts in the article surprised you? Why?
  2 Should fragrances be banned in some public places? If so, which?

GO BEYOND
A picture caption is a short text that usually appears under a picture. Write captions for the pictures in the text. Use information from the text.

>>> Workbook, page 53

GRAMMAR Passives (present, past and future)

>>> Use the past, present and future passives to talk about senses

READ >>> Grammar in context

1 Read about Molly's breakfast. Answer the question at the end of the text.

When Molly had breakfast this morning, her senses were working hard. First, visual messages **were sent** to her brain. (*Eggs on toast! They look good, but maybe they're bad.*) Then some cells which **are found** in the nose sent another message. (*They smell OK up here!*) Finally, the thousands of taste buds that **are located** on the tongue sent a final message. (*They taste really nice!*) When all the messages **were received** by her brain, she **was given** the OK to eat them. Unfortunately Molly has a cold. Tomorrow she**'ll be given** eggs again, but she **won't be given** the OK by her brain. Why not?

STUDY

2 Complete the explanations with words from the text in Exercise 1.

Passives (present, past and future)

Use:
When the action is more important than the person/thing that does the action.

Form:
Positive and negative

be	+ past participle
Present simple: am/are/is (not)	found
	located
Past simple: was/were (not)	
Future: _____ / _____ be	

Questions
are/is/were/was + you/he, etc + past participle
will + you/she, etc + be + past participle
by
by + the person/thing that did the action
See GRAMMAR DATABASE, page 124.

>>> Workbook, pages 54–55

PRACTISE

3 Complete the news story with the future passive form of the verbs.

A new fast-food restaurant, *Sixth Sense*, (1) *will be opened* (open) by superstar singer Justin next Tuesday. At the new restaurant, customers (2) _____ (not allow) to see the food they eat. All the food (3) _____ (serve) in the dark. *Sixth Sense* chef, Gerard LePong, says people (4) _____ (give) the chance to experience fast food in a new way. I asked Gerard: '(5) _____ (people / tell) what they're eating?' His answer was 'No. If you eat at *Sixth Sense*, you (6) _____ (not show) the menu until after you've eaten. Enjoy!'

4 Complete the sentences with the correct passive form of the verbs.
1 In the past, most fruit and vegetables *were sold* (sell) in markets.
2 They _____ (choose) for their taste and not for the way they looked.
3 In the UK, these days most fruit and vegetables _____ (sell) in supermarkets.
4 They _____ (often / reject) by supermarkets because they don't look good.
5 The supermarkets say that if they start putting ugly fruit on their shelves, it _____ (leave) on the shelves by customers.
6 But if tomorrow's fresh food _____ (grow) only to look good, its taste _____ (lose) forever.

5 Rewrite the sentences using the passive form of the verbs in blue.
1 In the US, people **spend** more than $100 billion on processed foods each year.
 In the US, more than $100 billion is spent on processed foods each year.
2 People often **choose** a product because of the photo on the packaging.
3 However, when they **prepare** the food, it can look very different.
4 Companies **receive** a lot of complaints each year.

SPEAK

6 Work in pairs. Compare the information in Exercises 4 and 5, talking about your country. How will people eat food in the future?

LISTENING AND VOCABULARY The power of colour

>>> Follow a conversation

SPEAK AND LISTEN

1 a **What do you associate each colour in the box with? Write the first word you think of. Then compare your words with your partner.**

| black | blue | brown | gold | green | grey |
| orange | pink | purple | red | silver | yellow |

black – night

b **Find as many of the colours as you can on the colour wheel.**

2 a **Read the tips in the HOW TO box.**

b **▶2.07 Listen to the interview with Amy Shore about the National Colour Wheel and order the topics.**
   a The ways in which different cultures interpret colours. ....
   b A survey carried out in Manchester. ....
   c The reasons for doing the new survey. ....
   d How people can take part in the survey. ....

3 **▶2.07 Listen again and choose the correct answers.**
   1 Amy Shore basically wants people to …
     A visit a website. B do a street survey. C visit Manchester.
   2 The main purpose of the survey is to …
     A know what colours mean. B make people more aware of colour.
     C create an international database.
   3 She gives an example of how white is associated with death in …
     A China. B countries with jungles. C the West.
   4 The presenter associates the colour green with …
     A grass. B the environment. C the country he was born in.

4 **Which tips in the HOW TO box did you use for help with Exercises 2b and 3? Tick (✓) them.**

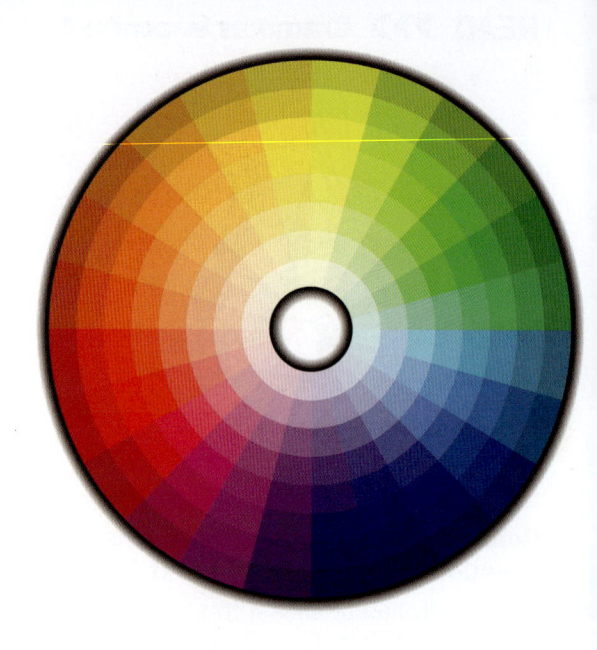

HOW TO
follow a conversation

☐ *Basically, …* and *The thing is, …* introduce an important point.

☐ *For example, …* and *For instance, …* introduce examples.

☐ *Although, Even though* and *However* add contrasting information.

REACT

5 **Work in pairs. Look at the colour wheel and answer the questions.**
   1 Which of the colours reflects the way you feel now?
   2 Which is your favourite colour? Why do you like it?
   3 Work in pairs. Complete the colours task. Student A looks at page 141. Student B looks at page 142.

WORK WITH WORDS

6 **Match the colour idioms and phrases (1–10) to the definitions (a–j).**

   1 as black as night   a suddenly feel angry
   2 black and white   b tell a small lie to make someone feel better
   3 as white as a sheet   c clear and simple
   4 get the green light   d very dark
   5 be in the red   e be sad or depressed
   6 once in a blue moon   f very pale, especially when frightened or ill
   7 out of the blue   g get permission to do something
   8 tell a white lie   h spend more money than you have
   9 feel blue   i very rarely
   10 see red   j suddenly and unexpectedly

7 **Work in pairs. Make a list of things that …**

   … make you see red.   … are black and white.
   … make you feel blue.   … only happen once in a blue moon.

GO BEYOND
Do the Words & Beyond exercise on page 134.

54

Workbook, pages 56–57

GRAMMAR (*In order*) *to* … , *so* (*that*) …

>>> Talk about the purpose of doing things

READ >>> Grammar in context

1 Read the story of braille. Do young people today still use it?

Blind people have restricted or no sight. They depend on their other senses in order to live independently. They use their sense of touch to read braille. A form of Braille was used by Napoleon's soldiers so that they could communicate silently at night. But it was a French teenager called Louis Braille who developed the idea so blind people could use it. These days, however, young people prefer using electronic screen readers so that they don't have to use braille.

STUDY

2 Read the explanations and underline examples in Exercise 1. Do they refer to now (in general) or to the past?

(In order) to … , so (that) …

Use:
To explain why somebody does, did or will do something.

Form:
(in order) to + infinitive
in order to is more formal than *to*
so (that) + subject…
  + *can*/present simple = now, in general
  + *can/will*/present simple = in the future
  + *could/would*/past simple = in the past

See GRAMMAR DATABASE, page 124.

PRACTISE

3 Choose the correct option to complete the sentences.

1. When he was 10, Louis Braille went to one of the first schools for the blind *in order* / *so that* he could study with other blind boys.
2. At that time, blind people used their fingers *to* / *so* feel the shape of normal letters.
3. A soldier called Charles Barbier visited the school *in order* / *so that* to demonstrate a system he'd created for soldiers.
4. He created his system *in order* / *so that* soldiers could pass messages at night.
5. Louis adapted Barbier's system *to* / *so* make it possible for blind people to read and write.
6. Over the years, the system has been adapted *in order* / *so that* it can be used in almost every language.

4 ▶2.08 Complete the conversation with *to* or *so*. Then listen and check your answers.

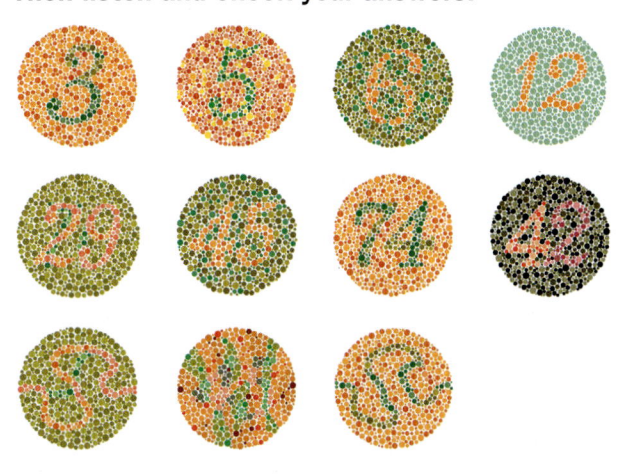

Mike: We're talking to Jacquie today (1) _____ we can learn something about being colour-blind. How did you find out you were colour-blind, Jacquie?

Jacquie: My art teacher asked me to stay after class one day (2) _____ talk to me. She thought it was strange that I had painted the sky purple. I did a test (3) _____ find out if I was colour-blind.

Mike: What's the test like?

Jacquie: They show you a circle with lots of coloured dots (4) _____ find out if you can see a number in the dots. They also do the test (5) _____ they can discover which type of colour-blindness you have.

Mike: Is it a problem being colour-blind?

Jacquie: Not really. But I usually buy clothes with a friend (6) _____ I don't choose colours that look bad together.

5 Complete the sentences in your own words using *in order to/to* or *so that/so*.

1. I use my phone's touchscreen …
2. Lifts have braille on the buttons …
3. You try clothes before you buy them …
4. We often use our sense of touch …
5. Signs often use the colour red …
6. You enter your PIN number in a cash machine …

SPEAK

6 Work in pairs. Answer the questions.

1. Why do we need each of the five senses?
2. If you had to live without one of the senses, which would you choose and why?

> We need our sense of smell in order to/so that …

> If I had to live without a sense, I'd choose my sense of … because …

Workbook, page 58

LANGUAGE & BEYOND

>>> **Recognise non-verbal communication**

SPEAK AND READ

1 Work in pairs. Choose one of the phrases in the box. Communicate the phrase to your partner without speaking. Can your partner understand you?

> Be quiet.   Do you know the time?   I can't hear you.   I'm hungry.
> I'm tired.   It tastes disgusting.   OK.   What's that smell?

2 Read about body language. Based on your experience, tick (✓) the points (1–6) you think are true. Then compare your answers with your partner.

DO

3 Work in groups. In turns, demonstrate the examples of body language in Exercise 2. Think of other examples. What do they mean?

REFLECT

4 Discuss the questions with your class. Do you agree with the REFLECTION POINT ?
   1 How accurate do you think the article is?
   2 In what situations might someone not read a person's body language correctly?
   3 How aware are you of your own body language? Do you ever try and control or change it? If so, in what situations?

EXTEND

5 Work in groups. Create a scene from a silent film.
   1 Think of a situation for the scene and who the characters are.
   2 Decide what happens in the scene. Think about how the characters feel and how they can express this with body language.
   3 Rehearse your scene and then perform it for the rest of the class. Can the other students describe what happens?

COMMUNICATE & COOPERATE

We often use gestures, facial expressions and eye movements to communicate with each other. Although we often do this deliberately in order to say something specific, our expressions and body movements also communicate things we don't mean to say. Look at these examples.

1 To find out if someone is telling the truth, look at their movements. If they touch things a lot while they are talking, then they might be lying. ☐

2 How much does someone like you? The closer they stand to you, the more they possibly like you. ☐

3 The way a person stands can say a lot about their character. If they stand with their arms folded, they might be trying to build a wall between you and them. ☐

4 We communicate best when we look each other in the eye. If someone looks down while they are talking, they might be hiding something. ☐

5 If someone moves their head to one side while you're talking to them, it can mean that they're interested. ☐

6 When someone 'mirrors' your body language and does the same movements as you, this means they might like you or they want you to like them. ☐

REFLECTION POINT

Sometimes our body language can reveal a lot about the way we think and feel. However, there might be other reasons for our expressions and body movements. So it isn't always accurate.

Workbook, page 61

SPEAKING At the chemist's

>>> Ask for help with words

SPEAK

1 Work in pairs. Look at the photos and answer the questions.

1 What's wrong with the people in the photos?
2 What should they do?
3 Which of the situations have you been in?

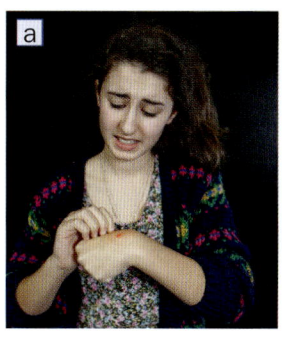

WATCH OR LISTEN

2 ▶2.09 Watch or listen to the scenes. Which problem in Exercise 1 is not talked about in the scenes?

1
Finn: Are you all right there?
Bella: I need something for my (1) _____ . I've got … I'm not sure how to say it in English. It's a pain.
Finn: You mean (2) _____ ?
Bella: Yes. Is this the right thing for a (3) _____ ?
Finn: Yes, it is.
Bella: Also I don't understand what this means. Can you help me?
Finn: Let me see. Ah … sunset yellow. It's a colour they use in the medicine.
Bella: I see. Does this sign mean that it is bad for you?
Finn: It can be bad for some people. Are you allergic to anything?
Bella: No, I don't think so.
Finn: Then you're probably OK.

2
Ruby: Can I help you?
Emma: Yes. I need some of that cream you put on your (4) _____ . I don't know what it's called. It's a special cream for keeping (5) _____ away.
Ruby: Do you mean (6) _____ repellent?
Emma: I think so.
Ruby: This one is very good.
Emma: What does 'light fragrance' mean?
Ruby: It means the lotion has a fragrance, but it's not very strong. Here. Smell it.
Emma: You called it a lotion. What's the difference between a lotion and a cream?
Ruby: A cream is thicker than a lotion.
Emma: OK. Thank you. I'll take it.

3 ▶2.09 Watch or listen again and write the missing words.

4 a Read the tips in the HOW TO box.

b ▶2.10 Complete the phrases from the conversation. Then listen and repeat. Pay attention to which words are stressed.
1 I'm not _____ how to say it in English.
2 I don't understand what this _____ .
3 I don't know what it's _____ .
4 It's a special cream _____ keeping insects away.
5 What's the _____ between a lotion and a cream?

5 Match the phrases in Exercise 4b to the tips in Exercise 4a.

ACT

6 🗣 Work in pairs. Complete the tasks.
1 Think of another product you buy at the chemist's.
2 Role-play a conversation between a shop assistant at a chemist's and a customer. The customer doesn't know the name of the object and needs help with words.
3 Change roles and repeat steps 1 and 2.

HOW TO
ask for help with words

When you don't know the name of something:
- Say that you don't know the word.
- Explain what it's for (*it's for* + verb + *-ing*).

When you don't understand a word:
- Say that you don't understand.
- Ask the other person for more information.

PHRASEBOOK ▶2.11

Explaining what you need

I need something for … / It's for …

I need some of that cream/liquid/stuff …

I'm not sure how to say it in English.

I don't know what it's called.

Asking for help

I don't understand what this means.

Does that mean … ?

Is this the right thing for … ?

What's the difference between … and …?

Workbook, page 59

57

WRITING A place I really like

>>> Link similar ideas

SPEAK AND READ

1 🔊 **Work in pairs. Look at the photo and describe it. What similar places do you know?**

2 **Read the description. Which part of the description doesn't fit the photo?**

PHRASE BYTES

It's a photo of …
It reminds me of …
I don't know anywhere like this.

> My grandmother lives in a big, old house in Scotland. We go to stay there three or four times a year. Other relatives often come too, so the house is always full of people.
> The house is in the middle of nowhere, and there aren't any shops or cinemas nearby, but we never get bored. There are hills to climb and a huge forest to explore. And there's the sea as well.
> We spend hours on the beach. I love the feeling of the wind on my face and the sand under my feet. I also love swimming, although the sea is freezing!
> My gran is not only one of the coolest people on the planet, but she's also an amazing cook. There's always the smell of cooking and baking in the house. At night it sometimes feels quite scary because it's so dark and quiet. But I love my grandmother's house.

✓ **Get it right**
quite = fairly but not very
quiet = with very little noise

3 a **Read the tips in the HOW TO box.**

HOW TO
link similar ideas

- Use *and* to join two parts of a sentence.
- Use *also*, *too* and *as well* to add another fact.
- Use *also* after *be* and *can*, but before other verbs.
- Use *too* and *as well* at the end of a sentence.
- Use *not only* + *but also* to say that two things are true.

b **Underline examples of all the linking words in the description in Exercise 2.**

PRACTISE

4 **Rewrite the sentences using the words in brackets.**
1 There's a park near my house. I go there once or twice a week. (**and**)
2 It's a good place to meet friends. It's a good place to do sports. (**not only + but also**)
3 There are some basketball courts. There's an area for skateboarding. (**also**)
4 Once a month there's a market. They have concerts in the summer. (**too**)
5 I go there to have fun. I sometimes go there to read. (**as well**)
6 You see lots of different people there. People take their pets there. (**too**)

PLAN

5 **You're going to write a description about a place you really like. Make a plan for your description.**

WRITING PLAN

1 **Give some basic information about the place.**
Where is it? What is it? When do you go there?

2 **Describe the place in more detail.**
What's the place like? What do you do there?

3 **Use your senses.**
How does the place make you feel? What can you see and hear?

4 **Explain why it's special.**
Is there anything you don't like about the place? Why is the place so special?

WRITE AND CHECK

6 **Use your plan and write your description. Then check it. Tick (✓) the things in the plan.**

SHARE

7 **Swap your description with a partner. Which place would you most like to visit? Why?**

>>> Workbook, pages 60–61

UNIT REVIEW 5

VOCABULARY The senses

1 Complete Casper Wright's introduction to his video game with the words in the box.

| feel | hear | hearing | listening | look | see |
| sight | smell | sounds | taste | touch | watch |

Don't just sit and (1) _____ boring TV, with SensaWorld you can use your sense of (2) _____ to (3) _____ our amazing 3D visuals. Stop (4) _____ to boring music and really use your sense of (5) _____. You'll be amazed when you (6) _____ the sound effects in the game. It (7) _____ incredible! And that's not all. (8) _____ at these other great features! With SensaWorld you can use your fingers to (9) _____ and (10) _____ the objects around you. And with our special five senses system you can (11) _____ fragrances and (12) _____ food. With SensaWorld you really are part of the action.

___/12

Colour idioms

2 Complete the conversation from the game with colours.

Sally: Hello? I can't see anything, it's as (1) _____ as night here.
Avatar: Why are you here? People only come here once in a (2) _____ moon. You look as (3) _____ as a sheet.
Sally: Are you … a ghost?
Avatar: Maybe. Nothing's ever (4) _____ and white in SensaWorld. Do I look like a ghost?
Sally: No … no. You look very well.
Avatar: Are you telling (5) _____ lies? Don't make me angry. I see (6) _____ very easily.
Sally: I'm sorry.
Avatar: I'm the creator of SensaWorld. Life was good when I got the (7) _____ light to make SensaWorld. But then I had money problems, and soon I was in the (8) _____. Then out of the (9) _____ I had an idea. I could escape the real world and live inside SensaWorld. But I feel sad and (10) _____ being _____ alone in a virtual world.

___/10

GRAMMAR Passive tenses

3 Complete the encyclopaedia entry with the passive forms of the verbs.

SensaWorld (1) _____ (create) by the inventor Casper Wright in 2011. He (2) _____ (inspire) by science fiction films. In 2012, he (3) _____ (interview) by a newspaper and said: 'I want to create a video game that (4) _____ (use) by young people for the next 100 years. I think in the future players (5) _____ (connect) to other players on other planets.' Soon after giving the interview, Casper Wright (6) _____ (report) missing by his family. Today the game (7) _____ (play) by millions of people around the world. Casper Wright (8) _____ (remember) for a very long time.

___/16

(in order) to … , so (that) …

4 Write the SensaWorld rules using *in order to/to* or *so that/so*.

HOW TO PLAY SENSAWORLD

1 In SensaWorld, you use your senses _____ complete tasks.
2 You complete the tasks _____ you can collect points.
3 You collect points _____ exchange them for tickets.
4 You need the tickets _____ travel to the next world.
5 You are given a wallet _____ you won't lose your tickets.
6 You need your tickets _____ you'll be able to get home.

___/12

Your score: ___/50

SKILLS CHECK

✓✓✓ Yes, I can. No problem!
✓✓   Yes, I can. But I need a bit of help.
✓   Yes, I can. But I need a lot of help.

I can use pictures to help me understand. _____
I can follow a conversation. _____
I can recognise non-verbal communication. _____
I can ask for help with words at the chemist's. _____
I can link similar ideas when I write. _____

▶▶▶ Workbook, pages 62–63

6 SELLING POWER

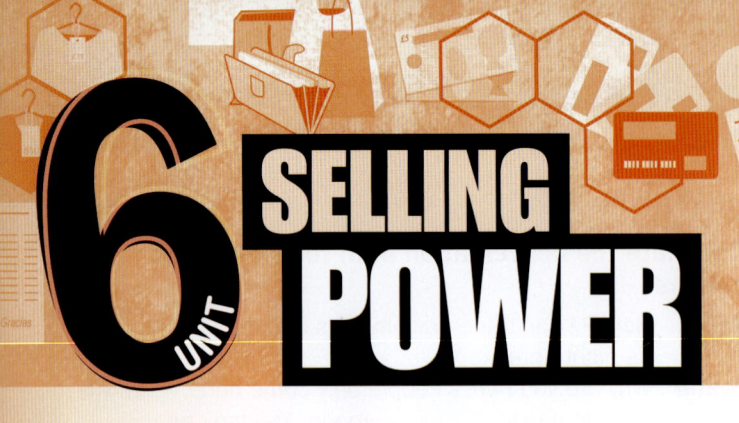

IN THE PICTURE In a shop

>>> Talk about shopping

WORK WITH WORDS

1 **RECALL** Work in pairs. Do the tasks. You have three minutes.

   a Add at least eight shops to the list.   *baker's*

   b Complete the phrases with the words in the box.

   | buy   cheap   cost   expensive   pay for   the price |
   | save   sell   spend |

   1 ask _____
   2 be _____ / _____
   3 _____ / _____ / _____ an item
   4 _____ / _____ / _____ money

2 Look at the shop in the big picture. What sort of shop is it and what does it sell?

3 ▶2.12 Listen to two conversations in the shop. Complete how much the two people pay.

   Assistant: These T-shirts are on special offer. Three for two. And this scarf is in the sale. Are the T-shirts the right size? You can try on clothes over there.
   Shopper: They're fine, thanks.
   Assistant: OK, that's _____. Keep the receipt if you want to exchange an item, or return an item and get a refund.

   Shopper: Hi, this bag is a bit dirty. Can I get a discount?
   Assistant: Erm, well I can make it 10 euros cheaper. OK? … So that's _____. … Do you want to pay in cash or pay by card?
   Shopper: Cash, please.

4 ▶2.13 Listen and repeat the phrases in orange in Exercise 3. Then match them to the definitions 1–10.

   1 use 'plastic' money to buy something
      pay by card
   2 swap something for a different size or colour _____
   3 check if something is the right size _____
   4 not throw away the document that shows you paid _____
   5 use 'real' money to buy something _____
   6 take something back _____
   7 cheaper than usual for a short time _____
   8 cheaper at a certain time of year, eg at the end of summer _____
   9 get some money off the price _____
   10 get your money back _____

5 a ▶2.14 **PRONOUNCE** Listen to the sounds in these words. Which one is longer? Listen again and repeat.

      /æ/ cash   bag   /ɑː/ card   scarf

   b ▶2.15 Listen and choose the word you hear. Then listen and repeat both words.

      1 ant / aren't   2 chat / chart   3 had / hard   4 jazz / jars   5 pack / park

60

6 **THE MOVING PICTURE** ▶ Watch Shay, Sebastian, Roisin and Tyler talking about shopping. Who likes shopping? How and where do they shop?

SPEAK

7 Read the shopaholic questionnaire. Work in pairs. Ask and answer the questions. Explain your reasons or give examples.

The shopaholic questionnaire

1. Do you like shopping?
2. How often do you go shopping and who with?
3. Do you prefer big shopping centres, smaller shops or markets?
4. What things do you usually buy?
5. Do you enjoy trying on clothes?
6. Do you often exchange or return items?
7. Do you often buy things in the sale or on special offer?
8. Do you ever ask for a discount?
9. Do you ever shop for products online?

GO BEYOND

Do the Words & Beyond exercise on page 135.

Workbook, page 64

READING What's it for?

>>> Identify the tone of written comments

SPEAK AND READ

1 **Work in pairs. Look at the photos and answer the questions.**
   1 Which photo do you like best? Why?
   2 What do you think they might be advertising?

2 ▶2.16 **Read the website comments. Find out if any people agree with your predictions and opinions.**

ZAC'S BIG CHALLENGE: One challenge a day for a year

Home | Blog | About

Challenge #122: Guess the ad

I love watching those TV shows and videos with funny adverts from around the world. So for today's challenge I've tried to design three ads with amusing photos. Your challenge is to tell me your ideas: what product the pictures might be for and why. (You can check out my ads tomorrow.)

💬 **8 Comments on Challenge #122: Guess the ad**

LNQ says
Wow, great idea for a challenge, Zac 😊. Ad 1 must be for glasses – they're all wearing glasses with similar black frames.
REPLY

angel15 says
No, it can't be glasses - that would be too obvious. It could be toothpaste.
REPLY

JedSW says
This ad might be for a clothes shop. They're all wearing a similar style of clothes.
REPLY

PT199 says
Ugh! Is this how you dress JedSW? If so, you are totally uncool!!! Those awful clothes must be from the 1970s!
REPLY

OMG says
I totally love the second ad. Good choice! It must be for healthy eating – eat more vegetables and fruit. There are five of them, so it might be to do with the campaign to eat five portions of fruit and vegetables a day.
REPLY

angel15 says
Definitely fruit and vegetables. But why are the banana and the carrot hiding?
REPLY

Jay says
Ad 3 might be for holidays. It looks like a really beautiful place.
REPLY

TC says
Hey stupid. Are you even looking at the photo? What about that rocket thing on the man's back? What does that have to do with holidays? Perhaps it's for train travel – 'Why not take the train? It's faster, easier and more comfortable.'
REPLY

3 a **Read the tips in the HOW TO box.**

  b **Read the website comments again.**
   1 Which are positive about the challenge or ads?
   2 Which are rude about other people's comments?
   3 Who is puzzled?

4 **Which tips in the HOW TO box did you use for help with Exercise 3b? Tick (✓) them.**

HOW TO
identify the tone of written comments

☐ Look for question marks (?) for uncertainty and exclamation marks (!) for emphasis.
☐ Look for exclamations like *oh*, *wow* and *ugh*. They express strong feelings.
☐ Look for positive and negative symbols.
☐ Look for positive and negative comments about other people or their ideas.

REACT

5 **Work in pairs. What do you think? Tell your partner.**
   1 What are your favourite TV/internet/magazine adverts? Describe them.
   2 Have you ever bought a product because you saw it in an advert? Why?/Why not? If you have, what was it and was it as good as the advert said?

GO BEYOND
Write your own slogan (an advertising phrase or sentence) for each photo.

>>> Workbook, page 65

GRAMMAR Possibility and impossibility

>>> Make logical guesses

READ AND LISTEN >>> Grammar in context

1 ▶2.17 Look at the photos of two products from adverts. Read and listen to the conversation. What do you think the objects are?

Nate: OK, I think the first one shows those things on the top of a cooker where you cook food.
Maizy: No, they **can't** be. Look at the colour. They **must** be buttons … yes, I'm sure they're buttons. It **could** be a gadget, but I don't know exactly what it is.
Nate: Hmm. The second one **might** be a piece of kitchen equipment, but I'm not sure.
Maizy: Mmm, it **may** be.

STUDY

2 Complete the explanations with the words in orange from Exercise 1.

Possibility and impossibility

can't, could, may, might and *must*
Use: To make logical guesses and say if you think things are possible or not.

- Use *could*, _____ , _____ when you're not sure if something is possible.
- Use _____ when you're sure something is true or possible.
- Use _____ when you think something is impossible.

Form:
could/must/can't, etc + infinitive (without *to*)

See GRAMMAR DATABASE, page 125.

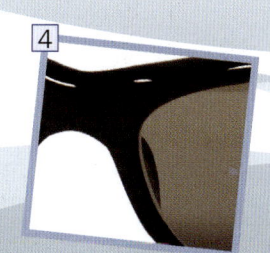

PRACTISE

3 a Complete the sentences with the products in the box.

| car | cheese | mobile | ring |
| shampoo | spaghetti | | |

1 It's a _____ . – No, It can't be. It's only got two wheels!
2 It's a _____ . – Yes, it must be. It's round and made of gold.
3 It's _____ . – Mmm, it could be. It's in a bottle.
4 It's _____ . – Yes, it must be. It's long and thin.
5 It's a _____ . – Mmm, it might be. It's got a screen.
6 It's _____ . – No, it can't be. It's pink!

b Work in pairs. Think of two products and write short explanations. Read them to another pair. Can they guess your explanation?

It's long and made of wood.   *It might be a …*

4 Complete the conversations with the correct verbs. Use *can/must/might/may/could* in the affirmative or negative.

Anna: What's that sound? It sounds like water.
Kristen: Mmm, it (1) _____ be rain. But it sounds as if it's inside.
Anna: No, it (2) _____ be rain. It isn't raining – look. It (3) _____ be the washing machine.
Kristen: What's that smell? Phew! It's really strong.
Anna: I'm not sure. It (4) _____ be those flowers over there.
Kristen: No, it (5) _____ be the flowers, they're plastic. Look, there's my brother. It (6) _____ be his new fragrance!

SPEAK

5 Work in pairs. Decide what the objects are in the photos below. Use the conversations in Exercise 4 to help you. Check your answers on page 142.

Workbook, pages 66–67

63

LISTENING AND VOCABULARY Smart shopping

>>> Understand the speaker's intention

SPEAK AND LISTEN

1 Work in pairs. Answer the questions.
1. What sort of shops and services can you find in shopping centres in your area?
2. What are the advantages and disadvantages of large shopping centres?
3. Give an example of something that you bought but didn't plan to buy or couldn't really afford. Explain why you bought it.

2 a Read the tips in the **HOW TO** box.

b ▶2.18 Listen to the interview. Choose the correct answer.

The interviewer wants to …
A advertise shops at Towngreen Centre.
B encourage shoppers to spend more.
C help shoppers to understand why they spend.

> **HOW TO**
> understand the speaker's intention
> - Listen for the main message.
> - Listen for expressions that give an opinion or suggestion.
> - Decide what you have learned and/or how you feel after listening.

3 ▶2.18 Listen again. For each question, tick (✓) the correct answer.

1. Shops and shopping centres are designed so you …
   A find things as quickly as possible.
   B stay as long as possible.
   C buy popular items.
2. Special offers are usually …
   A front left.
   B back right.
   C front right.
3. Expensive items are on …
   A shelves at eye level.
   B lower shelves.
   C higher shelves.
4. Shops and shopping centres use tricks of …
   A sight.
   B sight and smell.
   C sight, smell and touch.

REACT

4 Work in pairs. Answer the questions about the interview.
1. Did you know about any of these tricks? What did you find most interesting?
2. Do you think James Lewis's advice to shoppers at the end is good advice?

WORK WITH WORDS

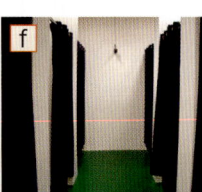

5 ▶2.19 Match the words for things and people in a shop (1–12) to the photos (a–l). Listen and check.

1 trolley   3 checkout   5 shop window   7 exit   9 store detective   11 changing room
2 shelf   4 basket   6 escalator   8 cash desk 10 department   12 customer

SPEAK

6 Work in pairs. Design your dream shop. Decide what the shop sells (all your favourite items and products) and give it a name. Make a plan of where things are. Present your shop to another pair. Which shop do you like best? Why?

> **GO BEYOND**
> Do the Words & Beyond exercise on page 135.

Workbook, pages 68–69

GRAMMAR Indirect questions

>>> Ask polite questions

READ AND LISTEN >>> Grammar in context

1 ▶2.20 Read and listen to the conversation. What and where is the shop Stefano wants to go to? What time does it close?

Stefano: Hello, *do you have any idea* where I can buy a computer mouse?
Mrs Foster: Well, there are two electronics shops – Electronic World and Black's.
Stefano: *Could you tell me* how I can find Electronic World, please?
Mrs Foster: Sure, it's on level two, about five shops down after the escalator.
Stefano: *Would you mind* showing me where it is on the map?
Mrs Foster: Erm, here it is, just here.
Stefano: *Do you know* if the shop closes late today?
Mrs Foster: All the shops close at 7pm.

STUDY

2 Complete the explanations with words from Exercise 1.

Indirect questions
Use: To be more polite and more formal.
Form: Indirect questions start with an expression like this: *Do you have* _____ ... *Could you* _____ ... *Would you mind* _____ ... *Do you* _____ ...
Word order: In a direct question, the verb comes before the subject: *Where **can I** buy a mouse?* In an indirect question, the verb comes after the subject: *Do you have any idea* where **I can** buy a mouse?
See GRAMMAR DATABASE, page 125.

PRACTISE

3 Write direct questions for the other three questions in Exercise 1.

4 a Make these questions more polite. Use the phrases in orange in Exercise 1.
   1 Where's the lift?
   2 Which level is the food area on?
   3 How do I find Top Fashion?
   4 Where are the toilets?
   5 How long does it take to SuperSport?
   6 Where can I find a chemist's?

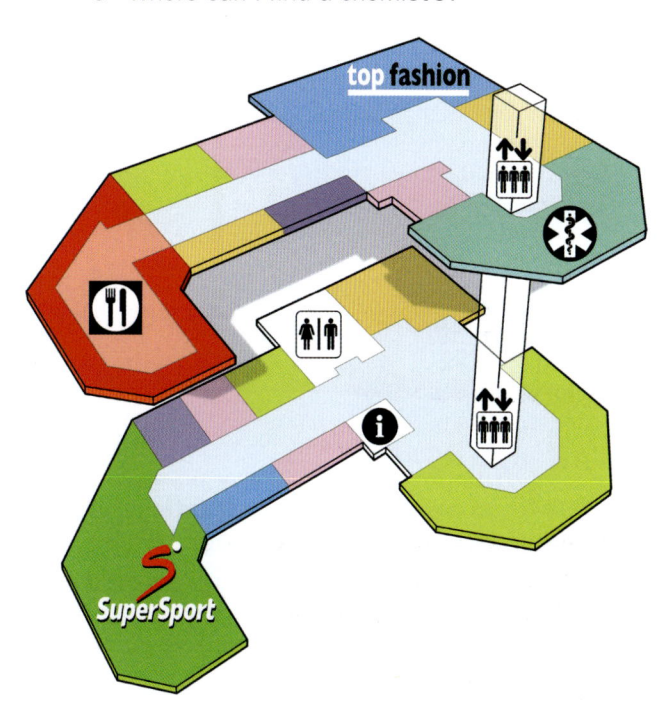

   b Work in pairs. You're at the information desk ⓘ in the shopping centre. Ask and answer the questions in Exercise 4a using the map.

SPEAK

5 a Work in pairs. You've finished shopping and want to relax. Student B looks at the cinema information on page 142. Student A asks the person at the ticket desk (Student B) indirect questions to find out this information:

   how much / tickets / cost?
   discount / students?
   take / drinks in?

   b Now find out about a fashion show. Student A looks at the information on page 141. Student B asks a shop assistant (Student A) indirect questions to find out this information:

   what time / fashion show?
   for men or women?
   how much / show?

Workbook, page 70

LANGUAGE & BEYOND

1
Bartek: Where shall we go?
Seth: (Thinks: *I want to go to the park.*) Er … I don't know – I don't mind.
Bartek: OK, let's go to the shopping centre.
Seth: (Thinks: *I don't want to go to the shopping centre.*) Yeah, sure, whatever.

2
Bartek: Where shall we go?
Seth: I'd like to go to the park and play basketball. Is that OK with you?
Bartek: Erm yeah … What about the shopping centre?
Seth: No, we went to the shopping centre yesterday. I'd like to go to the park today.

3
Bartek: Where shall we go?
Seth: I want to go to the park.
Bartek: Or what about …
Seth: I said I want to go to the park. OK?

»> Be assertive

SPEAK AND READ

1 ▶ 2.21 Read and listen to the situations. Describe Seth in each situation with one of these words.
- A aggressive = is angry and doesn't respect the other person's wishes
- B passive = accepts the other person's wishes but doesn't agree with them
- C assertive = is confident and respects the other person's wishes

2 Tick (✓) the actions that are assertive.
- always agree with somebody
- be calm and not emotional
- listen to other people
- say what you want
- shout and be rude
- repeat your wishes
- stand very close to somebody (inside their personal space)
- look at the floor
- stand up straight
- make eye contact
- speak slowly and clearly

DO

3 🔊 You are first in the queue at a cash desk. Another person walks in front of you. In pairs, role-play the situation in three different ways: aggressive, passive and assertive.

4 How did you feel in each situation? Was it difficult to be assertive? Why?/Why not? Tell your partner.

REFLECT

5 Discuss the questions with your class. Do you agree with the **REFLECTION POINT**?
1. Do you know someone who's assertive? What makes him/her assertive?
2. Why is it sometimes hard to be assertive?
3. Can you think of situations when you couldn't be assertive?

EXTEND

6 Work in pairs. Decide how to be assertive in the situations on page 142.

PHRASE BYTES

Excuse me, there's a queue.

Hey you, get to the back of the queue!

Er, can you please get in the queue?

So? Do you have a problem?

Oh, sorry.

REFLECTION POINT

Know what you want and act assertively (but not aggressively) to get it. This will help you feel better and get on with other people more easily.

COMMUNICATE & COOPERATE

Workbook, page 73

SPEAKING At the cash desk

>>> Return goods and make a complaint

SPEAK

1 Look at what people say when they take things back to a shop. What products could these phrases be about?

1. They're the wrong size. / They don't fit.
2. It doesn't suit me. / It doesn't look right.
3. I've changed my mind.
4. There's a mark on it. / There's a hole in it.
5. It doesn't work. / It's broken.

WATCH OR LISTEN

2 a ▶ 2.22 Watch or listen to the scenes. What is each person returning and why?

1.
Alice: I'm afraid this jumper is the _____. I'd like to change it for a smaller one.
Assistant: That's fine. Do you have your receipt?
Alice: Yes, here you are.
Assistant: OK ... there you go.
Alice: Thank you very much.

2.
Assistant: How can I help you?
Bella: I'd like to return this DVD player. It _____. The sound isn't right.
Assistant: Are you sure? Maybe you haven't read the instructions properly.
Bella: I'm sure. I'd like a refund, please.

3.
Finn: I'd like to return this T-shirt.
Assistant: Is there anything wrong with it?
Finn: No, _____. It doesn't suit me.

4.
Max: I'd like to return this shirt. I'm afraid there's a _____.
Assistant: Erm ... I can give you a discount.
Max: No, thank you. Here's my receipt. I'd like a refund.
Assistant: Would you like to exchange it for something else?
Max: No, thank you. I'd like a refund.

HOW TO
be polite

- Use *I'd like* ... to make a polite request.
- Use *I'm afraid* ... to make a polite complaint.
- Use *Thank you very much* to thank somebody politely.
- Use *No, thank you* to refuse something politely.

b ▶ 2.22 Complete the conversations. Use Exercise 1 to help you. Watch or listen again and check.

3 ▶ 2.23 Listen and repeat all the phrases in Exercise 1. Pay attention to which words are stressed.

4 a Read the tips in the **HOW TO** box.

b Underline polite phrases in the conversations.

PHRASEBOOK ▶ 2.24

Return goods

I'd like to return ...

I'd like a refund / to change it.

I'm afraid ...

... it's the wrong size. / It doesn't fit.

... it doesn't suit me. / It doesn't look right. / I've changed my mind.

Make a complaint

I'm afraid ...

There's a mark on it. / There's a hole in it.

It doesn't work. / It's broken.

ACT

5 👥 Work in pairs. Act out two conversations. Student A is the shop assistant, and Student B is the customer. The customer wants an exchange or a refund. Be polite but assertive.

>>> Workbook, page 71

WRITING We look forward to hearing from you

>>> Use polite phrases in formal emails and letters

SPEAK AND READ

1 **Read the survey. Work in pairs. Ask and answer the questions in the survey.**

2 **Read the letter and finish the sentences.**
The survey was written by …
It was written to …

> Dear Class 9a,
>
> We are writing to ask for help with a survey about brands. We would be grateful if you could tell us what you buy and where you shop. (Please see the attached questions.)
>
> Thank you for your help. We look forward to hearing from you.
>
> Yours sincerely,
>
> Class 8b, Westwood High School

Survey ABOUT BRANDS

1 *Could you tell us where you shop and why?*
– What are your favourite shops and why?
– Which is most important: the product or the price?

2 *Would you mind telling us how you feel about brands?*
– Do you only buy certain brands? Which brands and why?
– Do you think brands are more important for electronics, clothes or sports equipment?

3 *Could you tell us about your last buy?*
– What was the last thing that you bought?
– Why did you buy it?

✓ Get it right

Use *what* in general questions when a lot of different answers are possible.

Use *which* when there is a choice, or to ask about a specific group of things.

3 a **Read the tips in the HOW TO box.**

HOW TO
use polite phrases in formal emails or letters

Use …
- *I am / We are writing to ask (for … / if you can …)* to say why you are writing.
- *I/We would be grateful if you could …* to make a formal request.
- *Thank you for your help* for polite thanks.
- *I/We look forward to hearing from you* to say you expect a reply.
- *Yours sincerely* as a formal greeting at the end.

b **Find the phrases in the letter in Exercise 2. How do the first two phrases finish?**

PRACTISE

4 **Make this email sound more polite and formal.**

> Dear Class Teacher,
>
> We want to know if your students can answer our questionnaire. It would be really cool if they could help us.
>
> Thanks a lot! Write soon!
>
> Class 8b, Westwood High School

PLAN

5 **Work in pairs or small groups. You're going to write a survey about advertising for another class (in your school or another school). Make a plan for your letter and survey.**

WRITING PLAN

1 **Write a short formal email or letter about your survey.**
Explain why you're writing and what your survey is about.
Use indirect questions and formal phrases from the HOW TO box.

2 **Write your survey questions.**
Think about: what makes good adverts, the effect of adverts, advertising by famous people, adverts on the internet, music in adverts, …

3 **Include some indirect questions.**

WRITE AND CHECK

6 **Use your plan and write your email and survey questions. Then check them. Tick (✓) the things in the plan.**

SHARE

7 **Send your email and survey to another class. Write a short summary of the replies to your survey and present it to the class.**

Workbook, pages 72–73

UNIT REVIEW 6

VOCABULARY Shopping

1 Complete the poster with the words in the box.

a discount   a refund   by card   in cash   exchange
special offer   the receipt   the sale   try on   return

Buy, buy, buy!

Lots of items are on (1) _____!
Next week everything is in (2) _____ – 50% off!
Note you can only pay in the shop (3) _____ (very sorry, no cards).
Visit our online shop. Pay (4) _____ on our secure site.
(5) _____ clothes in your own home.
You can (6) _____ an item if it doesn't fit, and (7) _____ it for a different size or get (8) _____. Just keep (9) _____!
Get (10) _____ of 10% when you spend more than €50!

___/10

Things and people in a shop

2 Complete the shop notices.

At Sid's Superstore the (1) c_____ really is king! There are no silly rules here!
Please touch things in the (2) s_____ w_____.
Children: please sit on the (3) c_____ d_____ and play games on the (4) e_____.
You don't need to use a (5) b_____ or (6) t_____ for shopping items.
The (7) s_____ d_____ is there to help you.
Don't put things back on the right (8) s_____.
You can have any number of items at the fast (9) c_____.
Just leave clothes in the (10) c_____ r_____.
Dogs welcome in the food (11) d_____.
Leave through the entrance and not the (12) e_____, if you prefer.

___/12

GRAMMAR
Possibility and impossibility

3 Choose the correct verbs to complete the conversation.

Lucy: What's that?
Ben: Erm. I'm not sure. It (1) *must / might* be a kid's toy. Or it (2) *must / may* be something for a pet.
Lucy: No, it (3) *can't / could* be; it's too big.
Ben: It (4) *could / must* be something for fitness training. Yes, it (5) *can't / must* be to build arm muscles.
Lucy: Mmm, it (6) *might / can't* be. But why is it that horrible colour?
Ben: That (7) *can't / must* be why it's on special offer. Let's ask the shop assistant. He (8) *must / can't* know.
Lucy: Excuse me, what's that?
Assistant: I'm afraid I've no idea. But you can get three for two.

___/16

Indirect questions

4 Put the words in order to make questions.

1 is / the shoe department / Do you know / where / ?
  _____

2 costs / this shampoo / how much / Do you have any idea / ?
  _____

3 what time / Could you tell me / closes / the shop / ?
  _____

4 I need / Do you know / which floor / for the café / ?
  _____

5 starts / when / Would you mind telling me / the sale / ?
  _____

6 is / the shop manager / Could you tell me / who / ?
  _____

___/12

Your score: ___/50

SKILLS CHECK

✓✓✓ Yes, I can. No problem!
✓✓ Yes, I can. But I need a bit of help.
✓ Yes, I can. But I need a lot of help.

I can identify the tone of written comments. _____
I can understand the speaker's intention. _____
I can be assertive. _____
I can return goods and make a complaint. _____
I can use polite phrases in formal emails and letters. _____

Workbook, pages 74–75

PROGRESS CHECK

READ

1 Look at each sign and text. What does it say? Choose the correct summary, A, B or C.

NO ENTRANCE WITH DOGS OR OTHER ANIMALS.
Guide dogs for the blind are permitted to enter with their owners.

1 What animals can come into the shopping centre?
  A All animals with their owners.
  B Dogs with their owners.
  C Dogs with blind people.

Dear Mr Simms
I can't remember where we're playing on Saturday. Would you mind sending the details again?
Thank you
Jordan Scott

SportFit sports shoes are sold out. They might be available next week.

2 Why is Jordan writing to Mr Simms?
  A He wants to watch the match.
  B He needs some information about the match.
  C He wants to buy tickets for the match.

3 When can you buy SportFit shoes?
  A Not next week.
  B Maybe next week.
  C Definitely next week.

Where are you???? I've been here for half an hour!! 😞😞 Suri

NO REFUNDS OR EXCHANGES after 30 days or without a receipt.

4 How is Suri feeling?
  A She's angry.
  B She's embarrassed.
  C She's excited.

5 When can customers return or exchange something?
  A After 30 days with a receipt.
  B Before 30 days with a receipt.
  C Before 30 days without a receipt.

EXAM TIPS

- match short texts to summaries
  - Look at each text. What type of text is it?
  - Read the text. What is its general meaning?
  - Read the three summaries carefully.
  - Look for specific information in the text to help choose your answer.
- use pictures to help you understand
  See page 52
- identify the tone of written comments
  See page 62

Reading: _____ /10

PROGRESS CHECK

LISTEN

2 ▶2.25 You will hear a conversation between Ellen and Kenji about sense of smell. Decide if each sentence is correct (tick *A*) or incorrect (tick *B*).

	A	B
1 Ellen says she likes the smell of strong fragrances.		
2 Kenji wants to get something at the chemist so that Ellen feels better.		
3 Kenji has a strong sense of smell.		
4 There's a strong smell of cheese.		
5 Kenji disagrees that the shopping centre smells bad.		

Listening: _____ /10

EXAM TIPS

answer true/false questions
- Read the sentences carefully before you listen.
- Every part of the sentence must be true: listen carefully for the details.
- When you listen again, check your answers.
- If you don't know, guess – you have a 50% chance!

follow a conversation
See page 54

ask for help with words
See page 57

understand the speaker's intention
See page 64

WRITE

3 For each question, complete the second sentence so that it means the same as the first. Use no more than three words.

1. They'll probably open the new shopping centre next month.
   The new shopping centre _____ opened next month.
2. I'm going shopping to buy some new shoes.
   I'm going shopping _____ I can buy some new shoes.
3. I'm sure that's the right shop.
   That _____ be the right shop.
4. Could you tell me what time you close?
   Would you _____ me what time you close?

_____ /4

4 You want to ask for more information about a Saturday job in 'Top Fashion'. Write a short formal email to Ms Smith (35–45 words).

- Tell Ms Smith that you want to ask about the job.
- Ask about the working hours and the hourly pay.
- Thank her and finish your email.

_____ /6

Writing: _____ /10

Progress check score _____ /30

EXAM TIPS

use polite phrases in formal emails or letters
See page 68

link similar ideas
See page 58

Download extra speaking activities from www.macmillanbeyond.com

TRADITION AND CHANGE

IN THE PICTURE Traditional ways

>>> Talk about traditional and modern ways of living

WORK WITH WORDS

1 **RECALL** Work in pairs. Do the tasks. You have two minutes.

a Complete the names of the appliances you find in a modern house.

1 l _i_ ght
2 l __ mp
3 __ r __ n
4 c __ k __ r
5 fr __ dg __
6 d __ shw __ sh __ r
7 w __ sh __ ng m __ ch __ n
8 v __ c __ m cl __ n __ r

b Explain the difference between each pair of household jobs. Then think of two more jobs.

1 *lay the table* and *clear the table*
2 *do the washing* and *do the washing-up*
3 *sort the recycling* and *take out the rubbish*
4 *clean the floor* and *vacuum the floor*

2 Try and match eight of the activities to the photos.

bake bread _1_	build a house ___	chop wood ___
grow food ___	knit clothes ___	make furniture ___
make your own entertainment ___		milk a cow ___
sew clothes ___	travel by horse and cart ___	
use gas lights ___	wash clothes by hand ___	

3 a ▶2.26 Listen and check your answers to Exercise 2.

b Which four activities are not in the photos? Work in pairs. Mime the activities.

4 ▶2.27 Listen and repeat all the activities in Exercise 2.

5 Work in pairs. Read the statistics on the right and answer the questions.

1 How many people live on our planet?
2 How many people wash their clothes by hand?
3 Which statistic surprises you the most? Why?

6 **THE MOVING PICTURE** ▶ Watch the video and make a list of the activities you see.

The lines that divide us

On our planet …
Two billion people live under the **poverty line**.
They have less than $2 a day.

Three billion people live between the **poverty line** and the **wash line**.
They have less than $40 a day.
They have electricity but no washing machine.

One billion people live between the **wash line** and the **air line**.
They have less than $80 a day and have a washing machine.

One billion people live above the **air line**.
They have more than $80 a day and can buy gadgets and air tickets.

SPEAK

7 a Complete the survey with all the activities in Exercise 2. Then answer the questions.

Traditional ways survey

Have you ever done these things?

Have you ever …	Yes, I have.	No, but I know somebody who has.	No, and I don't know anybody who has.
… milked a cow?			
… baked bread?			

b Work in pairs. Compare your answers to the survey. Ask each other for more information.

Have you ever milked a cow?

No, I haven't, but my grandmother has. She grew up on a farm.

Have you ever baked bread?

Yes, I have. I help my mother bake bread every weekend.

GO BEYOND

Do the Words & Beyond exercise on page 136.

Workbook, page 76

73

READING Living in the past

>>> Make notes

SPEAK AND READ

1   a   Work in pairs. Look at the advert. What do you think it's for? What can you see in the photos?

    b   ▶2.28 Read the first section to check your answers.

1880: Could you live in the past?

The series
Life-Like Productions is looking for young people who are interested in participating in a new TV series called *1880*. Over eight weekly episodes, eight teenagers will live on a farm that recreates life in the late 19th century. Could you live without your phone, your gadgets and your social network? Could you live with cameras following you 24/7?

The past
How did teenagers use to live in late 19th-century America? Here's what series creator Susie Markham says: 'In 1880, most Americans led a rural existence. Children used to help with household jobs and farm work as soon as they could, so life for teens used to be much tougher. Houses didn't use to have running water or electricity, so people did everything by hand – fetch water, cook, clean, wash clothes, even build houses. They used to make their own entertainment too. As for school, students of all ages often studied in one room, and few studied beyond the age of 13.'

The cast
We're looking for a genuine mix of people to share life on the farm. You might love technology, or feel that modern life is too complicated. Whoever you are, you need to be prepared for surprises.

The audition
Auditions will take place in New York and San Francisco on April 30th. To take part, you must be aged between 15 and 19. It doesn't matter how much acting experience you have. You will be put in groups and asked to act out a short scenario that we will give you on the day. On the day of the audition you will need to provide proof of your age. Your parent or guardian will also need to give you permission to attend by signing the Permissions Form at our website.

The website
For further information and the Permissions Form, go to www.lifelikeproductions.com

2   a   Read the tips in the **HOW TO** box.

    b   You see the advert on a wall and think a friend might be interested. Read it all. Make notes about the series and how to apply for an audition.

3   Which tips in the **HOW TO** box did you use for help with Exercise 2b? Tick (✓) them.

4   ▶2.29 Listen and answer the questions you hear by looking at your notes. Don't look at the advert.

HOW TO
make notes
- ☐ Decide what information you need.
- ☐ Write headings or questions to help you organise your notes.
- ☐ Write only the most important words and ideas.
- ☐ Use or invent abbreviations like *info* (information).

REACT

5   Work in pairs. What do you think? Tell your partner and give reasons for your answers.
    1   What was hardest about life in the USA in 1880?
    2   What was positive about life at that time?
    3   Would you like to take part in the programme? Why?/Why not?

GO BEYOND
What comes after these verbs in the advert: *participating in*, *recreates*, *live without*, *led*, *help with*, *be prepared for*, *provide*, *signing*?
Check your answers.

GRAMMAR *Used to*

>>> Talk about habits and situations in the past

READ AND LISTEN >>> Grammar in context

1 ▶ 2.30 How much housework do you think people did in the 19th century – more, less or the same as today? Read and listen to part of an interview to check your prediction.

Jan: Housework in the 19th century used to be very hard. People used to use wood stoves, for example. They used to light the stove in the morning and had to keep adding wood during the day.

May: So did people use to spend more time on housework?

Jan: No, they didn't, surprisingly. Housework used to take about 50 hours a week, like today. Cooking took longer, but they didn't use to spend as much time on cleaning and shopping.

STUDY

2 Complete the explanations. Use the interview in Exercise 1 to help you.

Used to
Use:
To talk about situations or habits in the past.
Form:
Positive and negative
_____ / didn't use to + infinitive
Questions and short answers
did + I/you, etc + _____ + verb
Yes, I did. / No, they _____ .
See GRAMMAR DATABASE, page 126.

PRACTISE

3 ▶ 2.31 Complete another part of the interview in Exercise 1 with the correct form of *used to*. Then listen and check your answers.

Perhaps the hardest job that women (1) *used to do* (do) was washing clothes. Remember that houses (2) _____ (not have) running water. They (3) _____ (carry) the water for washing from outside the house, often from a well or stream. Doing a single load of washing (4) _____ (need) around 190 litres of water. So imagine how many visits to the well people (5) _____ (make) every day. Housework in those days (6) _____ (not take) more time, but it was extremely hard physical work.

4 Make the sentences true for your country. Complete them with *used to/didn't use to* and the verbs in the box.

| be | buy | cost | have | travel | use | ~~wash~~ | write |

100 years ago … most people (1) *used to wash* clothes by hand.
… most people (2) _____ by car.
50 years ago … most televisions (3) _____ in black and white.
… air travel (4) _____ a lot of money.
20 years ago … most people (5) _____ an internet connection at home.
… most people (6) _____ a mobile to take photos.
10 years ago … most people (7) _____ letters to friends.
… most people (8) _____ films on DVDs.

5 a ▶ 2.32 PRONOUNCE Repeat the sentences. Pay attention to how the 's' sounds.
1 People u/s/ed to wash clothes by hand.
2 Today people u/ʒ/ually u/z/e a washing machine.

b ▶ 2.33 Listen and write the words in three groups: /s/, /ʒ/ or /z/. Then listen and repeat.

| music | single | occasionally | clothes | habits |
| leisure | housework | houses | cost | decision |

/s/ u*s*ed to	/ʒ/ u*s*ually	/z/ to u*s*e

6 Write questions with *used to*.
1 your family / live / where you live now?
   Did your family use to live where you live now?
2 What games / you / play?
3 Who / your best friends / be?
4 What school / you / go / to?
5 you / help / with housework?

SPEAK

7 Work in pairs. Answer the questions in Exercise 6 about when you were six. Ask more questions.

— Did your family use to live where you live now?
— No, we didn't.
— Where did you use to live?
— We used to live in …

LISTENING AND VOCABULARY The pretty coloured snake

>>> Understand the situation

SPEAK AND LISTEN

1 Work in pairs. Think of at least three answers for each question. Then make a class list.
   1 Where can you read, hear or see fictional stories?
   2 Where can you read, hear or see true stories?

2 a Read the tips in the **HOW TO** box.

   b ▶2.34 Listen and answer the questions.
   1 Where are the people? Be specific.
   2 Is it a conversation, a talk or something else?
   3 What's the topic?
   4 Is the context the past, present or future?

3 Which tips in the **HOW TO** box did you use for help with Exercise 2b? Tick (✓) them.

4 ▶2.34 Look at the picture. Then listen again and complete the notes.
   1 In an allegory, events/characters represent …
   2 When the hunter first saw the snake, he gave it …
   3 When the hunter saw the snake again, it was …
   4 When the snake arrived, the tribe were …
   5 They shot the snake because …
   6 They hurt the snake, and it …

HOW TO
understand the situation

☐ Listen for sounds and other clues to know where people are.
☐ Listen to how people talk. Is it a conversation, a talk, an interview … ?
☐ Identify the topic. Listen for important words like nouns, adjectives and verbs.
☐ Listen for verbs. Are people talking about the past, present or future?

REACT

5 Work in pairs. Say what you think about the story and explain why. What do you think the snake represents?

WORK WITH WORDS

6 ▶2.35 Read and listen to the conversation. Then match the feelings in blue to the definitions (1–10).

Storyteller: How do the people in the story feel? Let's see what some of the younger members of our audience think.
Sam: I think the tribe's really proud to have such a good hunter. And maybe some other hunters are jealous because he's so good.
Sonia: The hunter feels sorry for the snake. It's hungry, and that makes him sad. He feels disappointed too. He thought it was a good animal.
Lou: The snake seems grateful for the food and satisfied when it's finished eating.
Mia: The tribe's really anxious when the snake arrives and upset when it kills people.
Matt: I think the snake's ashamed at the end. It didn't want to kill people. And the hunter feels guilty because he gave the snake food.

1 _____ : sad and sorry because you have done something very bad
2 _____ : happy about the good things you or somebody you know can do
3 _____ : sad because something bad has happened to somebody else
4 _____ : worried and frightened
5 _____ : very sad and/or angry
6 _____ : unhappy because someone does something better than you
7 _____ : wanting to say thank you
8 _____ : embarrassed because you have done something wrong
9 _____ : unhappy because something isn't as good as you expected
10 _____ : happy with something that has happened

7 ▶2.36 Listen and check your answers in Exercise 6. Then listen and repeat.

8 Write four sentences about people you know using adjectives from Exercise 6. Then read your sentences to a partner, but don't say the adjective. Can he or she guess the feeling?

GO BEYOND

Do the Words & Beyond exercise on page 136.

>>> Workbook, pages 80–81

GRAMMAR Past perfect simple

>>> Talk about things that happened before another time in the past

READ AND LISTEN >>> Grammar in context

1 ▶2.37 Read and listen to the conversation. Who's Mr Casey? Why didn't Petra speak to him?

Petra: Guess who I saw at the story-telling festival. Mr Casey.
Luke: Our first primary school teacher? **Had** he **changed** much?
Petra: Yes, he **had**. I didn't recognise him at first because he**'d shaved** his beard off.
Luke: Did you say hello?
Petra: No, he**'d** just **started** speaking when I arrived, and I **hadn't had** lunch yet. And when I went back later, he**'d** already **gone**.

STUDY

2 The verbs in blue in Exercise 1 are in the past perfect simple. Complete the explanations.

Past perfect simple

Use:
To show that an action happened before another action or time in the past. Use the past simple for the other action/time.

past perfect
─────●──────────●──────
          past simple

Form:
Positive and negative
had/_____ + past participle
The contracted form of *had* is _____ .

Questions and short answers
had + *I/you*, etc + past participle
Yes, I had. / No, he _____ .

Words and expressions:
After _____ for an explanation.
With *before, just, yet* and _____ .

See GRAMMAR DATABASE, page 126.

PRACTISE

3 ▶2.38 Complete the story with the past perfect simple form of the verbs. Then listen and check your answers.

'My grandmother (1) _had died_ (die) by the time I was born, so I never met her, but I've heard lots of stories about her. She lived in a small village and (2) _____ (never / travel) more than 30 miles in any direction. One day my father went to see her with the mobile phone he (3) _____ (just / buy). He was excited about showing it to her because he was sure she (4) _____ (not see) one before. But he was disappointed when he found out that she (5) _____ (already / get) one. She (6) _____ (ask) a neighbour to buy one of the new 'pocket phones' in the nearest town. 'What's your number?' she asked when he got out his mobile. 'I'll add you to my contacts list.'

4 ▶2.39 Choose the correct options to complete the conversation. Then listen and check your answers.

Jiya: This happened a couple of years ago. I was going home on the bus, and I (1) *fell / 'd fallen* asleep.
Ross: Where (2) *did you go / had you been*?
Jiya: To a friend's house. But I (3) *stayed / 'd stayed* up the night before to revise for exams, so I (4) *was / 'd been* really tired. Anyway, when I (5) *woke / 'd woken* up, I saw that I (6) *missed / 'd missed* my stop. We were nearly at the end of the line.
Ross: So what (7) *did you do / had you done*?
Jiya: I got off at the next stop, but the last bus in the other direction (8) *already went / had already gone*, so I had to walk home. It took me two hours.

WRITE AND SPEAK

5 a Choose three of the feelings. Think of a time when you had those feelings and write a sentence to explain why.

I was worried because I hadn't done my homework.
I was excited because I'd never been on a plane before.

| embarrassed | excited | exhausted | guilty |
| proud | upset | worried | |

b Work in pairs. Tell each other the story of how you felt and why. Ask each other questions to find out more information.

Workbook, page 82

77

LANGUAGE & BEYOND

Elders in different cultures

Different cultures see their elders in different ways. In many Asian, African and Latin American cultures, elders are respected for their wisdom – the ability to use their knowledge and experience to give good advice. They also have a role in teaching their children about the traditions and values of their culture. Elderly people often live with their children, who look after them. This contrasts with many western cultures, where family members often live in different places, and elderly people often live alone or in old people's homes.

How are elders seen in your country? Read the statements and circle Yes (*Y*), No (*N*) or It depends (*D*).

		Y	N	D
1	People value the experience elderly people have.	○	○	○
2	Families ask their oldest members for help with decisions.	○	○	○
3	Old age is seen as a positive time in somebody's life.	○	○	○
4	Most elderly people live with their children or family.	○	○	○
5	It's common for grandparents to look after their grandchildren.	○	○	○
6	Young people give their seats to elderly people on public transport.	○	○	○
7	You often see elderly people speaking on TV.	○	○	○

>>> Value your elders

SPEAK AND READ

1 **Work in pairs. Talk about the elderly people you know. Answer the questions below.**
   1 Who are they? Neighbours? Grandparents? Other relatives?
   2 How often do you see them?
   3 What do you usually talk about when you see them?

2 **Read the article above. How do people in *your* country see elders?**

3 **Choose your reaction to the statements (1–7) in the article.**

4 **Compare your reactions with the rest of the class. If your answer is *No*, or *It depends*, explain why.**

DO

5 **Copy and complete the profile about an elderly person that you feel close to.**

6 **Work in pairs. Tell each other about the person in your profile and ask each other for more information.**

Name: _____
Relationship with me: _____
Hobbies and interests: _____
How often I see him/her: _____
What he/she did before he/she retired: _____
Things he's/she's done in his/her life: _____
Things we talk about: _____
Things I have learned from him/her: _____
Things I admire about him/her: _____
Why I feel close to him/her: _____

REFLECT

7 **Discuss the questions with your class. Do you agree with the REFLECTION POINT?**
   1 Do you think people in your country generally value their elders? Why?/Why not?
   2 How do elderly people feel when they spend time talking to young people? Why?
   3 What have you learned from the elderly people you know well?

EXTEND

8 a **Think of some advice you would like to have from an elderly person.**
   b **Ask two elderly people you know for their advice. Is their advice similar or different? Which advice is best? Why?**

REFLECTION POINT

It's important to value your elders. Their experience means they have a lot of good advice to give, and it makes them feel proud when younger people listen to them.

RESPECT OTHERS

Workbook, page 85

SPEAKING At the library

›› Join and use a library

SPEAK

1 Work in pairs. Answer the questions about the things in the box.

> borrow books/magazines/CDs/DVDs/video games
> find a quiet place to study   use a computer/the internet

1 Which things can you do in your school library?
2 Which things can you do at your nearest public library?

WATCH OR LISTEN

2 ▶2.40 Watch or listen to the scene. What two things does Jack want to do at the library?

3 ▶2.40 Try to complete the questions in the conversation. Then watch or listen again to check or complete your answers.

4 ▶2.41 Listen and repeat the questions.

5 a Read the tips in the HOW TO box.

HOW TO
react to information

- Say *OK./Good./Great.* if you're happy with the information.
- Say *Right./Oh, right.* if there's a possible problem.
- Use *So* + a question/*Does that mean …?* to check you understand.

b Underline examples of the words and expressions in the HOW TO box in the conversation.

ACT

6 Work in pairs. Role-play a conversation at a library information desk.
 – Student B: You want to join and use the library. Ask questions and complete the table below.
 – Student A: You're the librarian. Answer your partner's questions with the information on page 141.

How to join the library if you're under 18
1
2

Borrowing from the library

Item	How long?	Charge	Charge if returned late
Books			
Music CDs			
DVDs and games			

Librarian:	Good morning.
Jack:	Hello. I'd like to join the library. How do you (1) _____?
Librarian:	You need to fill in a membership form.
Jack:	OK, and how old do you (2) _____?
Librarian:	You can join at any age, but you need to give the name of a parent or guardian if you're under 18.
Jack:	Good. And how much does it (3) _____?
Librarian:	It's free if you live or study locally.
Jack:	Right. I'm staying with my grandmother for a month. Does that mean I can't join?
Librarian:	No, that's not a problem.
Jack:	Great. Could you (4) _____, please?
Librarian:	Of course. Here you are.
Jack:	I've filled in the form. Do I (5) _____ anything else?
Librarian:	Can I just have a look? No, that all seems fine.
Jack:	So can I (6) _____ now?
Librarian:	We just need a photo for your library card.
Jack:	Oh, right. Is there any way I can just check my emails?
Librarian:	I'm afraid the computers are all busy.

PHRASEBOOK ▶2.42

Join a library

How do you become a member / use the internet … ?

How much does it cost to join/borrow … ?

How old do you have to be?

Do I have to do anything else / live locally … ?

Could you give me a form / give me some help with … , please?

Can I use a computer / borrow a DVD … now?

React to information

OK. / Good. / Great. / Right. / Oh, right.

Does that mean … ?

So … ?

Workbook, page 83

WRITING Telling tales

>>> Say how and when things happen in a story

SPEAK AND READ

1 **Work in pairs. Tell a story together.**
   1 Think of three traditional stories.
   2 Choose one of the stories and tell it together. Help each other to remember what happens.

2 **Read a short version of a traditional story from Europe. Do you know the girl's name?**

3 a **Read the tips in the HOW TO box.**

One-minute tales

Once upon a time there was a girl called … . One day she was taking some cakes to her grandma's house in the forest. Suddenly, a wolf appeared from behind a tree. The wolf asked where she was going. 'Why not pick some flowers for grandma?' he suggested. Meanwhile, the wolf ran to grandma's house, ate her, then got into bed. Later, when the girl arrived, he ate her too. After that he fell asleep and started snoring loudly. Just then, a hunter passed by and heard the snoring. He opened the door and as soon as he saw the wolf, he knew he had eaten grandma. He cut open his stomach and to his surprise the girl came out, followed by grandma. At first grandma looked very ill, but in the end she recovered and ate the cakes.

HOW TO
say how and when things happen in a story

- *Once upon a time* starts a story.
- *One day* introduces the first event.
- *then/after that* says what happened next
- *later* = at some time in the future
- *as soon as* = immediately after
- *suddenly* = very quickly
- *meanwhile* = at the same time
- *at first* = in the beginning
- *in the end* = finally, after some time

b **Underline the words and expressions in the HOW TO box in the story.**

PRACTISE

4 **Complete a traditional story from China with words and expressions from the HOW TO box.**

Once upon a time there was an old man who used to go fishing on a lake. One evening, he went fishing after dinner. He threw his line into the water and (1) _____ fell asleep. (2) _____, he woke up. There was a fish on the line. (3) _____ he saw it, he knew it was special. It was made of gold, and it said: 'If you let me go, I'll give you a golden line.' (4) _____ the old man didn't believe him, but he put his line into the water, and it turned to gold. 'Now let me go,' said the fish. But the man put the fish in a bucket.
(5) _____, he started pulling up the line.
(6) _____, the line was so heavy that the boat sank. The man died, and the fish swam away.

PLAN

5 **You're going to write a short version of a traditional story. Make a plan for your story.**

WRITING PLAN
1 **Think of a traditional story.**
It could be from your country or from another part of the world.

2 **Tell the story in no more than 140 words.**
How does the story start? What happens next? How does it end?

3 **Use time expressions to say how and when things happened.**
Look at the tips in the HOW TO box.

WRITE AND CHECK

6 **Use your plan and write your story. Then check it. Tick (✓) the things in the plan.**

SHARE

7 **Swap your story with a partner. Which story did you enjoy reading the most? Why?**

Workbook, pages 84–85

80

UNIT REVIEW 7

VOCABULARY Traditional activities

1 The words in the advert are all in the wrong place. Write the correct verbs under the advert. Use the correct forms.

Do you know how to (1) **wash** bread and (2) **milk** food? Have you ever (3) **baked** clothes by hand and (4) **made** a cow? In the past, people had to (5) **travel** a sweater if they wanted a new one, (6) **grow** holes in their shirts and (7) **sew** their own furniture. People (8) **used** by horse and cart, and (9) **made** gas lights at night. And when the day's work was done, they (10) **knitted** their own entertainment.

Come to Mrs Daly's Trad Camp and learn how people used to do things!

1 _____ 5 _____ 9 _____
2 _____ 6 _____ 10 _____
3 _____ 7 _____
4 _____ 8 _____   ___/10

Feelings

2 Complete the website with adjectives.

COMMENTS

Lidia
I was really (1) a_____s before I went, but I had a great time and came home really (2) s_____d with how things went. I'm (3) g_____l to my parents for giving me this experience.

Albert
I'm really (4) d_____d with myself. I didn't do anything well, and I feel a bit (5) g_____y for making more work for the others. Some of them looked a little (6) u_____t at the end.

Alana
I'm really (7) p_____d because I was good at everything. So good that the others seemed (8) j_____s of me. I'm (9) s_____y for them, because they really wanted to be as good as me, but they shouldn't be (10) a_____d because they tried really hard.   ___/10

GRAMMAR Used to

3 Complete the interview with the *used to* form of the verbs and short answers.

Interviewer: Why did you set up Trad Camp?
Mrs Daly: Well, when I was a kid, we (1) _____ (do) everything by hand. We (2) _____ (not have) machines to help us.
Interviewer: (3) _____ (you / help) around the house?
Mrs Daly: Yes, I (4) _____. Even young children (5) _____ (have) housework to do. I started when I was three years old!
Interviewer: And (6) _____ (the children / complain)?
Mrs Daly: No, they (7) _____. They just (8) _____ (do) it. Children today don't know what work is!   ___/16

Past perfect simple

4 Complete the second part of the interview with the past perfect simple or the past simple form of the verbs and short answers.

Interviewer: So tell me more about Trad Camp.
Mrs Daly: Well, I (1) _____ (start) Trad Camp in 1992 because I thought young people (2) _____ (forget) the value of good old hard work.
Interviewer: (3) _____ (you / try) to start a business before that?
Mrs Daly: Yes, I had. Twice. But they (4) _____ (not work) because I (5) _____ (not do) enough research. I (6) _____ (not understand) that although the old ways of doing things (7) _____ (be) better, you can't make a business work these days if you don't have a website!   ___/14

Your score: ___/50

SKILLS CHECK

✓✓✓ Yes, I can. No problem!
✓✓ Yes, I can. But I need a bit of help.
✓   Yes, I can. But I need a lot of help.

I can make notes when I read. _____
I can understand the situation when I listen. _____
I can value my elders. _____
I can join and use a library. _____
I can say how and when things happen in a story. _____

Workbook, pages 86–87

81

UNIT 8 SHE SAID, HE SAID

IN THE PICTURE In the news

>>> Talk about people working in the media

WORK WITH WORDS

1 **RECALL** Work in pairs. Do the tasks. You have three minutes.

   a Complete the names of things we read.

1	.... rtoon	8	.... em
2	.... cipe	9	.... ofile
3	.... port	10	.... ticle
4	.... tter	11	.... ory
5	.... cture .... ption	12	.... iz
6	.... og	13	.... les
7	.... terview	14	.... rvey

   b Find an example in this book of three of the things in the list.

2 ▶3.01 Write the media jobs in the correct category. Listen and check. Then listen and repeat.

   author   blogger   cartoonist   designer   editor
   gossip columnist   graphic artist   journalist
   photographer   printer   publisher   reporter

People who write	People who work with visuals	People who work behind the scenes

3 Choose the correct people from Exercise 2 to complete the sentences about a newspaper.

   1 The *printer / publisher* owns the newspaper and employs a lot of people.
   2 The *reporter / journalist* reports the news while the *reporter / journalist* investigates the news.
   3 The *designer / photographer* takes pictures to illustrate the stories. The *graphic artist / cartoonist* creates other visuals, like graphs and diagrams.
   4 The *author / editor* decides which stories to include in tomorrow's paper.
   5 The *designer / photographer* creates the final pages.
   6 The *printer / cartoonist* adds some visual fun to the news while the *gossip columnist / blogger* writes funny things about famous people. Today he's writing about the famous *author / reporter* of a bestselling book.
   7 When the newspaper is ready to print, it goes to the *printer / publisher*.
   8 While the paper is being printed, the *designer / blogger* is writing for the digital edition of the paper.

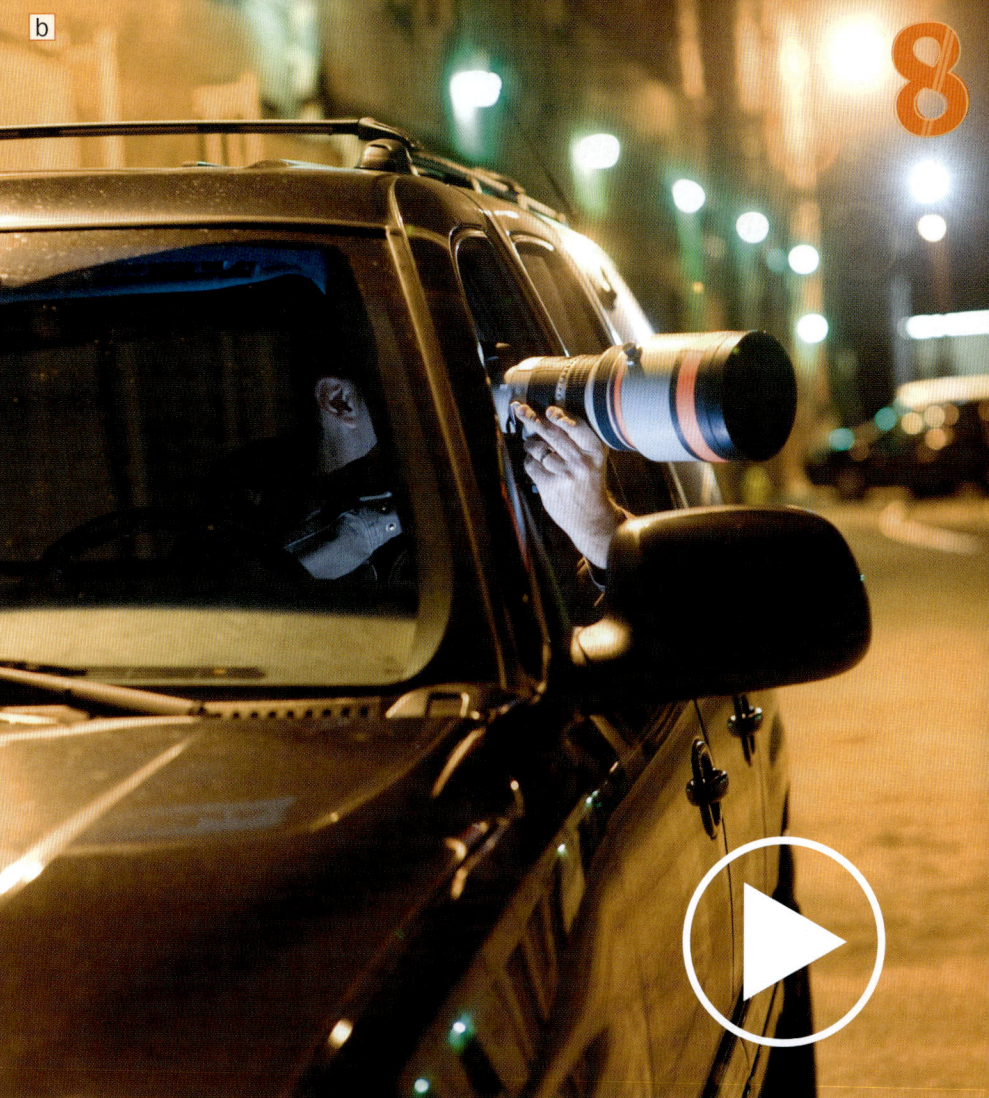

4 Which of the people in Exercise 2 can you see in the photos?

5 ▶3.02 Listen to a designer talk about the photos. Which photos is she talking about?

1 .... 3 .... 5 ....
2 .... 4 .... 6 ....

6 a ▶3.03 **PRONOUNCE** Listen and repeat the word. Pay attention to the <u>stressed</u> syllable and the /ə/ sound in the unstressed syllable.

/ə/ auth<u>or</u>

b ▶3.04 Listen to the other words in the box in Exercise 2. Underline the stressed syllables, and circle the syllables that have the /ə/ sound. Then listen and repeat.

7 **THE MOVING PICTURE** ▶ Watch the video. Which of the people from Exercise 2 do you see?

SPEAK

8 Work in pairs. Ask and answer the questions in the survey on media habits.

PHRASE BYTES

I hardly ever/rarely/occasionally …

I was looking for … / I wanted to find …

I'd prefer to be the … because … / Being a … must be …

Really? But surely …

I'd want to publish …

Media habits

1 Which magazines or comics do you read?
2 Which cartoons or cartoonists do you like?
3 When was the last time you looked at a newspaper? What part(s) did you look at (eg sports, TV, news)?
4 What was the last book or story you read? Who is your favourite author and why?
5 Which media job would you most like to do? Why?
6 If you were a publisher, what type of magazine would you like to publish and why?

GO BEYOND

Do the Words & Beyond exercise on page 137.

Workbook, page 88

READING Media culture

>>> Recognise formal and informal writing

SPEAK AND READ

1 **Work in pairs. Answer the questions.**
   1 Which famous people do you like in music, television, sport or film?
   2 What facts do you know about their lives?
   3 Where did you find the information?

2 a **Read the tips in the HOW TO box.**

   b ▶3.05 **Read each text then match it to the correct publication (1–3).**
      1 A showbiz blog   2 A celebrity magazine   3 A serious newspaper

A
A young Hollywood celebrity has spoken about being a victim of the paparazzi. In an interview with the *Los Angeles Times*, the 26-year-old actor said: 'Today's media culture is a dangerous monster.' Currently promoting his latest film, the star has also been in the news for personal reasons. Separating public and personal life has always been difficult for film and music stars. On the one hand, they want media attention in order to help promote their careers. On the other hand, they want the media to respect their privacy.
One magazine has suggested that the actor should move to France, where there are stricter privacy laws. In the United States however, the paparazzi can take photographs of anyone if they are in a public place, including the children of celebrities.
Sue Jakes, the respected journalist, told me that some photographers often scare celebrity children to make them cry. She said that an emotional or embarrassing photograph was easier to sell.
Maybe it's time to stop this form of 'journalism'. It's easy to do – just stop buying celebrity magazines.

B
Hot young star ▓▓▓▓▓ has told a newspaper that I am a monster! What did I do?! Did I hurt his feelings when I suggested that the 26-year-old actor's relationship was over? Or was it last week's embarrassing photo in our 'They're only human' feature?
If you don't like being famous, go to France, *chéri*! But please stop saying terrible things about the people who helped to make you a star.
By the way, an anonymous source told me that she had seen ▓▓▓▓▓ having dinner with a famous singer at one of the city's top restaurants. Hello? If you don't want to be photographed, eat at home! Well, my old friend, from now on I will respect your privacy by hiding your name on my blog and on the pages of all the celeb magazines that I write for (including this one). I will refer to you as ▓▓▓▓▓. Let's see how you feel when your name stops appearing in print!

3 **Choose the best title for each of the texts.**
   1 'Celebrity children complain about paparazzi'
   2 'Star tells me to leave him alone!'
   3 'Can public figures have private lives?'
   4 'Anonymous monster attacks Hollywood star!!'

4 **Which tips in the HOW TO box did you use for help with Exercises 2b and 3? Tick (✓) them.**

5 **Read the sentences and circle A (text A) or B (text B).**
   1 *A / B* includes a quote by the actor.
   2 *A / B* includes the views of an expert.
   3 *A / B* includes a fact that is wrong.
   4 *A / B* includes information given by an anonymous person.
   5 *A / B* says that the actor should move to France.
   6 *A / B* thinks we can do something to change the situation.

REACT

6 **Work in pairs. What do you think? Tell your partner.**
   1 Which of the texts is more interesting? Give reasons for your answer.
   2 Why is text A probably more accurate than text B?
   3 Why do people like reading about the lives of famous people?
   4 How can famous people have private lives?

HOW TO
recognise formal and informal writing

In formal writing, look for …
☐ longer sentences with formal words and phrases (*on the one hand*, *however*).
☐ full verbs (*I will*, *do not*).
☐ correct use of punctuation.

In informal writing, look for …
☐ shorter sentences with spoken English phrases (*well*, *By the way*).
☐ contractions (*I'll*, *don't*).
☐ extra punctuation to add emphasis, especially exclamation marks.

GO BEYOND
Read the two texts again and find two more differences between them.

>>> Workbook, page 89

GRAMMAR Reported speech

>>> Report what people say

READ AND LISTEN >>> Grammar in context

1 ▶3.06 Read and listen to the conversation. Who is Lucy's new photographer?

Harry: Jack! I'm surprised to see you. Where's Lucy? I told her that I'd meet her here at seven. We're doing a story for the school magazine.
Jack: Lucy told me she didn't want to see you. I told her that I could talk to you.
Harry: I don't understand. We arranged to meet here yesterday. I've brought my camera.
Jack: She said that she'd found another photographer. She said she was going to do the story with him. Hello? … Yes, I'll tell him … Yes, I can be there in five minutes.
Harry: Was that Lucy?
Jack: Yes. She said she was sorry. She also said that she was waiting for her new photographer.

STUDY

2 Complete the explanations. Use Exercise 1 to help you.

Reported speech

Use:
To report something that somebody said.
Direct speech: *She said: 'I'm sorry.'*
Reported speech: *She said she was sorry. / She told me/him, etc (+ that) she was sorry.*

Form:
Tense changes
Use the past forms of the verbs:
'<u>I'm</u> sorry.' ➤ She said (that) she was sorry.
'I <u>don't want</u> to see him,' ➤ Lucy told me (that) she _____ to see you.

Other changes
Pronouns and possessive adjectives change in reported speech:
'<u>I'm</u> surprised to see _____.'
Harry said that he was surprised to see **him**.

See GRAMMAR DATABASE, page 127.

PRACTISE

3 Write the sentences from Exercise 1 in reported speech with *said*.
1 Harry: 'I'm surprised to see you.'
   He said that he was surprised to see him.
2 Harry: 'We're doing a story for the school magazine.'
3 Harry: 'I don't understand.'
4 Harry: 'I've brought my camera.'
5 Jack: 'I'll tell him.'
6 Jack: 'I can be there in five minutes.'

4 Write the sentences from Exercise 1 in direct speech.
1 Lucy told me that she didn't want to see you.
   Lucy to Jack:
   '*I don't want to see him.*'
2 I told her that I'd meet her here at seven.
   Harry to Lucy:
   '   ,'
3 I told her that I could talk to you.
   Jack to Lucy:
   '   ,'
4 She said that she'd found another photographer.
   Lucy to Jack:
   '   ,'
5 She also said she was going to do the story with him.
   Lucy to Jack:
   '   ,'
6 She also said that she was waiting for her new photographer.
   Lucy to Jack:
   '   ,'

5 Complete the sentences about yourself.

Your life in six sentences
1 **Food:** For breakfast, I usually have …
2 **Entertainment:** The last film I saw was …
3 **Plans:** Next weekend, I'm going to …
4 **Dreams:** One day I hope I'll …
5 **Now:** At the moment I'm feeling …
6 **Skills:** I can't …, but I can …

SPEAK

6 Work in pairs. Read out your sentences from Exercise 5. Take notes about your partner and then tell the class what she or he said.

> She said that she usually had … for breakfast.

> She told me that the last film …

Workbook, pages 90–91

LISTENING AND VOCABULARY Picture stories

>>> Infer meaning

SPEAK AND LISTEN

1 Work in pairs. Describe what you can see in the pictures.

2 ▶3.07 Listen and tick (✓) the correct picture to answer each question.

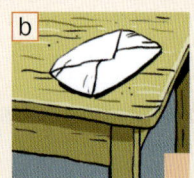

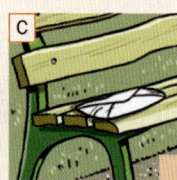

3 a Read the tips in the HOW TO box.

b ▶3.07 Listen to the scenes again and choose the correct option in the sentences.
  1 The police officer is *happy / unhappy* that the reporter called.
  2 The actor *likes / doesn't like* talking about her next project.
  3 The reporter *is / isn't* sure the witness remembers what she saw.
  4 The athlete feels *very happy / a bit disappointed* after the race.
  5 The reporter and his source *trust / don't trust* each other.
  6 In the same scene, the *reporter / reporter's source* switches off the recorder.

c Which tips in the HOW TO box did you use for help with Exercise 3b? Tick (✓) them.

REACT

4 Work in pairs. Act one of the scenes in Exercise 2 in your own words, reflecting the feelings of the characters.

WORK WITH WORDS

5 ▶3.08 Complete the sentences with the correct form of the reporting verbs in the box. Then listen and check.

| add | admit | claim | confirm | deny | promise |

Police officer: You said you wouldn't call me again, remember?
Reporter: I know. It's the last time. I (1) _____ .
Reporter: Can you (2) _____ the stories about you and rap star Dustin Dredd?
Reporter: In your original statement you (3) _____ that you saw three men?
Witness: That's right. I (4) _____ it sounds strange.
Athlete: Can I just (5) _____ one more thing? I couldn't have done this without the support of everyone back home.
Source: If you use my name, I'll (6) _____ I ever spoke to you.

6 ▶3.09 Complete the sentences. Then listen and repeat the verbs from Exercises 5 and 6.
  1 The police officer **suggested** that they meet at …
  2 The witness **insisted** that she saw …
  3 The athlete **explained** how he felt …
  4 The reporter **agreed** to switch off …

1 When will the journalist meet the police officer?
   a   b   c

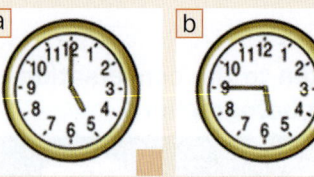

2 What type of film is the star going to make next?
   a   b   c

3 What did the witness see?
   a   b   c

4 In which place did the athlete finish the race?
   a   b   c

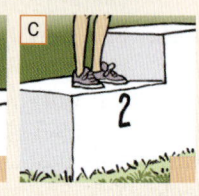

5 Where's the letter?
   a   b   c

HOW TO
infer meaning

People often don't say directly what they think and feel.
☐ Listen to <u>how</u> people talk. How people say things often tells you what they really think.
☐ Identify the <u>relationship</u> between speakers. People often don't say things directly when they don't know or don't trust the other person.

GO BEYOND
Do the Words & Beyond exercise on page 137.

Workbook, pages 92–93

GRAMMAR Reported questions

>>> Report what people ask

READ >>> Grammar in context

1 Read the news report. What kind of job does Johan have?

When I met Johan after the game, I asked him why he was leaving the club. He explained that it was for personal reasons. I then asked him how the other players had reacted. At first, he denied that there had been any problems on or off the pitch, but when I asked him if he was still friends with Pepe, he refused to comment. I asked him whether he had any immediate plans and he said that he was talking to a club in Spain. I asked him which club he was talking to, but he wouldn't say. As he was leaving, I asked him if he could say something to his fans. He promised that he'd come back one day.

STUDY

2 Complete the explanations with examples from Exercise 1.

Reported questions

Use:
To report a question that somebody asked.
Direct question: 'Why **are you leaving** the club?'
Reported question: I asked him why **he was leaving** the club.

Form: *wh-* questions
asked + person + question word + *I/you*, etc + verb:
I asked him how _____.
I asked him which _____.

Form: *yes/no* questions
asked + person + *if/whether* + *I/you*, etc + verb:
I asked him if _____.
I asked him whether _____.

Other changes:
Change verb tenses, pronouns, possessive adjectives, time expressions and adverbs of place if necessary (see page 85).

See GRAMMAR DATABASE, page 127.

PRACTISE

3 Write the reported questions in orange in Exercise 1 as direct questions.
'Why are you leaving the club?'

4 Read the journalist's notes and write her questions in reported speech.

1 Janet Mills (politician): 'Have you spoken to the minister?' *I asked her if she'd spoken to the minister.*
2 Justin (singer): 'Can you play any instruments?'
3 Cyclops (pop group): 'When will you play in Britain again?'
4 Mrs Mills (witness): 'Did you see what happened?'
5 Jeff Manners (athlete): 'How are you feeling?'
6 Mary Webb and Jack Landon (actors): 'Are you excited about the film?'

5 a Look at the information you were asked for in an oral exam. Write the direct and reported questions.

1 Where / from?
   'Where are you from?' /
   They asked me where I was from.
2 What / school / go to?
3 How long / study English?
4 ever / visit / the UK?
5 like / go to the cinema?
6 What / do / next weekend?

b Answer the questions in reported speech.
I told them I was from Mexico City.

6 Complete the tasks. Choose the type of reporter you'd like to be.
- sports reporter
- entertainment reporter
- news reporter

Write the name of a famous person you'd like to interview. Write five questions you'd like to ask the famous person.

SPEAK AND WRITE

7 Work in pairs. Complete the tasks. Your partner is the famous person you chose in Exercise 6. Ask your partner the five questions you prepared. Make a note of their answers. Write a short report of the interview using reported questions and reported speech. Read your report to the class.

Workbook, page 94

87

LANGUAGE & BEYOND

Anonymous
is a student in another class at the school.
'A friend told me that Laura had been excluded from school. Another friend said that Laura had used a phone camera to take photos of Beth's homework and copied it at home. I heard a long time ago that she'd copied other people's homework.'

Chris
is Laura's best friend. 'I know Laura better than anyone. She told me that she didn't copy Beth's homework, and I believe her. She admitted that she'd copied some school work from the internet in the past, but she said she'd never copy another student's work.'

Stefan
is Beth's friend. 'Beth told me that she'd seen Laura copying her homework in the break. She asked me if I could tell the teacher. She said that the teacher wouldn't believe her. Last year, someone said Beth had stolen a phone. Beth denied it, but no-one found the phone.'

Maite
is in Laura's class. 'I don't know Laura very well, but I think she's a good person. People claim that she stole someone's homework, but why would she do it? She helped me last month when I was having problems with history. She knows a lot. She's clever. She doesn't have to cheat.'

>>> **Compare and evaluate information that you read or hear**

SPEAK AND READ

1. ▶3.10 Work in pairs. Read and listen to the four people. What's the situation?

2. After reading and listening, do you think Laura is innocent or guilty? Why? Discuss your opinions.

DO

3. Work in groups. Answer the questions. Which speaker(s) …
   1. share the same opinion?
   2. might be influenced by their relationship with the people involved?
   3. don't agree about some facts?
   4. don't give their name or the name(s) of their sources?
   5. include information that is possibly out of date?

4. Order the speakers from the *least* to the *most* reliable, giving reasons for your choices.

REFLECT

5. Discuss the questions with your class. Do you agree with the REFLECTION POINT ?
   1. Why was it important to have more than one source for information in the situation in Exercise 1?
   2. Why are multiple sources important when you look for facts?
   3. How often do you use the internet to find information for school work? How often do you compare the information from different sources?

EXTEND

6. Work in groups. Write five tips for using the internet to find factual information. Use Exercise 3 to help you.
   Always check your information at more than two different sites.

PHRASE BYTES
I don't believe much of what … says because …
She/He isn't very reliable because …
… is much more reliable than …

REFLECTION POINT
It's important to find more than one source for information in order to compare and evaluate the different sources and information.

SPEAKING Excuse me …

>>> Interrupt someone

SPEAK

1 Work in pairs. Describe the picture. What's the situation?

WATCH OR LISTEN

2 ▶3.11 Watch or listen to the first scene and check your answer to Exercise 1.

Dad:	What time do you call this?
Leo:	I …
Mum:	You promised you'd be back by eight.
Dad:	We've been worried.
Leo:	(1) _____ ?
Dad:	You should've phoned us and …
Leo:	(2) _____ I did phone you. I got voicemail.
Mum:	What? Where's my phone?

3 ▶3.12 Watch or listen to the second scene. Where was the phone?

Ethan:	Then what happened?
Ruby:	My mom and dad are just the same.
Leo:	(3) _____ , let me finish.
Ruby:	If I'm late home, they get real mad.
Leo:	(4) _____ . I haven't finished the story.
Ethan:	My dad is always losing his phone. It drives Mum up the wall.
Leo:	(5) _____ . Will you let me tell the story?
Ruby:	OK. Keep your shirt on.
Leo:	Thanks. The phone was …

4 a ▶3.13 Watch or listen to both conversations again and write the correct phrases in the spaces.

b ▶3.14 Listen and repeat the phrases. Pay attention to intonation.

5 Read the sentences. Match them to sentences from the conversations with the same meaning.
1 It makes Mum extremely angry.
2 I heard the answering machine.
3 They get very angry.
4 You're very late.
5 Calm down.

6 Work in groups of three. Practise saying the conversations.

ACT

7 Work in groups of three. Complete the tasks. Read the conversation in Exercise 2 and decide what happens next. What do the people say? How do they find the phone? Write the conversation and include at least three interrupting phrases. Give each person in the group one of the parts and perform the scene for the class.

PHRASEBOOK ▶3.15

Interrupting phrases

Can I say something?

Excuse me …

Hang on a second/minute/moment.

(I'm) sorry to interrupt, but …

(I'm) sorry for interrupting, but …

Wait a second/minute/moment.

Workbook, page 95

89

WRITING School news

>>> Use correct punctuation

SPEAK AND READ

1 Work in pairs. Put the words in order to make newspaper headlines.

2 Match the news story to the correct headline in Exercise 1.

3 Complete the punctuation rules with the words in the box.

| apostrophes   capital letters   commas |
| exclamation marks   full stops |
| question marks |

1 Use _____ for names, nationalities, titles, days of the week and professions, titles of books, etc.
2 Use _____ at the end of sentences.
3 Use _____ for short forms of verbs and possessive s.
4 Use _____ at the end of direct questions.
5 Use _____ in lists, to separate phrases and with direct speech.
6 Use _____ to indicate surprise or to add emphasis.

1 IMPROVE / RESULTS / EXAM / SPANISH

2 TEACHER / WELCOMES / SCHOOL / NEW

3 PROBLEMS / BICYCLE / CONTINUE /

This term a new Spanish teacher has started working at the school. Rosa Martínez, from Granada in Andalucía, has a lot of exciting interests: going to the cinema, the theatre and museums; taking photos of people, buildings and wildlife; and improving her English! When I met her yesterday, I asked her if she was looking forward to meeting her new students. 'Of course,' she said, 'I'm really excited to be here.'

4 a Read the tips in the **HOW TO** box.

HOW TO

use correct punctuation

- Use a colon (:) to start a list or a quote.
- Use a semicolon (;) to separate longer phrases in a list.
- Use dots (…) to show that a sentence or quote isn't complete.
- Use single (' ') or double (" ") quotation marks for direct speech.

b Work in pairs. Find examples of the punctuation in the news story and explain how it is used.

PRACTISE

5 Check and correct the punctuation and spelling in another news story from the school magazine.

This year the drama group is going to perform a musical version of William Shakespeares play *romeo and juliet*. Are you intrested in acting if you are, come to the auditions on friday. Mrs jones the director of the show told me i am looking for poeple who luv doing all these things singing in the shower dancing to diffrent types of music and performing in public,

PLAN

6 Work in pairs. You're going to write a news story about your school for the school magazine. Choose a topic and make a plan for your story.

WRITING PLAN

1 **Write a short news story**
Explain the main points of your news story at the beginning.
Use direct and indirect speech.

2 **Use examples of different punctuation.**
Include some of the punctuation from Exercise 3 and the **HOW TO** box.

3 **Give your news story a headline.**
Look at the sample headlines in Exercise 1 and write a similar headline.

4 **Check the punctuation and spelling.**
Read your story carefully, then give it to another person to check.

WRITE AND CHECK

7 Use your plan and write your news story. Then check it. Tick (✓) the things in the plan.

SHARE

8 Swap your story with other students.

UNIT REVIEW 8

VOCABULARY Print and digital media jobs

1 Complete the text with the missing words.

Meet Bill Hearst. He's the (1) p_____ of the *Billington Post*. Bill also writes for the paper. In fact, he's the paper's top (2) r_____. Actually, he's the paper's only real (3) j_____. Bill is also the paper's award-winning (4) p_____. When Bill has written a story, he gives it to his (5) e_____, who's called Bill. Bill then gives the story to Bill, the (6) d_____, who prepares the page. If the story needs some other visuals, he contacts Bill, the (7) g_____ a_____.

Write the missing letters in some of Bill's other jobs.

8 c__rt__n__st
9 g__ss__p c__l__mn__st
10 pr__nt__r
11 bl__gg__r
12 __th__r

___/12

Reporting verbs

2 a Choose the correct options in each newspaper story.

1 'It's not me!' Yesterday Hearst *admitted / denied* that he was the thief.
2 'OK. It was me!' Today Hearst *admitted / suggested* that he'd stolen his dad's biscuit.
3 'I'll do it soon.' Last week, Hearst *added / promised* that he'd do the washing-up soon.
4 'You're right!' Today Hearst *agreed / denied* that he still hadn't done the washing-up.
5 'It's true! I don't like them.' Hearst also *confirmed / explained* that he didn't like carrots.

b Match the verbs in the box to the correct definitions.

| add | claim | explain | insist | suggest |

1 _____ : to help somebody understand something
2 _____ : to offer an idea or a plan
3 _____ : to say something more about the same thing
4 _____ : to say something is true
5 _____ : to continue saying that something is true

___/10

GRAMMAR Reported speech

3 a Write the quotes in reported speech.

1 The President: 'I will make the world a better place.'
2 Actor: 'I'm making a film in Brazil now.'
3 Policewoman: 'I saw the thief here yesterday.'
4 Pop group to Bill: 'We're going to play six concerts next week.'
5 Mum to Bill: 'You're the best editor in the world.'
6 Athletes to reporters: 'We love your country.'

b Choose the correct option to complete the sentences.

1 I *said / told* Bill that he needed to find more reporters.
2 But Bill *said / told* he enjoyed writing all the stories.
3 His mum and dad *said / told* him he should do a sport.

___/18

Reported questions

4 Report the questions, using pronouns in place of names.

1 Bill to his parents: 'Can I go out tonight?'
2 Dad to Bill: 'Have you done your homework?'
3 Mum to Bill: 'Where are you going?'
4 Bill to Mum: 'Do I have to tell you?'
5 Mum and Dad to Bill: 'What time will you be home?'

___/10

Your score: ___/50

SKILLS CHECK

✓✓✓ Yes, I can. No problem!
✓✓ Yes, I can. But I need a bit of help.
✓ Yes, I can. But I need a lot of help.

I can recognise formal and informal writing. _____
I can infer meaning when I listen. _____
I can compare and evaluate information that I read or hear. _____
I can interrupt someone. _____
I can use correct punctuation when I write. _____

Workbook, pages 98–99

91

PROGRESS CHECK

READ

1 Read the text and the questions below. For each question, choose A, B, C or D.

1 In the essay, the style of writing is …
   A all formal.
   B all informal.
   C informal with a few formal sentences.
   D formal with a few informal sentences.

2 What does Tara say about health?
   A Around the world, people live longer than they used to.
   B People live longer than they used to in some parts of the world.
   C In some countries, people live shorter lives than in the past.
   D In the United States, people live shorter lives than in most countries.

3 Her grandfather thinks that teenagers …
   A don't have as much fun as in the past.
   B have too many possessions.
   C aren't as grateful as they used to be.
   D are more anxious about work.

4 Tara has written the essay …
   A based on her personal knowledge.
   B after reading a magazine article.
   C using a variety of sources.
   D using just one main source of information.

5 How might Tara end her essay?

   A In conclusion, in most aspects, life was much better in the past than it is today.

   B My conclusion is that life isn't as much fun as it was in the past.

   C In conclusion, life was better in the past in some ways but much worse in others.

   D To conclude, people are more satisfied with life today than in the past.

EXAM TIPS

answer multiple-choice questions
- Read all the questions carefully and then read the text.
- Read each question again and read all the choices.
- Decide which choices are definitely wrong.
- Look at the text again to help you choose the correct answer.

recognise formal and informal writing
See page 84

Tara

People often claim that life was better in the past. But is this true? In this essay I'm going to look at how things have changed in different areas of life.

In my opinion, health is much better than it used to be. Statistics confirm that, in general, people live longer today than they used to. According to the United Nations, here in the United States, the average man and woman live until they are about 75 and 80 years old. In 1900, they lived until they were about 46 and 48. However, there are still countries today where life expectancy is as low as around 45 and 47.

I asked my granddaddy if he thought life was better for teenagers in the past. He said that he felt sorry for young people today. He admitted that life was much harder when he was a boy – his family lived on a farm, used gas lights and grew their own food – but he suggested that people were happier, partly because they made their own entertainment.

I'm not sure my younger brother would agree with him. When I suggested to him that life was more fun in the past, he said: 'You've got to be joking. Look at all this stuff – my laptop, phone. Can you imagine how life was before the internet? Boring!'

What about the environment? There didn't use to be so much pollution in the past because there were fewer people. However, we are more aware of how important it is to protect the environment today.

Reading: _____ /10

92

PROGRESS CHECK 7&8

LISTEN

2 ▶3.16 You will hear a radio reporter presenting a news story. Listen and write the missing information in the spaces.

NEWS REPORT

REPORTER: Karen White
LOCATION: Paris, France

SUMMARY:
Film star Veronica Payne denies giving up her career, giving money to charity and going to live (1) _____ close to Venezuela.

OTHER NAMES AND FACTS:
Veronica has signed a contract to make a new (2) _____ film called *Beyond*.
Heidi Williams is a Hollywood gossip columnist and (3) _____ .
New biography claims Veronica wants to live a simple life, making furniture, baking bread and (4) _____ .
Veronica plans to take legal action against the (5) _____ of *My Life*.

Listening: _____ /10

WRITE

3 Write a story (about 100 words) with the following first sentence:

> I had just got off the bus when my phone rang.

Writing: _____ /10

Progress check score _____ /30

EXAM TIPS

- listen and complete notes
  See page 27
- understand the situation
  See page 76
- infer meaning
  See page 86

EXAM TIPS

- write a story
  - Read the task carefully.
  - Think of the main events in your story.
  - Use the past simple, past continuous and past perfect to tell your story.
  - Use time expressions to order the events in your story.
  - Check punctuation and the number of words.
- say how and when things happen in a story
  See page 80
- use correct punctuation
  See page 90

Download extra speaking activities from www.macmillanbeyond.com

UNIT 9 LEARNING JOURNEYS

IN THE PICTURE At school

>>> Talk about different types of school

WORK WITH WORDS

1 **RECALL** Work in pairs. Do the tasks. You have two minutes.

   a Make a list of at least eight school subjects.

   b Complete the word in each definition.
      1 An e_____ is an important test at school.
      2 Some people study at u_____ when they leave school.
      3 There are normally three t_____ in the school year.
      4 A c_____ is a complete series of lessons in a subject.

2 Work in pairs. Look at the words in the box. Can you put any words in the table?

elementary   high   homeschooling   kindergarten
middle   ~~nursery~~   primary   secondary

Age	UK	US	
3–4	(1) _nursery_ school	(4) _____	
5			(6) _____
6			
7	(2) _____ school	(5) _____ school	Grades 1–5
8			
9			
10			
11			
12		(7) _____ school	Grades 6–8
13			
14	(3) _____ school		
15		(8) _____ school	Grades 9–12
16			
17			

3 ▶3.17 Listen to Finn from the UK and Ruby from the US talking about their education systems. Check or complete your answers to Exercise 2.

4 ▶3.17 Try to complete the other school options. Listen again to Finn and Ruby if necessary.

boarding   homeschooling   private   public   state

It's free: (1) _____ school (UK), (2) _____ school (US).
You pay: (3) _____ school. You live there: (4) _____ school.
You study at home: (5) _____ .

94

5 ▶3.18 **Listen and repeat the different types of school.**

6 a **Work in pairs. Look at each of the photos and answer the questions.**
   1 Where do you think the photo was taken?
   2 What type of school do you think it is?

   b ▶3.19 **Listen to the messages and check your answers.**

PHRASE BYTES

I think our system's more like the US/UK system because …

Yes, except that we / we don't …

I think the biggest difference is that …

7 **THE MOVING PICTURE** ▶ Watch Leo, Bella, Ruby and Finn talking about their schools. What types of school do they go to? How big is their school? Do they like it?

SPEAK

8 ◯ **Work in pairs. Compare the education system in your country with the US and UK systems. Which one is most similar to yours? What are the biggest differences?**

GO BEYOND

Do the Words & Beyond exercise on page 138.

Workbook, page 100

READING School journeys

>>> Understand referring words

SPEAK AND READ

1 a Work in pairs. Answer the questions about school days.
   1 What time do you have to get up?
   2 How do you get to school? Give details.
   3 How long does the journey take?

   b Compare your answers to Exercise 1a with the class. Who has the most difficult journey? Who has the longest journey?

2 ▶3.20 Where do you think the children in the photos are from? Quickly read the article to check your predictions.

GLOBAL FOCUS
Scary school runs

For this month's *Global Focus*, we searched the net to find some of the world's most difficult school journeys. These are the toughest **ones** we found. Is yours tougher? Write and tell us about it.

It's 4am, and 14-year-old Edison's getting up. **He** lives in a small village by the River Napo in the Amazon rainforest in Ecuador. There are very few roads **here**, so he has to go to class on the school canoe. The canoe stops at various places along the river to pick up students. When it rains the river can quickly rise by two metres. **This** makes the journey very dangerous, so his parents ask **him** to look after his younger brothers. If the weather's really bad, the school tells everybody to stay at home.

High in the Zanskar Valley in northern India, Anil and Dache are preparing for a long and extremely dangerous journey. In winter, snow closes their school, but it's spring now, and the new term starts soon. Their father tells them to follow him as they start a six-day trek up a frozen river or the steep, icy banks next to it. They do **this** in temperatures that are often below zero. There's a constant risk of avalanches, and the ice could break at any moment, throwing **them** into the freezing water. They're literally risking their lives to get to school.

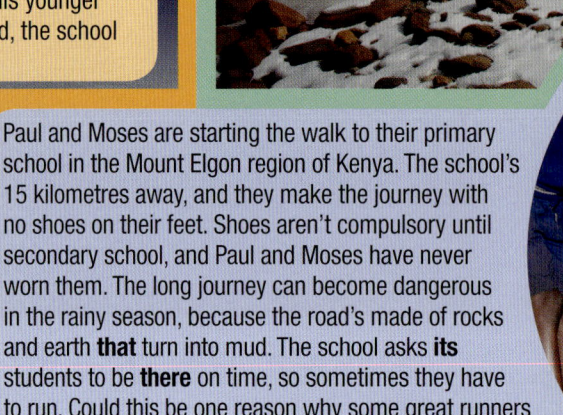

Paul and Moses are starting the walk to their primary school in the Mount Elgon region of Kenya. The school's 15 kilometres away, and they make the journey with no shoes on their feet. Shoes aren't compulsory until secondary school, and Paul and Moses have never worn them. The long journey can become dangerous in the rainy season, because the road's made of rocks and earth **that** turn into mud. The school asks **its** students to be **there** on time, so sometimes they have to run. Could this be one reason why some great runners have come from this part of Kenya?

3 Read the article more slowly. Write the name or names.
   1 _____ have a very dangerous journey to school.
   2 _____ takes transport to school.
   3 _____ don't have to wear shoes to school.
   4 _____ can't go to school in winter.
   5 _____ have a dangerous school journey when it rains.
   6 _____ need a parent's help to get to school.

4 a Read the tips in the **HOW TO** box.

   b What do the ten words in bold in the article refer to?

5 Which tips in the **HOW TO** box did you use for help with Exercise 4b? Tick (✓) them.

HOW TO
understand referring words

☐ *I, me, my*, etc refer back to people and things.

☐ *That, which, who*, etc add more information about the noun before.

☐ An adjective + *one/ones* refers back to a noun.

☐ *Here/There* refers back to a place.

☐ *This/that* at the start of a sentence refers back to the previous sentence.

REACT

6 Work in pairs. Put the three school journeys in order, from the *hardest* to the *easiest*. Explain your reasons and try to agree on the order.

GO BEYOND

Make a list of words in the text that describe the places where the students make their school journeys.

>>> Workbook, page 101

GRAMMAR Reported requests and commands

>>> Say what people ask and tell you to do

READ >>> Grammar in context

1 Read the diary extract. How does Denis get to school?

> Every school day is the same. First, Dad tells me to get up. Then, he tells me not to spend long in the shower. At breakfast, he asks me to eat quickly because it's time to go. I normally walk to school but if it's raining, I ask him for a lift. This morning the rain was really heavy and there was a huge traffic jam, so he asked me to get out and walk. 'If not, I'll be late to work,' he said. I arrived at school soaking wet, and the teacher told me to go home and change.

STUDY

2 Complete the explanations with examples from the diary extract in Exercise 1.

Reported requests and commands
Use: To report what people ask and tell you to do.   Form: requests   ask/asked + person + (not) to + infinitive: 'Can you eat quickly?' Dad asks.   He asks me _____.   Form: commands   tell/told + person + (not) to + infinitive: 'Don't spend long in the shower,' Dad tells me.   He tells me _____.   'Go home and change,' the teacher said.   The teacher told me _____.   Other changes: Change pronouns, possessive adjectives, time expressions and adverbs of place if necessary.   See GRAMMAR DATABASE, page 128.

3 Write another reported command and request from Exercise 1 in direct speech.
  1 Dad tells me to get up.
  2 I ask him for a lift.

PRACTISE

4 Complete the second sentence so that it means the same as the first. Use three words.
  1 'Could you be quiet, please?' the teacher asked us.
     The teacher asked _us to be_ quiet.
  2 'Can you give me more space?' Rob asked me.
     Rob _____ give him more space.
  3 'Denis, don't talk to Rob!' the teacher said.
     The teacher told me _____ to Rob.
  4 'Could you show me your homework?' I asked Rob.
     I _____ show me his homework.
  5 'Denis, stop copying Rob!' the teacher said.
     The teacher _____ stop copying Rob.
  6 'Don't open your books yet,' said the teacher.
     The teacher told us not _____ books yet.

5 a ▶3.21 **PRONOUNCE** Listen and underline the word that Rob stresses most. Why does he stress this word?

  Denis: The teacher told us to be quiet.
  Rob: No, she didn't. She told you to be quiet.

b ▶3.22 Listen and repeat the conversation.

6 Write the requests and commands in direct speech.
  1 When I got home from school, Dad asked me to tidy my room.
     '_Can/Could you tidy your room, please_?' asked Dad.
  2 He told me to stop playing computer games.
     '_____,' he told me.
  3 I asked him to make pizza for dinner.
     '_____?' I asked him.
  4 He told me to lay the table first.
     '_____,' he told me.
  5 I asked him to pass me the ketchup.
     '_____?' I asked him.
  6 He told me not to eat with my mouth open.
     '_____,' he told me.

WRITE AND SPEAK

7 a Write four to six sentences about things that people ask and tell you to do.

  My brother often asks me to turn my music down.

b Work in pairs. Compare your sentences. Say if your partner's sentences are true for you.

Workbook, pages 102–103

97

LISTENING AND VOCABULARY Circus school

>>> Understand spoken instructions

SPEAK AND LISTEN

1 Work in pairs. Look at the advert then answer the questions.
 1 Have you been to a circus? Tell your partner about it.
 2 If you went to a circus, what acts would you most want to see? Explain why.

2 ▶3.23 Listen to Emma talking about her circus school. Put the things she mentions in order.
 ___ School subjects
 ___ How she became interested in the circus
 ___ Her advice to others who want to be a circus performer
 ___ When she started at the school
 ___ The qualities you need to be a circus performer

3 ▶3.23 Listen again and answer the questions.
 1 Where does she live during the week?
 2 Why doesn't she find it hard to be away from home?
 3 Why do circus performers need to be self-confident and self-sufficient?
 4 Why is circus school a lot of work?
 5 When did she realise she wanted to perform in a circus?
 6 What's her advice for people who want to join a circus?

4 a Read the tips in the **HOW TO** box.

 b ▶3.24 Listen to Emma explaining how to juggle with two balls. Follow her instructions.

5 Which tips in the **HOW TO** box did you use for help with Exercise 4b? Tick (✓) them.

REACT

6 Work in pairs. Answer the questions.
 1 Would you like to go to a circus school? Why?/Why not?
 2 Which act do you think you'd be best at? Why?

WORK WITH WORDS

7 ▶3.25 Complete the definitions with the *self-* words in the boxes. Listen and check. Then listen and repeat.

 centred   confident   conscious   sufficient   taught

 1 If you're self-_____, you feel that you can do things well.
 2 If you're self-_____, you don't need help from others.
 3 If you're self-_____, you don't like people looking at you.
 4 If you're self-_____, you learned something without a teacher.
 5 If you're self-_____, you only think about what you want.

 control   defence   discipline   esteem   pity

 6 If you have self-_____, you always do the things you need to do.
 7 If you have self-_____, you can stay calm in stressful situations.
 8 If you have high self-_____, you value yourself.
 9 If you feel self-_____, you feel that your situation is worse than others.
 10 If you practise self-_____, you can defend yourself from attack.

8 Work in pairs. Tell your partner which words in Exercise 7 describe you and explain why.

THE FLY HIGH CIRCUS SCHOOL

Study circus arts along with your other school subjects at the Fly High Circus School.
For more information go to www.flyhighcs.org

TRAPEZE ARTISTS
JUGGLERS
TIGHTROPE WALKERS
ACROBATS
CLOWNS

HOW TO
understand spoken instructions

☐ Imperatives (*make*), or *you* + present simple (*you throw*) give instructions.

☐ Sequencers (*first*, *next*) tell you a new instruction is starting.

☐ *When* (*when you've done that*) tells you to complete one instruction before another.

☐ Adverbs (*comfortably*) tell you how to do something.

GO BEYOND

Do the Words & Beyond exercise on page 138.

Workbook, pages 104–105

GRAMMAR Reflexive pronouns; *each other*

>>> Use reflexive pronouns and *each other*

READ >>> Grammar in context

1 Read the introduction at a school website. Is your school like Spring Hills?

Welcome to Spring Hills Secondary School

Our school sees itself as a community, a place where students, teachers and parents work with each other to provide the best possible education for all. We also believe in learner independence, so we encourage every student to do things by himself or herself. At the same time, we recognise that teenagers need to express themselves. They are learning to understand themselves and each other too. That's why personal development is so important at Spring Hills. Healthy eating is also important. The canteen makes all its food itself with organic products.

STUDY

2 Complete the explanations with examples from the school website in Exercise 1.

Reflexive pronouns: *myself, yourself*, etc

Use:
For actions you do to or for yourself.
Reflexive pronouns are often used:

after the verbs *hurt, express, enjoy, teach, introduce*:
Teenagers need to express _____ .
after *by* to mean 'alone' or 'with no help'
We encourage every student to do things _____ .
to emphasise who does an action:
The canteen makes all its food _____ .

Form:
Singular: *myself, yourself, himself, herself, itself*
Plural: *ourselves, yourselves, themselves*

Each other

Use:
When each person does something to the other(s).
Students, teachers and parents _____ each other.

See GRAMMAR DATABASE, page 128.

PRACTISE

3 ▶3.26 Complete each conversation with the words in the boxes. Then listen and check.

1 | us | yourselves | each other |

Fran: Did you enjoy _____ at the school concert?
Nik: Yes, except for when you and Holly started arguing with _____ .
Tina: Yeah, it was embarrassing. Everyone was looking at _____ .

2 | us | ourselves | each other |

Nik: It looks like we'll have to finish the project _____ .
Tina: You're right. Fran isn't going to help _____ .
Nik: No, but I'm sure we'll finish quickly if we help _____ .

3 | them | themselves | each other |

Nik: Fran and Holly are friends again. Look. They're talking to _____ .
Tina: That's good. They were eating by _____ in the school canteen earlier.
Nik: Shall we go and say hello to _____ ?

4 Complete the opinions about education with a reflexive pronoun or *each other*.

1 'People can teach *themselves* to do things, but having a good teacher is always a better option.'
2 'Exams don't help students learn. They just encourage them to compete with _____ .'
3 'It's important for you to enjoy _____ at school. If you have fun, you learn more.'
4 'The problem with school is that teachers and students never really listen to _____ .'
5 'School teaches you a lot, but I learned the most important things in life by _____ .'
6 'I hope my daughter learns to think for _____ at school. Anyone can find facts on the internet.'

SPEAK

5 a Decide if you agree or disagree with the opinions in Exercise 4. Make notes on your reasons.

b 🔊 Work in pairs. Talk about the opinions in Exercise 4. Tell your partner why you agree or disagree with them.

PHRASE BYTES

I totally agree with the (first) opinion.
I'm not sure I agree with the (second) opinion …
I think that's true to a point, but …
That's completely wrong. It's obvious that …
What's the (third) opinion actually saying?

Workbook, page 106

LANGUAGE & BEYOND

Five steps to becoming more self-confident

Self-confident people believe in themselves and their abilities, and don't feel nervous or frightened about things. Some people are naturally self-confident, but everyone can learn to be more self-confident. Try these steps.

1 _____
What's making you feel insecure? Knowing why you feel nervous in certain situations is the first step to becoming more self-confident.
What stops you feeling more self-confident?

2 _____
It's good to talk to close friends or family members. You'll see that everyone feels insecure about something, even people who seem very self-confident.
Who are you going to talk to?

3 _____
Everyone has strong points – things they can do well. Focus on what you can do, not on your insecurities. And the next time someone gives you a compliment, say thank you and smile.
What strength are you most proud of?

4 _____
If you think things will go wrong, they often will. Try to avoid self-pity and have a positive attitude, even when you don't feel positive.
What positive lesson can you learn from a recent bad experience?

5 _____
Think of a situation that makes you feel nervous. Now choose a time to put yourself in that situation. Act as if you really feel confident and see what happens. You might find that being confident is not so difficult!
What situation are you going to choose?

>>> Learn to be more self-confident

SPEAK AND READ

1 Work in pairs. Discuss how people who aren't self-confident feel in these situations. What do they do?
- meeting new people
- needing to complain about something
- talking in front of others
- knowing the answer in class

2 Read an article with advice on becoming more self-confident. Match the headings (A–E) to the steps (1–5) in the article.
A Be positive   B Discuss it   C Know your strengths   D Recognise why   E Take a risk

DO

3 Think of a friend who isn't very self-confident. Write his/her answers to the questions in the article.

4 Work in pairs. Talk about the answers you wrote in Exercise 3. Will the five steps in the article help your friend? Why?/Why not?

REFLECT

5 Discuss the questions with your class. Do you agree with the **REFLECTION POINT**?
1 Do you think it's true that everybody feels insecure about something? Explain your answer.
2 How hard or easy is it to become more self-confident? Why?
3 What are the benefits of becoming more self-confident? Give details.

EXTEND

6 Work on the things that make you feel insecure. Answer the questions in the article for you, then put the five steps in the article into practice. Keep a record of your progress in a diary.

> **REFLECTION POINT**
> Everyone can learn to be more self-confident. If you become more self-confident, you'll start doing things that you don't do now, and you'll probably enjoy yourself more of the time.

Workbook, page 109

SPEAKING Go on!

>>> Persuade people to do things

SPEAK

1 Work in pairs. Answer the questions.
1. When was the last time you persuaded somebody to do something? Was it easy or difficult?
2. Do you think you're good at persuading people to do things? Why?/Why not?
3. When was the last time somebody persuaded you to do something? What happened?

WATCH OR LISTEN

2 ▶ 3.27 Watch or listen to the scene. What does Ruby persuade Finn to do?

3 ▶ 3.27 Put the words in order. Then use the sentences to complete the conversation. Watch or listen again and check.
1. speak / me / let / Will / to them / you
2. amazing / be / It'll
3. you're / Tell / instead / them / to Edinburgh / going
4. don't / if / come / won't / the same / you / It / be
5. opportunity / this / real / But / will / a / be

Ruby:	We've been invited to perform at the Edinburgh Festival.
Finn:	Yes, I've heard.
Ruby:	So are you coming?
Finn:	I can't.
Ruby:	Oh, come on! Be adventurous! (1) _____ .
Finn:	It's not that easy. I've got other plans.
Ruby:	(2) _____ . What could be better than performing in Edinburgh?
Finn:	I'd love to go, but Mum and Dad have planned a camping holiday.
Ruby:	So phone them. (3) _____ .
Finn:	I'd prefer not to. They'll only say no.
Ruby:	Don't be so pessimistic! (4) _____ .
Finn:	I'm sorry, I can't.
Ruby:	OK. (5) _____ ?
Finn:	No way! You've never met them!
Ruby:	Then phone them yourself. Go on, please! What have you got to lose?
Finn:	Oh, all right then. I'll try.
Ruby:	Yes!!

4 ▶ 3.28 Listen and repeat the missing sentences in Exercise 3. Pay attention to intonation.

5 ▶ 3.29 Underline five different imperatives that Ruby uses to try to persuade Finn. Listen and check. Then listen and repeat. Pay attention to intonation.

6 🗘 Try to complete how Finn says 'no' and then 'yes' to Ruby from memory. Then check your answers.
1. I'd _____
2. I'd _____
3. I'm _____
4. No _____
5. Oh, _____

ACT

7 🗘 Work in pairs. Prepare and practise the conversation between Finn and his mother or father. Then present it to other students.

PHRASEBOOK ▶ 3.30

Persuade people

Are you coming/going … ?

Will you let me / ask them … ?

Oh, come on! / Go on, please!

Be adventurous/brave.

Don't be pessimistic/boring.

It'll be amazing/fantastic.

What could be better than going/ seeing … ?

It won't be the same if you don't come.

What have you got to lose?

React to persuasion

I'd love to go / be there, but …

I'd prefer not to.

No way!

Oh, all right then.

>>> Workbook, page 107

101

WRITING Our school

Express reasons and results

SPEAK AND READ

1 Work in pairs. Discuss the type of information you can usually find from a school's website.

2 Read the school website page. Match each text (1–3) to a section at the top (Home, Location, etc).

3 a Read the tips in the **HOW TO** box.

HOW TO
express reasons and results

To express a reason:
- Use *because/as* + subject + verb to link two parts of a sentence.
- Use *because of* before a noun.

To express a result:
- Use *so* after a comma to link two parts of a sentence.
- Use *therefore* at the start of a sentence, after an auxiliary verb or before a main verb.
- Use *as a result* at the start of a sentence.

b Underline seven examples of reasons and results in the school website information.

PRACTISE

4 Choose the correct words to complete more information from the website. What section is it from?

(1) **As / So** it is a relatively new school, Fairfields has excellent facilities. (2) **So / As a result**, students do not need to travel to other schools to use a sports hall, swimming pool or library. The pool is heated and covered, (3) **so / therefore** it can be used all year round. (4) **Because / Because of** these facilities, students are prepared to travel large distances to study here. It is (5) **so / therefore** the most popular school in this part of the country.

Home   Location   History   Learning at FFSS   Canteen   Facilities

Welcome to
FAIRFIELDS
SECONDARY SCHOOL

Click on a section to find out more about us.

① Fairfields was opened in 1998, so we are a fairly new school. We had just 250 students in the beginning, but because the school was so popular, we expanded in 2003. As a result, around 750 students can now study with us.

② The school is situated just outside Fairfields, in an area famous for its farming, and it's therefore a quiet and safe place to study. Because of its location, the school has large playing fields and easy access to the river and farm land around the town.

③ As most of our students stay at the school for lunch, we have a large canteen. We are very aware of the need to provide a variety of healthy meals at lunchtime. Therefore, our meals are all made from the highest quality, local products.

PLAN

5 You're going to write information for two sections from a new website for your school. Make a plan for your website sections.

WRITING PLAN

1 **Choose two sections.**
Look at the sections from the Fairfields school website, or think of different ones.

2 **Decide what information to include.**
Make notes on things to include in each section. Ask your teacher for information if you need it.

3 **Use the correct linking words to introduce reasons and results.**
Look at the tips in the **HOW TO** box.

WRITE AND CHECK

6 Use your plan and write your website sections. Then check them. Tick (✓) the things in the plan.

SHARE

7 Swap your website sections with a partner. Is there any information missing from their sections?

Workbook, pages 108–109

UNIT REVIEW 9

VOCABULARY Types of school

1 Complete the information about a school with different types of school.

The All-In-One School caters for everyone. The west wing offers a US education. There's a (1) n_____ school for children under five, and a (2) k_____ for five-year-olds – the first grade of (3) e_____ school. When they're 11, students go to (4) m_____ school and then to (5) h_____ school. The east wing offers a UK education, starting with (6) p_____ school for five-year-olds, who go to (7) s_____ school when they're 11. We offer a free education in a (8) s_____ (UK) or (9) p_____ (US) school, but you can also pay for a (10) p_____ school education. We have a (11) b_____ school too, with bedrooms for 100 students. For parents who prefer to educate their children at home, we sell material for (12) h_____ .

___/12

Words with self-

2 Choose the correct options to complete the school's manifesto.

We teach (1) *self-pity* / *self-discipline*, the ability to do what needs doing, and (2) *self-control* / *self-defence*, the ability to remain calm. There's no place for negative thoughts, (3) *self-esteem* / *self-pity* or feeling (4) *self-taught* / *self-conscious*. Our students are positive. They have high (5) *self-control* / *self-esteem* and are (6) *self-confident* / *self-sufficient* when they meet new people. They are also (7) *self-centred* / *self-taught* in one foreign language so they learn to be (8) *self-conscious* / *self-sufficient*. However, our students learn to think of others too and not be (9) *self-confident* / *self-centred*. And all learn (10) *self-discipline* / *self-defence*, because you never know when you might need to fight an attacker.

___/10

GRAMMAR Reported requests and commands

3 Look at the speech bubbles (1–7). Then complete the email. Write four words in each space.

1 All of you run round the school 20 times!

2 Could you let me stop now, please?

3 Don't stop running!

Hi Sean,
The All-In-One School's like a military academy! Yesterday the PE teacher (1)_____ round the school 20 times. I (2)_____ me stop after 10 because I felt bad, but he (3)_____ stop running. Then he took my mobile. The first day they (4)_____ bring our mobiles to class, but I forgot. He heard it ringing, and he (5)_____ it to him. After the class, I (6)_____ it back, but he said no. Last night I emailed my parents. I (7)_____ and get me. They haven't answered yet.

4 Do not bring your mobile phones to class.

5 Give me your phone.

6 Could you give me my phone back?

7 Mum! Dad! Can you come and get me?

___/14

Reflexive pronouns; *each other*

4 Complete what a teacher says with reflexive pronouns (*myself*, *yourself*, etc) and *each other*.

1 'Dan and Bill, stop talking to _____.'
2 'Billy, clean that table. It won't clean _____.'
3 'Kim and Louise, are you sending _____ text messages?'
4 'Stop laughing, everyone. You're not here to enjoy _____.'
5 'Frank, can you get the nurse? Jon's hurt _____.'
6 'Michelle, let your classmates work out the answer by _____.'
7 'Silence, please! I can't hear _____ think.'

___/14

Your score: ___/50

SKILLS CHECK

✓✓✓	Yes, I can. No problem!
✓✓	Yes, I can. But I need a bit of help.
✓	Yes, I can. But I need a lot of help.

I can understand referring words when I read. ____
I can understand spoken instructions. ____
I can learn to be more self-confident. ____
I can persuade people to do things. ____
I can express reasons and results when I write. ____

Workbook, pages 110–111

103

UNIT 10 CHANGING FASHIONS

IN THE PICTURE In fashion

>>> Talk about changing fashions

WORK WITH WORDS

1 **RECALL** Work in pairs. Do the tasks. You have three minutes.

a Think of as many clothes and accessories as you can.

Clothes (incl. footwear)	Accessories
boots	belt

b Complete the sentences with the verbs in the box.

| fit   match   suit   try on   wear |

1 I'm going to _____ these jeans. I'm not sure about the size.
2 This T-shirt doesn't _____ this skirt.
3 These shorts _____ really well. They're exactly the right size.
4 I never _____ trainers.
5 These trousers don't _____ me. They're too old-fashioned.

2 a Look at the collage of western fashion from the 70s to the present. Put the labelled items and adjectives in the correct categories below.

Parts of clothes	Materials	Fit and look
collar	silk	patterned

b ▶3.31 Listen and check. Then listen and repeat the words.

3 ▶3.32 Listen to a report about fashion from the 1970s to the 2000s. Write the key word for each decade.

4 ▶3.32 Complete the sentences from the listening with a word from Exercise 2. Listen again and check.

1 Trousers had _____ high above the waist, were _____ at the top but wide after the knees.
2 Shirts were worn with the _____ turned up.
3 Trousers were _____ round the waist with huge side _____.
4 Jeans, T-shirts with short and long _____, trainers and hoodies came on the scene.
5 Hair became smooth, and _____ dark colours replaced bright _____ clothes.
6 Everybody from babies to grandparents wore _____.
7 Smart _____ shirts and soft _____ scarves were combined with jeans and trainers.
8 People became more eco-friendly and non-_____ bags and shoes and organic cotton started to appear in high street shops.

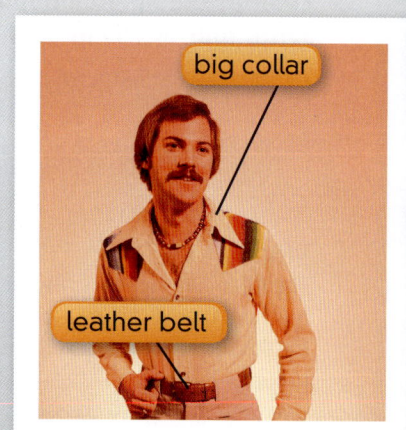

1970s

silk

patterned shirt with long sleeves

plain trousers

big collar

leather belt

104

1980s **1990s** **2000s** **10**

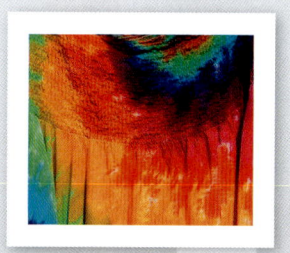

baggy wool jumper

button
denim

pocket

tight jeans

5 a ▶3.33 **PRONOUNCE** Listen to the /t/ and /d/ sounds in these words. Put your hand in front of your mouth and repeat: which sound produces more air?

tigh**t**   pocke**t**   **d**enim   pattern**ed**

b ▶3.34 Listen to these words and circle the one you hear. Then listen and repeat both words.

1 coat / code
2 feet / feed
3 hat / had
4 tight / tied
5 white / wide

6 Work in pairs. Take turns to give your opinion of the clothes in the collage.

I don't like the 70s shirt because the collar is too big and I don't like patterned clothes.

Actually, I like it. It's different.

7 **THE MOVING PICTURE** ▶ Watch Roisin, Sebastian, Shay and Tyler talking about their clothes. Which clothes do you like best? Why?

SPEAK

8 Work in groups. Brainstorm ideas for the fashion of the 2010s and 2020s. Think of popular clothes, their look and fit, parts of clothes and materials. Compare with another group.

GO BEYOND

Do the Words & Beyond exercise on page 139.

Workbook, page 112

READING Fashion statements

Understand paraphrase

SPEAK AND READ

1. Look at the statements about fashion and write *agree*, *disagree* or *not sure*. Then compare with your partner. Explain your opinion.
   a What you wear says a lot about you. _____
   b I don't care about fashion. _____
   c I like to wear the same clothes as my friends. _____

2. a Read the tips in the **HOW TO** box.

   b ▶3.35 You want to buy a fashion item for the four people below. Read descriptions A–F and match one description to each person.

HOW TO
understand paraphrase

In exams, matching tasks with different texts often use 'paraphrase': different ways of saying the same thing.

- [ ] Read all the texts quickly for the main ideas.
- [ ] Look for important words in one text. In the other texts, find synonyms or definitions.
- [ ] Look for words from the same word family (*comfort – comfortable*).
- [ ] Look for 'category' words for specific items (*jewellery – bracelet*).

Luna doesn't mind sacrificing comfort in order to stand out from the crowd.

Joe typically wears shorts, leather bracelets and a necklace. He usually goes barefoot.

Aldo isn't interested in brands or fashionable accessories. He likes slogans.

Ella likes comfortable outfits. She spends whole days in her nightwear.

A HOME TO SCHOOL
The word 'pyjama' comes from a Persian word for baggy cotton trousers. 'Pyjamas' (or 'PJs') have a jacket as well and are usually used for sleeping. Recently, however, some American schools banned pyjamas when students started wearing them to class.

B SPORT TO STREET
Trainers were designed for playing basketball, but were so comfortable that people started to wear them as everyday footwear. Now they're often an expensive fashion statement, and promoted by top celebrities.

C PRACTICAL TO FASHIONABLE
In the past, belts were mostly worn to carry weapons. But in 19th-century eastern Europe, soldiers used to wear tight leather belts in order to make their shoulders and chest look more powerful. Today, belts are mostly worn to hold jeans up or as a chic fashion accessory.

D STRANGE TO STRANGER
In the 16th and 17th centuries, 'chopines' protected feet from dirty streets. However, they were so high that people needed help to walk. Recent stylish (but uncomfortable) footwear designs for those who want to look different include high shoes without heels.

E POWER TO STYLE
The first jewellery was created from stone and bone. Expensive gold jewellery later became a way to show wealth. The use of new materials, such as plastic, has turned jewellery into a cheap fashion accessory.

F UNDERWEAR TO EVERYWHERE
Originally a T-shirt was underwear that was worn by sailors. Then American actors began to wear plain white T-shirts in films. They were such a hit that soon everybody was wearing them as informal clothes. Now T-shirts communicate messages too.

3. Which tips in the **HOW TO** box did you use for help with Exercise 2b? Tick (✓) them.

REACT

4. Work in pairs. Do the tasks, giving reasons.
   1. Explain which of the texts you found most interesting.
   2. Think of three comparatives to complete this sentence:

   I think fashion today is _____ than in the past.

GO BEYOND
Design a T-shirt slogan. It can be funny or serious.

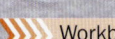

Workbook, page 113

GRAMMAR *So* and *such … that*

>>> Emphasise somebody's or something's qualities

READ >>> Grammar in context

1 Work in pairs. Look at the photos. Tell your partner what you think of the outfits. Then read the descriptions and find out what their owners thought of them.

I used to have a patterned shirt and some pink trousers. The shirt was so colourful that you needed sunglasses to look at it! But I thought it was such a cool outfit that I wore it all the time.

I once wore a red dress and shoes to a school party. I borrowed the shoes from my mum, and I felt so confident in them that I danced all night. But they had such high heels that my feet really hurt the next day.

STUDY

2 Complete the explanations with examples from Exercise 1.

So and such … that …

Use:
To emphasise somebody or something's qualities and the result of those qualities.

Form:
so + adjective
The shirt was _____ that …

such a/an + adjective + singular countable noun
I thought it was _____ that …

such + adjective + uncountable noun/plural noun
They had _____ that …

that …
Use *that* + clause for the result.

See GRAMMAR DATABASE, page 129.

PRACTISE

3 Match the two parts of the sentences.
1 My coat had such big pockets
2 My shirt was such a strange colour
3 My trainers were so comfortable
4 My trousers were so baggy
5 My T-shirt was so clean
6 My gloves were made of such thin material

a that I wore them every day.
b that it looked new.
c that my hands were still cold.
d that it didn't match anything.
e that I didn't need a bag.
f that I had to wear a big belt with them.

4 a Complete the sentences with *so* or *such (a/an)*.

- It's (1) _____ pity that the outfit didn't fit me. I looked so cool.
- The trousers were (2) _____ small that I could hardly breathe.
- The leather outfit in the shop was (3) _____ stylish that I had to buy it. 1
- One day I bent over (4) _____ far that I got a big hole at the back of my trousers.
- And the jacket had (5) _____ tight sleeves that I could hardly put it on.
- It was (6) _____ embarrassing moment that I went bright red.

b ▶3.36 Put the sentences in Exercise 4a in order to make a story. Listen and check.

5 Work in pairs. Student A looks at page 141. Student B looks at page 142. Read out the sentence beginnings in turn. Your partner completes the sentence with a *that* clause, using his/her own ideas.

WRITE

6 Write a short description (three to five sentences) of an outfit or an item that you once wore or used to have. Use Exercise 1 to help you. Work in pairs. Share your descriptions and say more about the outfit or item you described.

Workbook, pages 114–115

107

LISTENING AND VOCABULARY Materials and more

>>> Recognise formal and informal speech

SPEAK AND LISTEN

1 Work in pairs. Look at your clothes. Are they natural or man-made materials?

2 Try to complete the materials timeline with the words and phrases in the box.

> cotton   grasses   leaves   linen   smart materials
> the first man-made material   wool

3 ▶3.37 Listen to a video for a company that designs high-tech clothes. Check your answers from Exercise 2. Write three examples of what future clothes will do.

4 a Read the tips in the **HOW TO** box.

  b ▶3.37 Listen again. Tick (✓) the things in the **HOW TO** box when you hear examples. Which part of the video is formal and why?

REACT

5 Work in pairs. Discuss these questions.
  1 Which of the wearable technology possibilities do you find most interesting and why?
  2 Would you be interested in buying clothes with fragrances which can make you feel happier or more awake? Why?/Why not?

WORK WITH WORDS

6 Look at these expressions from the listening text. What type of words can we add -able to so that the adjectives mean 'you can do something'?

  wear**able** technology (= you can wear this technology)
  afford**able** clothes (= you can afford these clothes)

7 ▶3.38 Which verbs are the -able adjectives in the box from? Listen and check. Then listen and repeat.

> breakable   downloadable   enjoyable
> manageable   reasonable   recyclable   reliable
> respectable   suitable   valuable

WRITE AND SPEAK

8 Write a person or thing for each adjective in Exercises 6 and 7. Work in pairs. Show your partner your words. Your partner guesses the correct adjective.

GO BEYOND
Do the Words & Beyond exercise on page 139.

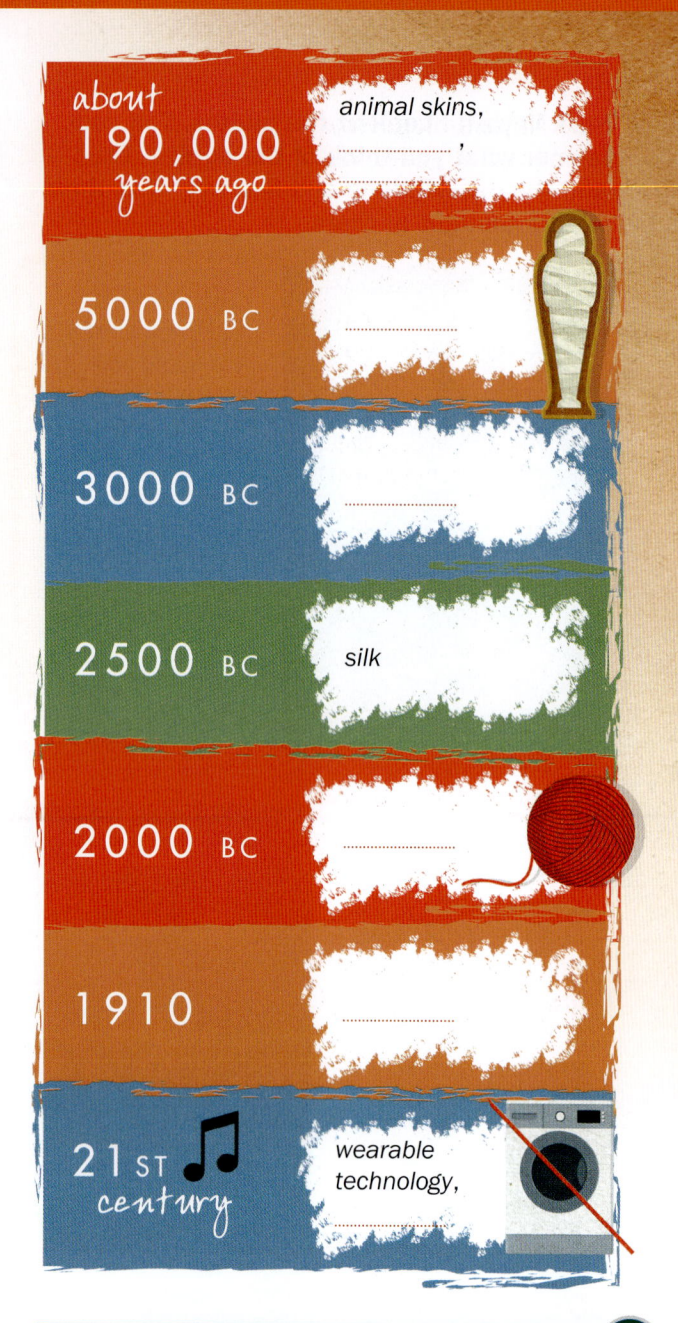

---

about 190,000 years ago — animal skins, ..., ...

5000 BC — ....

3000 BC — ....

2500 BC — silk

2000 BC — ....

1910 — ....

21st century — wearable technology, ...

HOW TO
recognise formal and informal speech

In formal speech, listen for ...
☐ longer sentences with full verbs (*we were not, we are*).
☐ longer or more formal words (*approximately* or *about*).
☐ slower, more careful pronunciation.

In informal speech, listen for ...
☐ shorter, simpler sentences with contractions (*they're, they'll*).
☐ simpler and more informal words (*stuff = things, dead cool = very cool*).
☐ less careful pronunciation (*wearin'* for *wearing*).

Workbook, pages 116–117

GRAMMAR Ability

>>> Talk about ability in the past, present and future

READ >>> Grammar in context

1 Read Nayla's blog. How did she become a fashion designer? Would you like to do this job?

> A lot of people ask me how I was able to become a fashion designer so young. You probably won't be able to guess! When I was small, my parents couldn't afford to buy me new clothes, so I wore my brother's old things. I hated them. So as soon as I could use a sewing machine, I started to make my own clothes.
>
> Later I studied fashion design in London. I wasn't able to get a scholarship and I had to borrow a lot of money. But now I'm able to do something I love as a job – and I can't imagine buying clothes in a shop again. I hope that I'll be able to help other young designers.

STUDY

2 Complete the explanations with negative forms.

Ability (1): *can, could*
Use: For ability in the present and past.
Form: can/_____ + infinitive could/_____ + infinitive

3 Read the explanations. Then underline examples of *be able to* in the present, past and future in Exercise 1.

Ability (2): *be able to*
Use: For ability in the present, past and future.
Form: *be able to* + infinitive

Present	am/is/are able to
Past	was/were able to
Future	will be able to

Specific achievements in the past:
Use *was/were able to* for past achievements:
I was able to become a fashion designer.
(NOT *I could become a fashion designer.*)
Use *wasn't/weren't able to* or *couldn't* for something you didn't achieve:
I wasn't able to/couldn't get a scholarship.

See GRAMMAR DATABASE, page 129.

PRACTISE

4 a Complete Nayla's sentences with the correct form of *be able to*.

Six things about me

1 I _____ (sew) when I was seven.
2 I _____ (stand) on my head for two minutes. It's part of my daily yoga routine.
3 I'd like to play a musical instrument, but I _____ (not learn) one in the next few years because I'm just too busy.
4 I _____ (not speak) any foreign languages, unfortunately.
5 I _____ (not cook) before I left home – and I still can't cook.
6 I hope that _____ (drive) soon. I'm taking my driving test next week.

b Can you do any of the things in Exercise 4a?

5 Read about Nayla and her brother when they were small. Circle the orange verb forms that can be replaced with *could*.

> When I was small my brother (1) **was able to do** most sports activities better than me. He (2) **was able to run** faster than me and he (3) **was able to learn** to ride a bike before me. But I (4) **was able to play** tennis better than him and one year I (5) **was able to beat** him and win the local tennis championship. That was my greatest achievement!

6 Write the questions with *can*, *could* or the correct form of *be able to*.

1 you / run / fast / when you were small?
2 When / you / ride a bike?
3 What two things / you / do well when you were small?
4 What two things / do well / now?
5 What / you / hope / you / do / in the future?

SPEAK

7 a Work in pairs. Ask and answer the questions in Exercise 6.

b Tell your partner about your greatest achievement. What were you able to do?

Workbook, page 118

LANGUAGE & BEYOND

>>> **Consider all the options**

Danny: I don't know which bag to buy. There are so many! What do you think?
Tyson: Let me look. Well, this one's leather, and it looks good. It's not very big, though.
Danny: This one's made from recycled water bottles. The label says it's 'a vegan, eco-friendly bag for people who care about the environment and animal rights'. The company also gives one euro for every bag to an environmental charity. … That's impressive, but the colour's a bit bright.
Tyson: This one's fair trade. The label says that it's 'made by workers who are given a fair price for their product'. It's expensive.
Danny: Mmm, I like that one the best. It looks as if it's good quality and it doesn't exploit people; both those things are important to me … But I don't have enough money for it.
Tyson: Well, if you wait until you get your allowance next week, you'll be able to buy it then.
Danny: I really need it for the match on Saturday.
Tyson: But it's better to get something that you like.
Danny: Yeah, you're right. I'll wait until next week.

SPEAK AND READ

1 **Do the tasks and tell a partner.**
   1 Think of two or three choices you have made in the last few days.
   2 Which choices did you find most difficult? Why? Tell a partner.

2 **Danny needs a new sports bag. Read the conversation and find out which bag (a–c) he chooses.**

3 a Make notes on the advantages and disadvantages of each bag.
   b Write what's important to Danny.

DO

4 **When you buy new clothes and accessories, which things are important to you? Tick (✓) them.**

   the price ☐
   the design, colour and style ☐
   the size and fit ☐
   the quality of the material and how it's made ☐
   fair trade ☐
   eco-friendly products/recycled materials ☐
   products or materials that are not cruel to animals ☐
   companies that give money to charity ☐

5 **Decide which sports bag you would choose. Explain your choice to a partner.**

REFLECT

6 **Discuss the questions with your class. Do you agree with the REFLECTION POINT ?**
   1 Are you sometimes afraid of making the wrong choice? Why?
   2 Do you consider all the options? How?
   3 Is it easier to make a choice with more or fewer options? Why?

EXTEND

7 **Make a list of five decisions where you think it's important to look at options before you decide. Then compare with a partner. Discuss why you think you chose similar or different things.**

> **REFLECTION POINT**
> Sometimes it's hard to make a decision. For important decisions, first look at all your options carefully, make a list of advantages and disadvantages, then think about what's important.

>>> Workbook, page 121

SPEAKING You look great!

>>> Give and react to compliments

SPEAK

1 Work in pairs. Answer these questions.
1. How often do you give somebody a compliment?
2. What do you usually compliment people on?
3. How do you feel when you get a compliment?

2 Look at the photos. What do you think Emma and Leo are complimenting Max and Alice on?

WATCH OR LISTEN

3 ▶3.39 Watch or listen to the scene and check your answers from Exercise 2.

> **Emma:** Hi Max. You look good today! What a great T-shirt!
> **Max:** (1) _____ . I got it on holiday. I chose it because it's organic cotton.
> **Emma:** Your hair looks nice as well. Have you had it cut?
> **Max:** Yes, I have. (2) I'm glad you _____ . (3) You look _____ .
> **Emma:** Thanks … So, are you going somewhere special?
> **Max:** Erm, … You know, that top really matches your eyes.
> **Emma:** Max, who are you meeting?
>
> **Leo:** Thanks for helping me with this homework. You're such a good friend.
> **Alice:** Thanks, (4) that's the nicest thing _____ . You know I'm always happy to help.
> **Leo:** I'm so bad at French that I'll never be able to remember all the tenses.
> **Alice:** But you're good at other things. Your drawings are fantastic.
> **Leo:** Thanks, (5) that's a really _____ . But yes, they are pretty good!

4 ▶3.39 Underline all the compliments in the conversations. Then watch or listen again and complete the expressions that Max, Alice and Leo use to accept and return compliments (1–5).

5 ▶3.40 Listen and repeat the underlined compliments in the conversation. Pay attention to stress and intonation. Then practise the conversations in pairs.

ACT

6 Work in pairs. Give, accept and return compliments. Compliments can be about appearance, personality or ability. Pay attention to stress and intonation.

PHRASEBOOK ▶3.41

Give a compliment
What a great T-shirt / cool shoes!
You look great/amazing … (in those jeans / that T-shirt …).
Your hair/outfit looks nice.
That dress/colour really matches your …
You're such a good friend/artist …
You're so good at art/cooking …
You're always so positive/patient …

Accept and return a compliment
Thanks.
Thanks, that's a really kind thing to say.
Thanks, that's the nicest thing I've heard for ages.
I'm glad you like it/them.
You look great too.

Workbook, page 119

WRITING For sale

>>> Refer to two options

SPEAK AND READ

1 🔊 **Work in pairs. Answer the questions.**
1. Do you ever sell things that you don't need any more? How?
2. Do you ever buy things second-hand? What kinds of things, and where do you buy them?

2 Read Jessie's advert. Complete the notes.

Item	Kit	Boots
size		
colour		
condition		
brand		
material		
other details		

PHRASE BYTES
I don't sell old things, I give them/ donate them to …
I sometimes sell clothes/old electrical stuff/ … online/in the local paper/ …
I often buy … in online auctions/in charity shops/at flea markets/ …

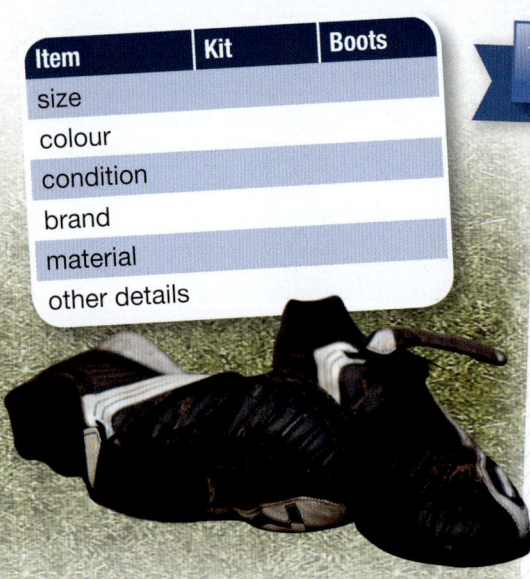

FOR SALE — England football kit and boots

Original England away unisex football kit and Kickit football boots for sale. The kit includes a dark blue cotton football shirt with short sleeves and a light blue collar, a pair of matching light blue shorts and long blue socks. The shirt and shorts are size 164, and the socks are one size. The football boots are black leather with white stripes and very comfortable. They're size 40, but such a small fit that they will fit people who are size 39. Both the kit and the boots have been worn quite a lot, but neither the kit nor the boots have any marks and are in good condition.

€25

The price is for everything, but if you want to buy either the kit or the boots separately, please contact me.

3 a Read the tips in the HOW TO box.

HOW TO
refer to two options
- Use *both … and …* in positive sentences to emphasise that two things are true.
- Use *neither … nor …* in negative sentences to emphasise that two things aren't true.
- Use *either … or …* to talk about two choices.

b In Jessie's advert, underline an example of each linking phrase from the HOW TO box.

PRACTISE

4 Complete these descriptions from other adverts with the correct linking phrases in Exercise 3a.
1. _____ the hat _____ the scarf has been worn at all and are brand new.
2. _____ the computer _____ the speakers are black and three years old.
3. You can wear the sweatshirt _____ on its own _____ with the jogging trousers.
4. _____ the bike _____ the helmet are suitable for ages 14–15.
5. _____ the phone _____ the case is breakable.
6. Please contact me _____ by phone _____ by email.

PLAN

5 You're going to write an online advert to sell some clothes, accessories or other items that you don't need. Think of two items and make a plan for your advert.

WRITING PLAN
1. **Write a heading with the items and the price.**
   Include only the most important information. ☐
2. **Describe the items.** ☐
   Use the headings in Exercise 2 to help you. Use *so/such … that* to emphasise particular qualities.
3. **Add any general comments about the items, notes or special contact details.** ☐
   Use the linking phrases in Exercise 3.

WRITE AND CHECK

6 Use your plan and write your advert. Then check it. Tick (✓) the things in the plan.

SHARE

7 Display your advert in the class. Note down the items that you think sound interesting.

Workbook, pages 120–121

UNIT REVIEW 10

VOCABULARY Fashion

1 Complete the labels on the fashions.

Rob and Rosie's **FASHION BLOG**

Take a look at these supercool fashions

A (1) p_____ green, (2) b_____ (3) w_____ dress with (4) p_____ (5) s_____s and a (6) big c_____.

(7) T_____, (8) d_____ trousers with (9) l_____ (10) p_____s, big (11) b_____s and a pink (12) s_____ belt.

___/12

Adjectives with -able

2 Choose the correct options in the tips.

1 Rude T-shirts – not *enjoyable* / *suitable* for school.
2 Gold front teeth – unusual, but *valuable* / *reasonable*.
3 Glass bags – *breakable* / *reliable*, but smart.
4 Plain white shirts – so *respectable* / *manageable*.
5 Silk socks – expensive, but *enjoyable* / *downloadable* to wear.
6 Orange plastic sunglasses – fun and *affordable* / *valuable*.
7 Flat leather sandals – *reasonable* / *breakable* summer footwear.
8 Paper underwear – not very soft, but 100% *recyclable* / *suitable*.
9 Yellow plastic coats – for when the weather is not *affordable* / *reliable*.
10 Wool swimming trunks – different, but not very *wearable* / *recyclable*.
11 Homemade clothes – easily *enjoyable* / *manageable* if you have a sewing machine.
12 Our blog articles – all *downloadable* / *respectable* for free.

___/12

GRAMMAR So/such (a/an) ... that

3 Complete with the phrases in the box.

such an uncool   such an amazing   such big
so 'in'   so warm   so fantastic

Fashion INs of the week

1 Pyjamas: That's right! Pyjamas are _____ now that you can wear them when you go out!
2 Plastic clothes: Lucy X looked _____ in her plastic dress that this is top of our list!
3 Hats: Hats are _____ accessory that everybody should wear them.

Fashion OUTs

4 Socks with sandals: If it's _____ that you can wear sandals, why wear socks??
5 Baby pink: This is _____ colour that nobody over 10 should wear it!
6 T-shirts with kittens: Yes, even if they have _____ eyes that your heart melts.   ___/12

Ability

4 Read the interview. Write the correct form of *able to*, *can/can't* or *could/couldn't*. If more than one form is possible, write both.

Us: As a child, (1) _____ (choose) your own clothes?
Lucy X: No, I (2) _____ (not pick) them when I was really young. But I just (3) _____ (not wear) pink T-shirts with kittens on. Then suddenly one birthday I (4) _____ (choose) something. I bought a red hat. Now, of course, I (5) _____ (buy) whatever I want. I (6) _____ (not wear) socks and sandals, though. That would be too shocking even for me. But I hope I (7) _____ (shock) people for a long time!

___/14

Your score: ___/50

SKILLS CHECK

✓✓✓ Yes, I can. No problem!
✓✓ Yes, I can. But I need a bit of help.
✓ Yes, I can. But I need a lot of help.

I can understand paraphrase. _____
I can recognise formal and informal speech. _____
I can consider all the options. _____
I can give and react to compliments. _____
I can refer to two options when I write. _____

▶▶▶ Workbook, pages 122–123

113

PROGRESS CHECK

READ

1 Read the text and choose the correct word for each space, A, B, C or D.

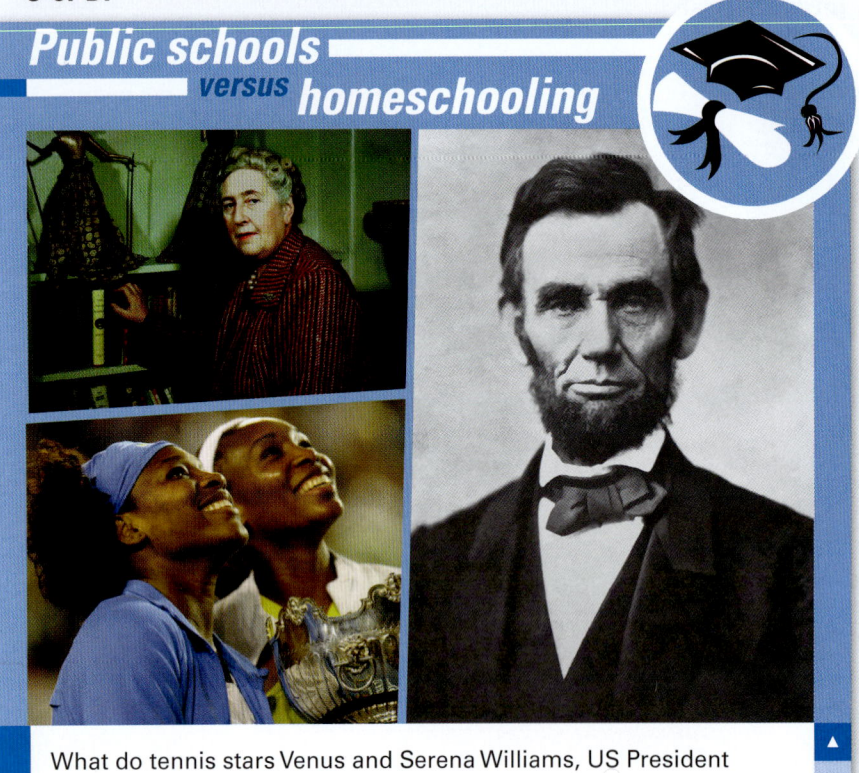

Public schools versus homeschooling

What do tennis stars Venus and Serena Williams, US President Abraham Lincoln and writer Agatha Christie have in common? They were all homeschooled. Homeschooling meant Venus and Serena were **(1)** _____ to combine classes with training. Lincoln didn't live near a school and was **(2)** _____ with help from his stepmother. And Agatha Christie was **(3)** _____ shy that her parents decided not to send her to school.

There are other reasons for homeschooling too. Some parents say public schools aren't a **(4)** _____ place for their children to learn. At home **(5)** _____ can have individual attention. Family members can also spend more time with **(6)** _____ other.

Others disagree. They say homeschooling for children is bad for **(7)** _____ their education and their personal development. Most parents are poor teachers **(8)** _____ they haven't been trained, and children learn **(9)** _____ social skills at school.

What do you think? Go to our forum and leave your opinion **(10)** _____ .

1	A can	B able	C could	D wanted
2	A self-centred	B self-conscious	C self-sufficient	D self-taught
3	A so	B very	C such	D as
4	A breakable	B manageable	C suitable	D recyclable
5	A there	B it	C them	D they
6	A the	B each	C one	D some
7	A either	B neither	C both	D or
8	A because	B so	C therefore	D result
9	A reasonable	B valuable	C respectable	D reliable
10	A yet	B in	C here	D there

Reading: _____ /10

EXAM TIPS

complete a multiple-choice gapped text

- Quickly read the text. What's it about? What's its aim?
- Read it again. Think what the word for each gap might be.
- Look at the choices. Is your word there?
- If not, look at the other choices. Which word fits best?

understand referring words
See page 96

PROGRESS CHECK 9 & 10

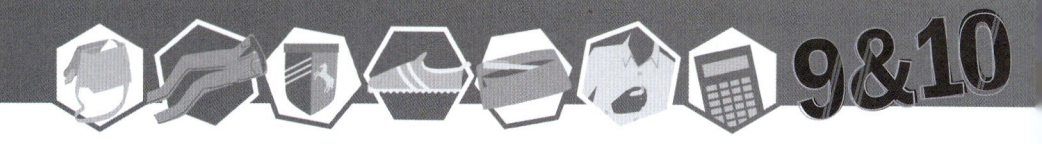

LISTEN

2 ▶3.42 **Listen and choose the correct picture for each question. Tick (✓) the box below it.**

1 Which top does the customer buy?
   A  B  C

2 What does John have to do first?
   A  B  C

3 Which picture is of James?
   A  B  C

4 When was Miss Jones the men's teacher?
   A  1990 B  1995 C 2004

5 Which picture shows Liam's homework?
   A  B  C

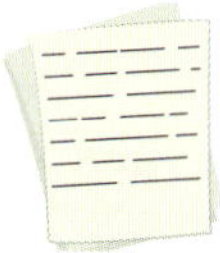

Listening: _____ /10

EXAM TIPS

answer multiple-choice questions with pictures
- Read the questions carefully before you listen.
- Look at the pictures: what English words and numbers do they show?
- Listen carefully for these words and numbers, and for the main ideas.
- When you listen again, check your answers.

understand spoken instructions
See page 98

recognise formal and informal speech
See page 108

WRITE

3 For each question, complete the second sentence so that it means the same as the first. Use no more than three words.

1 I knew you could download the app for free.
   I knew the app was _____ for free.
2 The instructions were so complicated that I couldn't follow them.
   It had _____ instructions that I couldn't follow them.
3 'Can you help me?' I asked Jake.
   I asked Jake _____ me.
4 In the end I managed to download it without any help.
   In the end I managed to download it by _____ .

_____ /4

4 Your penfriend Diego is going to spend a day at your school. Send him a message. (35–45 words)
- Say you're happy he can come to your school.
- Explain why you're happy.
- Your class wants to hear about school in the US. Tell him the options – a talk or an interview.

_____ /6

Writing: _____ /10

EXAM TIPS

express reasons and results
See page 102

refer to two options
See page 112

Progress check score _____ /30

Download extra speaking activities from www.macmillanbeyond.com

115

EXTRA READING Owl Hall

BEFORE YOU READ

1 Look at the cover of the book. What kind of story is *Owl Hall*?
   a a love story   b a mystery   c science fiction   d a thriller

2 Describe the characters in the pictures. What do you think their relationship is?

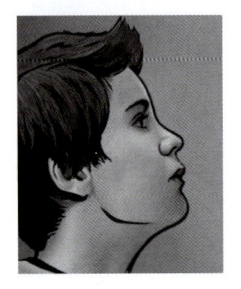

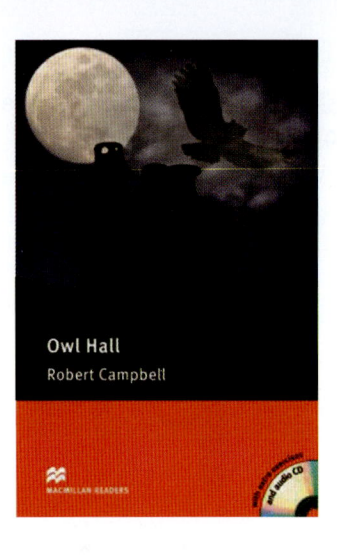

WHILE YOU READ

3 ▶3.43 Read the extract from *Owl Hall* and check your answers to Exercises 1 and 2. Is the extract from the beginning, middle or end of the story?

Kara looked out of the car window at the other cars driving past on the motorway. Where had they been? Where were they going? Who were the people sitting inside them and what were they thinking? Sometimes Mum passed the cars in front and Kara had time to look inside.

Kara smiled at a man and woman having an argument in a black Ford. They were probably arguing about something stupid. It's strange, Kara thought. People always argue about things that aren't important and then they don't talk about the things that *are* important. Why?

Then Mum drove faster and suddenly the man and woman were gone.

In the next car they passed, a couple were sitting in the front. They weren't talking but they looked relaxed and happy together. Maybe they were listening to the radio. A young girl and boy were sitting in the backseat. The girl was asleep and the boy was playing a video game. They looked like a happy family, Kara thought. They were probably going home after a day at the beach or a visit to a castle.

Kara had started thinking about her own dad when Mum said, 'We won't be on the motorway much longer.'

'Is it far?' Martin asked, yawning in the backseat.

Kara turned and looked into Martin's open mouth. She felt like she could see all the way down his throat to his stomach. It didn't look very nice.

Kara looked at Mum. 'Why can't we go on a *real* holiday?' she asked.

'This *is* a real holiday,' Mum replied. 'You'll love it.'

Kara didn't know where they were going for their holiday. It was Mum's surprise. Five days ago she had suddenly decided that they were going away for a week. Kara had imagined lying on a beach in Spain, dancing in the streets of Rio, shopping in New York. But when they drove past the airport, she realised that Mum had a different plan. Her mum's idea of a holiday was probably a week inside a caravan in a wet field outside a sad seaside town.

Kara's disappointment grew when they left the motorway and drove further into the countryside. They passed through a small town and some villages, but soon there were only fields around them and there were no other cars on the road. Then Mum stopped the car.

'Are we there?' Martin asked. 'I'm hungry.'

Kara looked out of the window but it was getting dark now and she couldn't see much. Mum took a map from under the seat and tried to find where they were.

'We're lost, aren't we?' Kara said.

'Not *very* lost,' Mum replied. But Kara didn't believe her.

Suddenly Martin kicked the back of Kara's seat. Kara turned and gave her brother one of her *I'm-going-to-kill-you* looks. Martin smiled at his sister at the same time as Mum started the car.

'Let's go on,' Mum said. 'I'm sure we'll find a road sign or a house … or a phone box.'

They drove slowly down the country roads. There were trees on both sides of the road. Then suddenly the trees disappeared and all they could see was the road in front of them.

116

'There it is!' Mum said suddenly.

The car turned left and they drove down a bumpy track, waking Martin up.

'Where are we?' Martin asked sleepily.

'We're here,' Mum said, looking at the wooden sign that hung next to a large metal gate. There was a picture of an owl on the sign and the name: 'Owl Hall.'

Mum smiled and turned to Kara. 'Please can you open the gate for me?' she said.

'Why *me*?' Kara said as she got out of the car, closing the door loudly behind her. It was cold outside and very quiet. Kara looked around her but she couldn't see far in the darkness. As she walked towards the gate she heard an owl calling and the noise of something moving in the bushes. Suddenly Kara thought she could feel someone or something watching her. 'It must be the owl,' she told herself as she reached the gate. Through the gate she could see the shapes of some small buildings and one large building. They had arrived but Kara didn't know where they were. She only knew two things. The place was called Owl Hall and something didn't feel right.

The gate creaked loudly as Kara opened it. Then she turned and waved to Mum in the car. Mum drove through the gates with Martin smiling in the backseat, and parked next to two other cars. As Kara was closing the gate, she thought she heard a voice whispering in her ear.

'Kara! Help me. Let me go!' the voice said.

But when Kara turned round, no one was there.

HOW TO

understand new words

See page 30

AFTER YOU READ

4 Copy the organiser. Then complete the information for the extract.

```
Title: _____
Main character: _____
Other characters: _____
Setting (place, time): _____
Story (most important events)
Event 1: _____
Event 2: _____
Event 3: _____
Event 4: _____
```

5 a **Look at the picture and complete the task.**

In the extract, part of the story is missing. What do you think happens in the missing part?

b ▶3.44 **Listen to the audio version to check your answer. How does Kara feel about the man?**

6 Write the answers to the questions in your own words.

1 What kind of person is Kara?
2 How would you describe Kara's relationship with her brother and mother?
3 Who do you think Howard is?

7 Read the dictionary entry and answer the questions.

1 What's the climax in the *Owl Hall* extract?
2 What 'mystery story' ingredients does the author include in the climax?
3 What do you think happens next? Make a note of your ideas.

climax

Noun [countable] informal

The most exciting or important moment in a story, event or situation, usually near the end.

Workbook, pages 124-125

EXTRA READING Robinson Crusoe

BEFORE YOU READ

1 **Look at the cover of the book and read the plot summaries. Which is a summary of *Robinson Crusoe*?**

a A boy, whose mother owns a small hotel, finds a map and goes to sea to find some treasure on an island.

b A young man ignores his father's advice and goes to sea. After a storm, he finds himself shipwrecked alone on an island.

c A teenager travels by ship with his family and some animals. The ship sinks and the boy finds himself alone with a tiger on a lifeboat.

WHILE YOU READ

2 ▶3.45 **Read the extract from *Robinson Crusoe* and check your answer to Exercise 1. Do you know the titles of the other two books?**

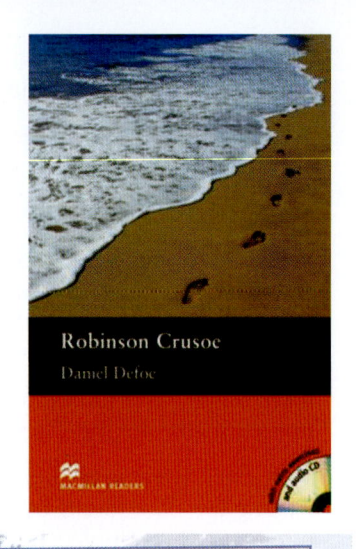

My name is Robinson Crusoe. I was born in 1632 in the city of York, in England. I came from a good family. My father was from Germany. He made his money as a merchant – buying and selling things – and came to live in York, where he married my mother.

I had two older brothers. One became a soldier and was killed in France. And I never knew what happened to my other brother – just as my mother and father never knew what happened to me.

I had a good education. I went to a good school, and learned a lot at home. My father wanted me to get a good job. But I had other ideas. I wanted to go to sea. I could not think about anything else, even though my parents and friends argued strongly against it. It was as if something was pushing me towards the terrible life that lay ahead of me. One day my father called me to his room and asked me why I wanted to leave his house, and England.

'People who go to sea are not like you,' he said. 'They either go because they have no money, or because they are very rich, and they want an adventure. You are lucky because you are neither rich nor poor. Poor people have to worry about finding food and somewhere to live. Rich people have to worry about looking after their money. You are in the best place, because you are in the middle. You can have a comfortable life if you stay at home.'

My father promised to do many things for me if I listened to him. With tears running down his face, he told me to remember my older brother. He had gone away to become a soldier and been killed.

'If you go to sea, you will have no one to help you,' he warned me.

I listened carefully to my father's words, and for a few days, I changed my mind about leaving home. But within a few weeks, I had decided to go away once more. I asked my mother to talk to my father. I told her that I wanted to go on one voyage. I said that if I did not like it, I would come home and work very hard.

But my mother was very upset. She said she would not talk to my father. She said she did not know how I could even think of going to sea. And she told me that she would not help me to do foolish things with my life. A year went by, and my parents would still not let me go to sea.

Then one day I went to the city of Hull and met a friend. His father was the captain of a ship which was sailing to London, and I decided to go with them, without even telling my mother or father.

When the ship left Hull, the wind began to blow and the sea turned rough. As I had never been to sea before, I was terrified, and became very seasick. Suddenly I thought about what I had done.

I remembered my mother and father's words, and felt terribly sorry for not listening to them. I promised to myself that if I lived, I would go straight home to my father and never go in a ship again.

The next day, the sea was a little calmer, but I still felt seasick. The following morning, however, when I got up, the sun was shining on a clear sea. I thought it was the most beautiful thing I had ever seen.

I completely forgot all the promises I had made when I felt so ill.

A few days later, when we came near the shore, a terrible storm blew up. The sea was very rough, and waves that were as high as mountains broke over the ship every few minutes.

118

This storm was nothing like the first one. Even the other men on the ship had faces full of fear. They said they had never seen anything like it. We all prayed for our lives.

In the middle of the night, one of the men told us that there was a leak in the ship – water was coming in. The men worked as hard as they could to get the water out, but everyone knew that the ship was going to sink. I felt as if my heart had died inside me. The captain told the men to fire guns to show other boats that we needed help. But the sea was too rough for a boat to come near.

At last, however, the storm started to die down a little, and a boat managed to come close to the ship. After trying many times, we finally pulled the boat near to our ship and climbed into it. As we rowed away, we saw our ship go down in the rough sea. I was so frightened I almost couldn't watch.

We rowed safely to the shore, where we were well looked after. There, we were given enough money to go on to London or back to Hull. I could have gone back home to Hull. My father would have been pleased to see me, and I could have had a quiet, happy life. But something inside me would not let me go back.

HOW TO
understand referring words
See page 96

AFTER YOU READ

3 Copy the organiser. Then make notes about the different characters in the extract. Think about their relationships, jobs, wishes and feelings. What do they do in the extract?

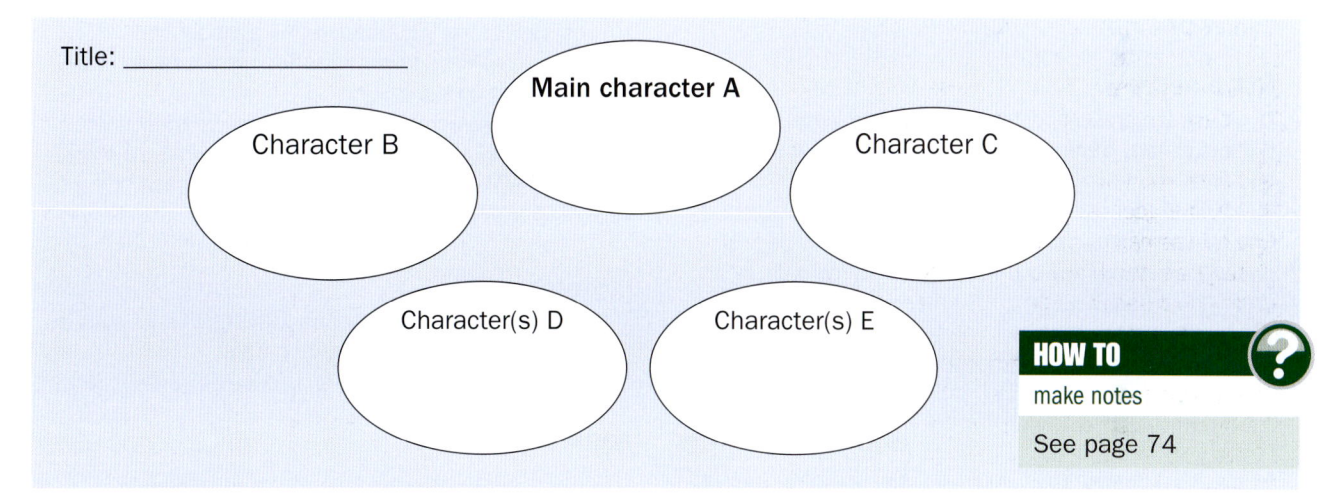

Title: _____

- Main character A
- Character B
- Character C
- Character(s) D
- Character(s) E

HOW TO
make notes
See page 74

4 Write the answers to the questions in your own words.
1 How did Crusoe's family feel about him going to sea? Why?
2 What event finally made him decide to go?
3 Why didn't Crusoe go home after the second storm at sea?

5 ▶3.46 Listen to an audio extract of one of the most famous parts of the book. What does Crusoe find and why is he frightened?

6 Read about *Robinson Crusoe* and answer the questions.
1 Novels are usually told in the first or third person. What are the advantages and disadvantages of telling a story in the first person?
2 What does Crusoe mean when he says: 'I never knew what happened to my other brother – just as my mother and father never knew what happened to me.'?
3 What do you think happens in the story? Does Crusoe ever return to England?

Robinson Crusoe was published in 1719, and many people think of it as the first English novel. The book is a fictional autobiography, told in the first person by the main character. Daniel Defoe may have got the idea from a true story about a man called Alexander Selkirk, who spent several years on an island.

Workbook, pages 126–127

GRAMMAR DATABASE 1

Present continuous and present simple

USE
Present continuous
- Use the present continuous to talk about things happening now or around now:
  *She **is preparing** for the Sunrise dance.*
  *In this photo the girl **isn't wearing** special clothes.*
  *What **are** these girls **doing**?*
- Use time expressions such as *now, right now, at the moment* and *these days* with the present continuous:
  *My sister's **preparing** the food for her party **at the moment**.*
- You can also use the present continuous to talk about temporary situations:
  *My brother has got a holiday job. He's **working** in a café.*

Present simple
- Use the present simple to talk about habits, routines and things that are generally true:
  *The celebration **starts** with a ceremony.*
- Use adverbs and expressions of frequency such as *usually, sometimes, every day* with the present simple:
  *The girls **usually wear** special clothes for their parties.*

State verbs
Don't use the present continuous with **state verbs**. Use the present simple. State verbs often express mental states and opinions (eg *believe, know, remember, think, understand*) and preferences (eg *hate, like, love, need, want*):
*She **wants** a big party.* (not *She is wanting* …)
*I **don't understand** what he's saying.*

FORM

	Present simple	Present continuous
Positive	I usually **wear** jeans to school.	I'm **wearing** jeans today.
	You/We/They usually **wear** jeans to school.	You're/We're/They're **wearing** jeans today.
	He/She usually **wears** jeans to school.	He's/She's **wearing** jeans today.
Negative	I **don't** usually **wear** jeans to school.	I'm not **wearing** jeans today.
	You/We/They **don't** usually **wear** jeans to school.	You/We/They **aren't wearing** jeans today.
	He/She **doesn't** usually **wear** jeans to school.	He/She **isn't wearing** jeans today.
Questions and short answers	Do I/you/we/they usually **wear** jeans to school? Yes, I/you/we/they **do**. No, I/you/we/they **don't**.	Am I **wearing** jeans today? Yes, I **am**. No, I'm not. Are you/we/they **wearing** jeans today? Yes, you/we/they **are**. No, you/we/they **aren't**.
	Does he/she usually **wear** jeans to school? Yes, he/she **does**. No, he/she **doesn't**.	Is he/she **wearing** jeans today? Yes, he/she **is**. No, he/she **isn't**.

Spelling of -ing forms
- If a verb ends in -e, remove the final -e before adding -ing: *take – taking   use – using*
- If a verb ends in a vowel (eg *a, i, o*) and a consonant (eg *m, p, t*), double the consonant before adding -ing: *swim – swimming   hit – hitting*
- If a verb ends in -l, double the -l: *travel – travelling*
- If a verb ends in -ie, change the -ie to -ying: *lie – lying*

Past simple and past continuous

USE
- Use the past simple for completed actions in the past:
  *My mum and dad **bought** me a new mobile.*
- Use the past continuous for actions in progress at a particular time in the past:
  *We **were walking** down the street one day.*
- Use the past simple and past continuous together to say something happened while another action was in progress. You usually use *while* before the continuous:
  *My dad bought it for me **while** we were staying in Rome.*
  You usually use *when* before the past simple:
  *We were walking down the street one day **when** I saw it in a shop window.*
- You can also use the past continuous to describe background events, often to set the scene in a story:
  *It **was raining**. I **was reading** a book in my bedroom when I suddenly heard a loud bang.*

State verbs
Don't use the past continuous with state verbs such as *know, like, need, understand* and *want*:
*I **didn't know** how to use it.* (not *I wasn't knowing* …)

FORM

	Past simple	Past continuous
Positive	I **walked** to work.	I **was walking** down the street.
	You/We/They **walked** to work.	You/We/They **were walking** down the street.
	He/She **walked** to school.	He/She/It **was walking** down the street.
Negative	I **didn't walk** to work.	I **wasn't walking** down the street.
	You/We/They **didn't walk** to work.	You/We/They **weren't walking** down the street.
	He/She **didn't walk** to work.	He/She **wasn't walking** down the street.
Questions and short answers	Did I **walk** to work? Yes, I **did**. / No, I didn't.	Was I **walking** down the street? Yes, I **was**. / No, I wasn't.
	Did you/we/they **walk** to work? Yes, you/we/they **did**. No, you/we/they didn't.	Were you/we/they **walking** down the street? Yes, you/we/they **were**. No, you/we/they **weren't**.
	Did he/she **walk** to work? Yes, he/she **did**. No, he/she **didn't**.	Was he/she walking down the street? Yes, he/she **was**. No, he/she **wasn't**.

GRAMMAR DATABASE

Present perfect (1)

USE
- Use the present perfect to talk about past actions when we don't know the exact time:
They've visited lots of countries.

ever
- Use the present perfect with *ever* to ask about an experience in your life:
Have you ever worked as a volunteer?

never
- Use the present perfect with *never* to say you have not done something in your life:
I've never been to Egypt.

just
- Use the present perfect with *just* to talk about very recent events:
She's just spent four weeks travelling round America.

already
- Use the present perfect with *already* to talk about actions completed before now:
They've already finished building the new school.

yet
- Use the present perfect with *yet* in questions to ask if an action is completed or not:
Have you finished your homework yet?
- Use the present perfect with *yet* in negative sentences to talk about an action that isn't completed:
I haven't written my essay yet.

Present perfect (2)

for and since
- Use the present perfect with *for* and *since* to answer the question *How long …?*
Use *for* with periods of time:
My brother's played in a band for three years.
Use *since* with dates and points in time:
We've lived in this house since I was two.
My dad's worked as a teacher since 1998.

FORM
Positive
- You form the present perfect with *have/has* + past participle of the verb:

| I/You/We/They | have | never | been | to the USA. |
| He/She | has | | | |

Short forms

| I've/You've/We've/They've | never | slept in a tent. |
| He's/She's | | |

Past participles
- Many verbs have irregular past participles. You have to learn these:
*make – **made**   write – **written**   see – **seen***
See page 140 for a list of irregular past participles.

Negative
- You form the present perfect negative with *have/has* + *not* + past participle of the verb:

| I/You/We/They | haven't (have not) | flown on an aeroplane. |
| He/She | hasn't (has not) | |

Questions and short answers
- You form questions in the present perfect with *have* + subject + past participle of the verb:

Questions			Short answers
Have	you/we/they	ever eaten Chinese food?	Yes, I/we/they **have**. No, I/we/they **haven't**.
Has	he/she		Yes, he/she **has**. No, he/she **hasn't**.

WATCH OUT! Don't use short forms in positive short answers:
Yes, I have. (not *Yes, I've.*)

The future

USE
- Use different future forms to express different types of activities.

Present continuous
- Use the present continuous for future arrangements:
We're going on holiday tomorrow.

Present simple
- Use the present simple for events on a timetable:
Our flight leaves at 12.

be going to
- Use *be going to* + infinitive for future plans and intentions:
I'm going to spend lots of time in the hotel pool.

will/won't
- Use *will/won't* for predictions about the future:
We will have a fantastic time!
We won't want to come home.
- Use *will definitely* when you're 100% sure:
We'll definitely try the local food.
- Use *will probably* when you're 75% sure:
We'll probably go on a boat trip.
- In affirmative sentences with *will*, the adverb (*probably/definitely*) comes AFTER *will*. In a negative sentence, the adverb comes BEFORE *won't*:
will + *definitely/probably* + infinitive
definitely/probably + *won't* + infinitive

be likely to
- Use *be likely to* talk about probable events in the future:
It's likely to be very hot!

GRAMMAR DATABASE

Verbs followed by -ing form or to + infinitive

USE
- When a verb comes after another verb, its form depends on the first verb.

FORM
- You can use the -ing form (eg *doing*) after these verbs:
  don't mind, enjoy, imagine, practise
  I **enjoy listening** to music.
  I **practise playing** the piano every day.
- You use *to* + infinitive (eg *to do*) after these verbs:
  decide, hope, learn, plan, want, inspire, wouldn't like
  My sister's **learning to play** the guitar.
  She'd also **like to sing** in a band one day.
- Some verbs can be followed by -ing or to with little or no difference in meaning such as:
  hate, like, love, prefer
  I prefer **dancing** to salsa music.
  I prefer **to dance** to salsa music.

WATCH OUT! Some verbs can be followed by -ing or to but the meaning changes:
forget, remember
I forgot **to shut** the door. (I didn't do it.)
I forget **shutting** the door. (I may have done it, but I don't remember.)
He doesn't remember **doing** his homework. (He did his homework but now he's forgotten he did it.)
He didn't remember **to do** his homework. (He forgot to do his homework.)
Remember! Some verbs change their spelling in the -ing form:
shop – **shopping**   use – **using**   travel – **travelling**

Comparison of adverbs

USE
- To compare how people or things do something, use comparatives and superlatives:
  She sings **better** than me.
  The Australian swimmer swam **the fastest**.
  Tom runs **as fast as** his brother.
  He **doesn't** practise **as hard as** his brother.
- To compare how two or more people or things do something, use comparatives.
- To compare one thing with all the others in a group, use superlatives.

FORM
Comparative adverbs
- Add -er at the end of short adverbs followed by *than*:
  He practises **harder than** the others.
- Use *more* with long adverbs that end in -ly followed by *than*:
  She swims **more quickly than** me.

Superlative adverbs
- Use *the* + *est* with short adverbs:
  She jumped **the highest** at the high jump competition.
- Use *the most* with long adverbs:
  The Russian gymnasts performed **the most confidently**.

Irregular adverbs
- Some adverbs have irregular comparative and superlative forms:

Adverb	Comparative	Superlative
well	better	the best
badly	worse	the worst
far	further	the furthest

(not) as ... as ...
- Use *as* + adverb + *as* to say two people or things do something the same:
  My sister can run **as fast as** me.
- Use *not as* + adverb + *as* to say two people or things don't do something the same:
  She can't jump **as high as** me.
  She doesn't sing **as loudly as** me.

GRAMMAR DATABASE

First conditional with *if/unless*

> **USE**
> - Use the first conditional to talk about the future. The *if*-clause describes a possible action in the future. The other clause describes its result:
> **If** I **don't finish** my homework, my parents **won't let** me go to the party.
> **If** you **don't go** to the party, I **won't go** either.

FORM

- Use the present simple in the *if*-clause and *will (not)* + infinitive in the result clause:
  if-clause (action)　　　　result clause
  If + present simple + (subject) + will (not) + infinitive
  If he **asks** me, I**'ll say** yes.
- Use the present simple in the *if*-clause and *may* or *might (not)* + infinitive in the result clause if you are not sure about the result:
  If Tom **goes** to the party, I **might not go**.
- Use *unless* with a positive verb in the *if*-clause to mean 'if ... not':
  Unless I **finish** my homework, my parents **won't let** me go to the party.
  (= If I don't finish my homework, my parents won't let me go to the party.)
- You can start the sentence with either clause:
  If you talk to them, they might let you go.
  They might let you go **if** you talk to them.

> **WATCH OUT!** If the *if* clause comes second, don't use a comma:
> I won't come to the party if you invite Tom.

Second conditional

> **USE**
> - Use the second conditional to talk about an unlikely or imaginary situation in the present or future and its result:
> **If** I **was** a parent, I**'d be** quite strict.
> **If** I **had** kids, I **wouldn't let** them stay up late in the week.

FORM

- Use the past simple after *if* or *unless* in the *if*-clause. Use *would (not)* + infinitive without *to* in the result clause. The contracted form of *would* is *'d*:
  　　　　if-clause　　　　　　　result clause
  If/unless + past simple + subject + would (not) + infinitive
  If I **won** the lottery, I**'d buy** a house with a swimming pool.
  Unless my kids **helped** with the housework, I **wouldn't give** them pocket money.
- To form questions, use *would* + subject + infinitive:
  Would you **be** strict **if** you **were** a parent?
  Yes, I **would**. / No, I **wouldn't**.
  What **would** you **do if** you **won** the lottery?
- You can use *If I was* or *If I were* for the first person:
  If I **was** a parent, I'd be quite strict.
  If I **were** a parent, I'd be easy-going.
- You can start the sentence with either clause:
  If I was president of our country, I'd ban all cars.
  I'd ban all cars **if** I was president of our country.
- Remember: if the *if*-clause comes second, don't use a comma.

GRAMMAR DATABASE

Passives (present, past and future)

USE
- Use the passive when the person or thing that did the action is unknown, obvious or less important than the subject of the sentence. Compare the two sentences:
  Active: *They make chocolate out of cocoa beans, milk and sugar.*
  Passive: *Chocolate is made out of cocoa beans, milk and sugar.*

FORM
Present simple passive
- Form the present simple passive with *am/are/is (not)* + past participle:
  *Chocolate **is enjoyed** by people all over the world.*
  *Cocoa beans **are grown** in hot countries such as Africa, and Central and South America.*
- To form questions in the present simple passive, put *am/is/are* before the subject:
  ***Are** chocolate bars **sold** in schools in your country?*
  *Yes, they **are**. / No, they **aren't**.*

Past simple passive
- Form the past simple passive with *was/were (not)* + past participle:
  *Chocolate **was brought** to Europe in the 16th century by Hernán Cortés.*
- To form questions in the past simple passive, put *was/were* before the subject:
  ***Was** sugar **added** to chocolate by the Europeans?*
  *Yes, it **was**. / No, it **wasn't**.*

Future passive
- Form the future passive with *will/won't be* + past participle:
  *Chocolate **won't be sold** in schools from next year.*
- To form questions in the future passive, put *will* before the subject:
  ***Will** chocolate **be produced** in this factory in the future?*
  *Yes, it **will**. / No, it **won't**.*
- To say who or what does the action, use *by*:
  *Many different types of chocolate bars are produced **by** thousands of chocolate companies.*

(In order) to ... , so (that) ...

USE
- Use *in order to ...* or *so that ...* to explain the reason why someone does, did or will do something:
  *I turned up the TV **in order to** hear it better.*
  *I turned up the TV **so that** I could hear it better.*

FORM
- Use *in order to ...* with the infinitive of the verb:
  *Lisa watches films without subtitles **in order to practise** her English.*
- You can also use the shorter form *to* + infinitive (without *in order*). It is more informal than *in order to*:
  *Lisa watches films without subtitles **to practise** her English.*
- Use *so that* + subject + verb when the reason is negative:
  *I always check my spelling **so that** I **don't** make any mistakes.*
- Use *so that* with *can*/present simple to talk about now or in general:
  *We learn foreign languages **so that** we **can** communicate with people from other countries.*
- Use *so that* with *can/will*/present simple to talk about the future:
  *Jared is studying hard **so that** he'll get a good job when he's older.*
- Use *so that* with *could/would*/past simple to talk about the past:
  *I turned on the light **so that** I **could** see.*
- You can use the shorter form of *so* without *that*:
  *I turned on the light **so** I could see.*

WATCH OUT! If the subject of the sentence changes, use *so (that)*, not *(in order) to*:
*Braille developed the idea **so (that)** blind people could use it.* (not *Braille developed the idea (in order) to blind people could use it.*)

124

GRAMMAR DATABASE

Possibility and impossibility

USE

- Use *can't, could, may, might* and *must* to make logical guesses and say whether you think things are possible or not.
- Use *could, may* or *might* when you're not sure if something is possible. These three modal verbs have a similar meaning:
  *What's that smell? It smells like something's burning. It **could** be the oven.* (= *It **may/might** be the oven.*)
- Use *can't* when you believe something is impossible:
  *It **can't** be the oven. It isn't switched on.*
- Use *must* when you're sure something is true or possible:
  *Look, there's smoke coming from over there. It **must** be the toaster.*
- *Can't* is the opposite of *must*:
  *It **can't** be the oven. It **must** be the toaster.*
- You can also use phrases such as *I'm (not) sure* to express how certain or uncertain you are about something:
  *I'm **sure** they're buttons.*

FORM

- Use an infinitive without *to* after *can't, could, may, might* and *must*:
  It must be …
  It could be …
  It may be …
  It might be …
  It can't be …

Indirect questions

USE

- Use indirect questions to be more polite and more formal:
  Direct question: *Where can I buy a mobile phone charger?*
  Indirect question: *Do you have any idea where I can buy a mobile phone charger?*

FORM

- Indirect questions start with an expression like these:
  Could you tell me …
  Would you mind telling me …
  Do you know …
  Do you have any idea …
- Form indirect *wh-* questions with indirect expression + *where/when*, etc + subject + verb:
  *Would you mind telling me **where** the café **is**?*
- Form indirect *yes/no* questions with indirect expression + *if/whether* + subject + verb:
  *Could you tell me **if** the chemist's **is** open?*
- The word order in indirect questions is different to direct questions:
  In a direct question, the verb comes *before* the subject:
  *Where **is** the mobile phone shop?*
  In an indirect question, the verb comes *after* the subject:
  *Do you know where the mobile phone shop **is**?*

WATCH OUT! You don't use *do/does/did* in indirect questions:
Direct question: *Where **does** the bus for the town centre **leave** from?*
Indirect question: *Could you tell me where the bus for the town centre **leaves** from?*
(not ~~Could you tell me where does the bus for the town centre leave from?~~)

- Be careful with the third person s in indirect questions:
  Direct question: *What time does the shopping centre **open**?*
  Indirect question: *Do you know what time the shopping centre **opens**?*

GRAMMAR DATABASE

Used to

USE
- Use *used to* + infinitive to talk about situations or habits in the past:
  *People **used to wash** their clothes by hand.*
- Don't use *used to* in the present; use adverbs of frequency:
  *I **usually cook** at the weekend.*

FORM
- The negative form of *used to* is *didn't use to* + infinitive:
  *They **didn't use to have** washing machines.*
  *She **didn't use to walk** to school.*
- To form questions, use *did* + subject + *use to* + infinitive:
  ***Did** people **use to have** less free time in the 19th century?*
  Yes, they did. / No, they didn't.

WATCH OUT!
Don't use *used to* in negative and question forms. Use *use to*:
*I didn't **use** to like chocolate.* (not *I didn't **used** to like chocolate.*)

Past perfect simple

USE
- Use the past perfect simple to show that an action happened before another action or time in the past. Use the past simple for the other action/time:
  *When I arrived, the film **had** already **started**.*

film started → I arrived

- You often use the past perfect simple after *because* to give an explanation:
  *I was exhausted **because** I'**d stayed** up very late the night before.*
- You often use the past perfect simple with the time expressions *already*, *before*, *just* and *yet*:
  *I didn't go to the cinema with them because I'**d already seen** that film.*
  *The band **had just finished** playing when I arrived.*

FORM
Positive
- Form the past perfect with *had* + past participle of the verb:
  *My brother **had** already **left** by the time I got there.*
- The contracted form of *had* is *'d*:
  *He'**d already gone** home.*
- To form the past participle of regular verbs, add *-ed*:
  design – designed   help – helped   start – started
- Many verbs have irregular past participles. You have to learn these. Some of these past participles are the same as the past simple.
  make – made   write – written   see – seen
  See page 140 for a list of irregular past participles.

Negative
- You form the past perfect negative with *had* + *not* + past participle of the verb:
  *The talk **hadn't started** yet.*

Questions and short answers
- You form questions in the past perfect with *had* + subject + past participle of the verb:
  ***Had** they **eaten** lunch before you arrived?*
  Yes, they had. / No, they hadn't.

WATCH OUT! Don't use short forms in positive short answers:
Yes, I had. (not *Yes, I'd.*)

GRAMMAR DATABASE

Reported speech

USE
- Use direct speech to repeat the exact words someone says:
  He said: 'I'm tired.'
- Use reported speech to repeat what someone says without using their exact words:
  He said he was tired.

FORM
- Use *said* or *told* in reported speech. You can use reported speech with or without *that*:
  He said (**that**) he was tired.
  It is more usual to include *that* in more formal speaking and writing.
- Use *told* + object pronoun if you say who the person is talking to:
  He told **me** that he was tired.
- Tenses usually change in reported speech:
  Ana: 'I've never been to London.'
  > Ana said she **had** never **been** to London.

Direct speech	Reported speech
present simple	past simple
present continuous	past continuous
present perfect	past perfect
past simple	past perfect
future with *going to*	*was going to*
future with *will*	*would*
can	could
may	might

- However, if the situation that is being reported is still true, the tense doesn't change:
  Jon: 'I'**m** a computer programmer.'
  > Jon said he'**s** a computer programmer.
- Pronouns and possessive adjectives change in reported speech:
  Liam: 'I'll phone you later.'
  > Liam said that **he** would phone **me** later.
- Time expressions and adverbs of place often change in reported speech:
  Lucy: 'I'm going to the cinema tonight.'
  > Lucy said she was going to the cinema **that night**.

Direct speech	Reported speech
now	then
today	that day
here	there
tonight	that night
yesterday	the day before
tomorrow	the next day
last week	the week before
next week	the following week

Reported questions

USE
- Use reported questions to report a direct question that someone asked.

FORM
- The word order in reported questions is different to direct questions. In reported questions, the verb comes after the subject:
  Mum: 'Where **are you** going?'
  > Mum asked him where **he was** going.
- Don't use *do/does/did* in reported questions:
  Mum: '**What do you want** for tea?'
  > Mum asked him **what he wanted** for tea.
- Form reported *wh-* questions with: *asked* + person + question word + *I/you*, etc + verb:
  Mum: 'When will you be back?'
  > Mum asked him when he would be back.
- Form reported *yes/no* questions with *asked* + person + *if/whether* + *I/you*, etc + verb:
  Mum: 'Have you finished your homework?'
  > She asked him **if** he had finished his homework.
- Don't use a question mark at the end of a reported question.
- Change verb tenses, pronouns, possessive adjectives, time expressions and adverbs of place if necessary (see above):
  Mum: 'Have **you** finished **your** homework?'
  > She asked him if **he** had finished **his** homework.

127

GRAMMAR DATABASE

9

Reported requests and commands

USE
- Use reported requests and commands to report what people ask and tell you to do.

FORM
- Requests use *Can/Could you ... ?* and commands use imperatives (*Go/Don't go*).
- To form reported requests, use *ask/asked* + object + *to* + infinitive:
  '**Can you** clear the table, please?' Dad asked.
  > Dad **asked me to** clear the table.
- To form reported commands, use *tell/told* + object + (*not*) *to* + infinitive:
  '**Turn** your music down,' he told me.
  > He **told me to** turn my music down.
- Change verb tenses, pronouns, possessive adjectives, time expressions and adverbs of place if necessary (see Grammar Database 8 on page 127).

Reflexive pronouns

USE
- Use a reflexive pronoun after a verb when its subject is the same as its object:
  I taught **myself** Japanese.
- Reflexive pronouns are often used after the verbs *hurt, express, enjoy, teach, introduce, cut, help*:
  Oh, dear. It looks like John's hurt **himself**.
  We really enjoyed **ourselves** at the end of term disco last night.
  Hello, can I introduce **myself**? My name's Tina.
- Reflexive pronouns are often used after *by* to mean 'alone' or 'with no help':
  I walked home **by myself**.
- Use reflexive pronouns to emphasise who does an action:
  Do you like your card? I made it **myself**.

FORM
Singular: *myself, yourself, himself, herself, itself*
Plural: *ourselves, yourselves, themselves*

> **WATCH OUT!**
> Don't use reflexive verbs after verbs that are reflexive in some other languages: *concentrate, dress, feel, relax, remember, sit down, stand up* and *wash*.
> Note that *wash* and *dress* can be used with a reflexive pronoun, but only for emphasis:
> You are old enough to dress yourself.
> Lucy is only two, but she can already wash herself in the bath.

each other
- Use *each other* to say that each person does something to the other(s):
  It's important that we all respect and help **each other**.
  My cousin lives in Australia. We email **each other** once a week.

128

GRAMMAR DATABASE

So and *such* ... *that* ...

USE

- Use *so* and *such* ... *that* ... to emphasise somebody or something's qualities and the results of those qualities:
  *The heels on her new shoes were **so high that** she found it difficult to walk.*
  *The weather was **so horrible that** we stayed indoors all day.*
  *T-shirts were **such a hit that** soon everybody began wearing them.*
  *It was **such a lovely day that** we spent the whole day in the park.*

FORM

- Use *so* + adjective:
  *It was **so cold** ...*
- Use *such a/an* + adjective + singular countable noun:
  *It was **such a cold day** ...*
- Use *such* + adjective + uncountable noun/plural noun:
  *It was **such cold weather** ...*
- Use *that* + clause to describe the clause.
  *... **that** I wore two jumpers, one coat, a hat, scarf and gloves!*
- We can leave out *that* in informal speaking and writing:
  *It was **so windy** my umbrella blew away!*
  *We had **such a terrible holiday** we came home early.*

Ability in the past, present and future

can, could

- Use *can* and *can't* + infinitive for ability in the present:
  *I **can** speak Spanish, but I **can't** speak Portuguese.*
- Use *could* and *couldn't* + infinitive for ability in the past:
  *I **could** play the violin when I was younger, but I **couldn't** play the piano.*

be able to

- Use *am/is/are able to* + infinitive for ability in the present:
  *I **am able to speak** several foreign languages.*
  However, *can* is more usual than *be able to* when talking about the present.
- Use *was/were able to* + infinitive for ability in the past:
  *I **was able to do** a handstand when I was younger. I can't now!*
- Use *will be able to* + infinitive for ability in the future:
  *I hope that I **will be able to have** an interesting career when I'm older.*
- We usually use *was/were able to*, and not *could*, for a specific achievement in the past (eg *I **was able to** become a fashion designer*, not *I could become a fashion designer.*).
- However, we use both *was/weren't able to* and *couldn't* for things we didn't manage to do on a specific occasion (eg *I **wasn't able to** get a scholarship. / I **couldn't** get a scholarship.*).

WORDS & BEYOND

UNIT 1

Page 6

RECALL

STAGES OF LIFE
baby
child
middle-aged person
parent
pensioner
teenager
university student
(young) adult

WORK WITH WORDS

TIP: To remember words, try to associate them with people or things you know well.

TASK: Make a list of people you know who are at each of the stages of life.

Pages 6 and 7

SPECIAL DAYS
get a driving licence
get a job
get married
go on a first date
go to university
have children
leave home
retire
start school
vote

GO BEYOND
1 Which things in the list have you already done? Write them down.
2 Which things would you like to do in the next five years?

Page 10

ADJECTIVES FOR DESCRIBING OBJECTS
antique
colourful
cotton
enormous
old-fashioned
square
tiny
unusual
useful
valuable

GO BEYOND
Think of five objects you have. Write a sentence describing each one. Use as many adjectives in the list as you can.

OTHER IMPORTANT WORDS

celebrate	diving	remind	turn + age
celebration	doll	ritual	vine
ceremony	election	second-hand	wooden
city offices	identical	stuff	work together
coming of age	miss (someone)	throw out	
crown (n)	packaging	traditional	

UNIT 2

Page 16

RECALL

METHODS OF TRANSPORT

AIR	RAIL	ROAD	SEA
helicopter	train	bike	boat
plane	tram	bus	ferry
	underground	car	ship
		coach	
		horse	
		motorbike	
		scooter	
		taxi	

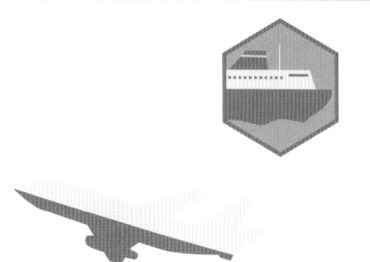

WORK WITH WORDS

TIP: When you learn a word, learn it with verbs and prepositions as phrases.

TASK: Can you use *in*, *on* (or both) with each method of transport? Use a dictionary or search online to check.

Pages 16 and 17

TRAVEL ITEMS

backpack
boarding pass
hairbrush
passport
scissors
shampoo
sleeping bag
suitcase
toothbrush
toothpaste
visa
wallet

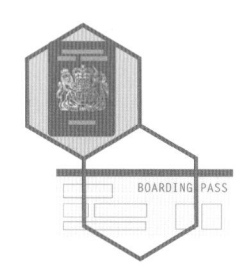

GO BEYOND

1. Which word in the list has a silent letter? Circle it.
2. Which word exists in its plural form only? How would you describe 'one' of this thing? Use a dictionary to check.

Page 20

TRAVEL

arrival
connection
delay
departure
destination
fare
passenger
reservation
route
seat

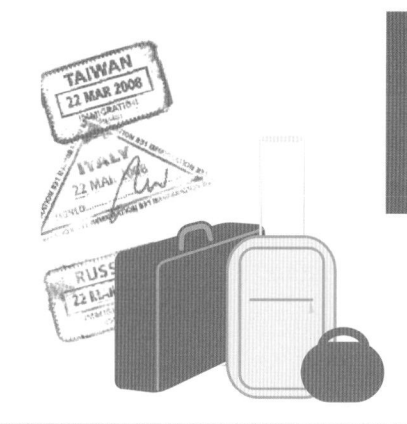

GO BEYOND

Write the verbs for the following nouns.
1. connection
2. delay
3. departure
4. reservation

OTHER IMPORTANT WORDS

abroad	check in (v)	distance	host family	material goods	take off
aid (n)	community	flight	invisible	natural disaster	trip (n)
attitude	compartment	gate	journey	passport control	voyage
baggage	crew	homeschooling	land (v)	queue (n)	
bubble	customs	homesick	luggage	sharp object	

131

WORDS & BEYOND

UNIT 3

Page 28
RECALL

TYPES OF MUSIC
classical
heavy metal
hip hop
pop
R&B
reggae
rock

INSTRUMENTS
drum
guitar
keyboard
piano
violin

PEOPLE
musician
singer

TYPES OF GROUP
band

PLACES & EVENTS
concert
concert hall
festival

WORK WITH WORDS

TIP: Listening to songs in English is a great way to improve your vocabulary.

TASK: Make a list of English song titles you know. Then write the name of the person or group who performs the song and the style of music.

Pages 28 and 29
MUSIC WORDS
audience
band
brass band
conductor
flute
folk
jazz
opera
orchestra
performance
trumpet
venue

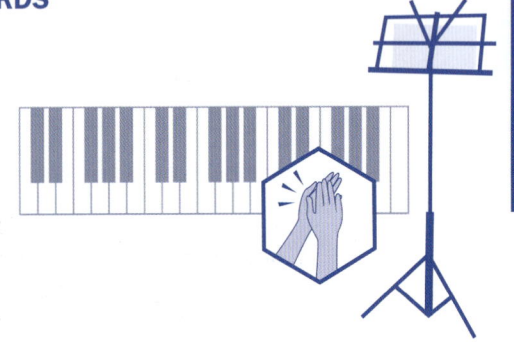

GO BEYOND
Add at least five more music words to the list.
1
2
3
4
5

Page 32
ADVERBS OF DEGREE
a bit
a lot
extremely
incredibly
pretty
quite
really
terribly
totally
very

GO BEYOND
Write the title of a film, a book and a TV programme you've watched recently. Give your opinion of each one using an adverb of degree.
1
2
3

OTHER IMPORTANT WORDS

audition (v)
aware
beat (n)
childhood
conductor

confidence
convey
creatively
criteria
distracting

extreme
focused
gesture (n)
grasp (n)
inspire

music theory
perform
powerful
rhythm
rubbish (adj)

stage (n)
steady
talent
tell off
wordless

UNIT 4

Page 38

RECALL

APPEARANCE

GENERAL
good-looking
old
short
tall
young

HAIR
dark
light
straight
wavy

EYES
big
small

MOUTH/NOSE
big
small

PERSONALITY
ambitious
brave
cheerful
competitive
confident
creative
emotional
generous
patient
polite
rude
serious
shy

WORK WITH WORDS

TIP: To help you remember new words, write definitions in English.

TASK: Choose three of the personality words from the list and write a definition in English.

Pages 38 and 39

PEOPLE AND RELATIONSHIPS

acquaintance
boyfriend/girlfriend
classmate
close friend
enemy
friend of a friend
guest
neighbour
old friend
online friend
relative
team-mate

GO BEYOND
Think of someone you know for each of the people and relationships, and write the name of the person, eg *Gerry Denis is a close friend*.

Page 42

EXTREME ADJECTIVES

amazing
ancient
awful
exhausted
fascinating
furious
huge
shocked
terrified
unbelievable

GO BEYOND
Divide the words into syllables, and then underline the stressed syllable, eg a-<u>maz</u>-ing. Practise saying the words.

OTHER IMPORTANT WORDS AND PHRASES

accept
argue
condition
cruise (n)
friendship
give somebody a hard time
good company
have something in common
honesty
point out
quality
recognise
respect (n) and (v)
row (n) and (v)
shame (n)
strict
suffer (from something)
support (n) and (v)
survey (n)
take an interest in someone/something
talk behind somebody's back
trust (n)

133

WORDS & BEYOND

UNIT 5

Page 50
RECALL

PARTS OF THE BODY
ankle
arm
back
chest
ear
eye
face
finger
foot
hand
head
knee
leg
mouth
neck
nose
shoulder
teeth
throat
thumb
toe

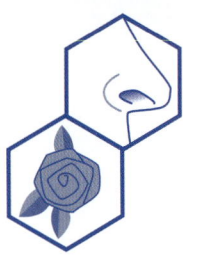

WORK WITH WORDS
TIP: Make drawings and label the parts to help you remember vocabulary.

TASK: Draw a human body and label the different parts without looking at the word list. How many words did you remember?

Pages 50 and 51

THE SENSES
hearing
sight
smell
taste
touch

SENSE VERBS
feel
hear
listen
look
see
sound
smell
taste
touch
watch

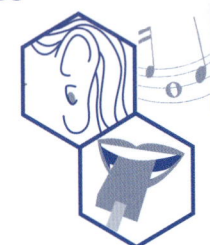

GO BEYOND
Match ten of the body parts above to the five senses. Then write sentences with the sense verbs, eg *We use our eyes to see.*

Page 54

COLOUR IDIOMS
as black as night
as white as a sheet
be in the red
black and white
feel blue
get the green light
once in a blue moon
out of the blue
see red
tell a white lie

GO BEYOND
Choose three idioms from the list. Write three sentences about you or the world today using the idioms.

OTHER IMPORTANT WORDS AND PHRASES
air freshener
allergic
ban (v)
blind (adj)
cell
chemist
cloud
complaint
crisps
formula
fragrance
incense (n)
independently
insect repellent
liquid
lotion
noisy
pale
perfume
processed foods
promote
restricted
signify
taste buds
tongue
unisex

134

UNIT 6

Page 60

RECALL

SHOPS
baker's
bookshop
butcher's
chemist's
clothes shop
department store
electronics shop
gift shop
newsagent's
pet shop
shoe shop
sports shop
supermarket
toy shop

SHOPPING PHRASES
ask the price
be cheap/expensive
buy/pay for/sell an item
cost/spend/save money

WORK WITH WORDS

TIP: Make networks with words: start with the word that you want to learn and add related words.

cake —— baker's —— bread
            |
       sandwiches

TASK: Choose two shops from the list. Make networks with the things that you can buy in each one.

Pages 60 and 61

SHOPPING
be in the sale
be on special offer
exchange an item
get a discount
get a refund
keep the receipt
pay by card
pay in cash
return an item
try on clothes

GO BEYOND
Choose three phrases from the list. For each one, write a question that you could ask a shop assistant.

Page 64

THINGS AND PEOPLE IN A SHOP
basket
cash desk
changing room
checkout
customer
department
escalator
exit
shelf
shop window
store detective
trolley

GO BEYOND
Complete these phrases with the correct words from the list.
go up on the _____
try on clothes in the _____
look in the _____ / on the _____
put things in your _____ / _____
pay at the _____ / _____

OTHER IMPORTANT WORDS
advertising
afford
aggressive
amusing
assertive
brand (n)
campaign (n)
challenge (n)
eye contact
fashion show
fit (v)
frame (n)
grin (v)
mind (v)
passive
product
shopaholic
size
slogan
suit (v)
the middle of nowhere
trick (n)
uncool

135

WORDS & BEYOND

UNIT 7

Page 72

RECALL

APPLIANCES
clock
computer
cooker
dishwasher
fridge
iron
kettle
lamp
light
phone
radio
vacuum cleaner
washing machine

HOUSEHOLD JOBS
clean the floor
clear the table
do the ironing
do the washing
do the washing-up
lay the table
load the dishwasher
make the bed
sort the recycling
take out the rubbish
tidy the room
vacuum

WORK WITH WORDS

TIP: Use ranking activities to help you remember new vocabulary.

TASK: Put the appliances in order, from the most important to the least important. Then rank the household jobs from the most to the least tiring.

Pages 72 and 73

TRADITIONAL ACTIVITIES
bake bread
build a house
chop wood
grow food
knit clothes
make furniture
make your own entertainment
milk a cow
sew clothes
travel by horse and cart
use gas lights
wash clothes by hand

GO BEYOND
Try to think of another noun you can use after each of the verbs in the activities.

Page 76

FEELINGS
anxious (about)
ashamed (about)
disappointed (with)
grateful (for)
guilty (about)
jealous (of)
proud (of)
satisfied (with)
sorry (for)
upset (about)

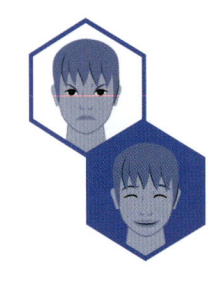

GO BEYOND
Divide the adjectives on the left into positive and negative feelings.

OTHER IMPORTANT WORDS
allegory
bow and arrow
elder (n)
fetch
fill in
genuine
hunter
light (v)
recreate
running water
rural
snore
statistics
stove
stream (n)
take part (in)
tribe
well (n)
wisdom

UNIT 8

Page 82

RECALL
THINGS WE READ
article
blog
cartoon
interview
letter
picture caption
poem
profile
quiz
recipe
report
rules
story
survey

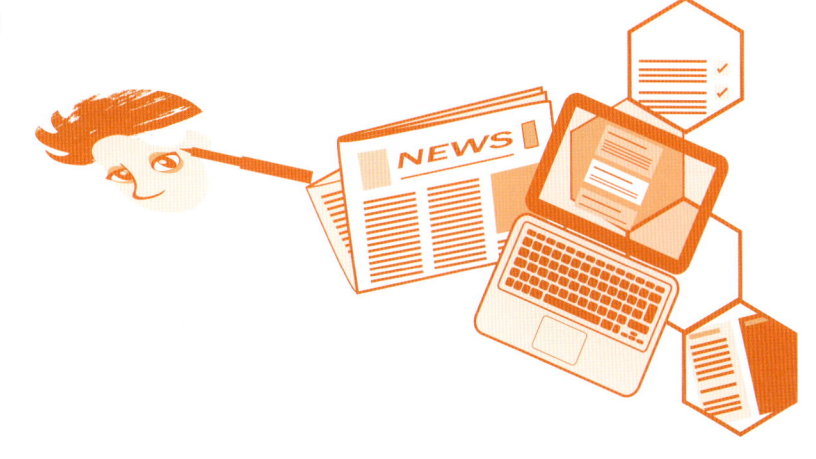

WORK WITH WORDS

TIP: Make a note of the stressed syllables when you learn new words.

TASK: Underline the stressed syllables in the words in the list. Check in a dictionary if necessary. Then practise saying the words.

Pages 82 and 83
PRINT AND DIGITAL MEDIA JOBS
author
blogger
cartoonist
designer
editor
gossip columnist
graphic artist
journalist
photographer
printer
publisher
reporter

GO BEYOND
Find the names of the publisher, authors, designer and printer of this book.
1
2
3
4

Page 86
REPORTING VERBS
add	deny
admit	explain
agree	insist
claim	promise
confirm	suggest

GO BEYOND
Use three of the verbs in the list to write sentences about three stories in the news.
1
2
3

OTHER IMPORTANT WORDS AND PHRASES

anonymous	employ	original	source
celebrity	exclude	paparazzi	statement
cheat (v)	explain	privacy	top (adj)
diagram	graph	quote (n)	victim
disappointed	headline	react	voicemail
drive someone up the wall	monster	refuse	witness

137

WORDS & BEYOND

UNIT 9

Page 94

RECALL

SCHOOL SUBJECTS
art
design & technology
drama
English
geography
history
IT (information technology)
languages
maths
music
PE (physical education)
science (physics, chemistry, biology)

STUDY WORDS
course
exam
term
university

WORK WITH WORDS

TIP: When you learn new nouns, writing your personal opinion can help you remember them, eg *I love geography because I have an interesting teacher.*

TASK: Choose five school subjects and write your opinion of them.

Pages 94 and 95
TYPES OF SCHOOL
boarding school
elementary school
high school
homeschooling
kindergarten
middle school
nursery school
primary school
private school
public school
secondary school
state school

GO BEYOND
Think of an example of as many of the different types of school as you can. Think about real schools or schools in books, films or TV programmes.

Page 98
WORDS WITH *SELF-*
self-centred
self-confident
self-conscious
self-control
self-defence
self-discipline
self-esteem
self-pity
self-sufficient
self-taught

GO BEYOND
Write sentences about people you know with five of the *self-* words.

OTHER IMPORTANT WORDS

acrobat	compliment	insecurity	rainy season	strength
adventurous	compulsory	juggle	rise	tightrope walker
avalanche	expand	juggler	school run	tough
banks	facilities	mud	soaking wet	trapeze artist
canoe	icy	pessimistic	steep	trek (n)
clown	insecure	pick up		

138

UNIT 10

Page 104

RECALL

CLOTHES AND FOOTWEAR
boots
coat
dress
hoody/hoodie
jacket
jeans
shirt
shoes
shorts
skirt
socks
sweater
swimming costume / trunks
tracksuit top/bottoms
trainers
trousers
T-shirt

ACCESSORIES
backpack
bag
belt
bracelet
earring
gloves
hat
jewellery
scarf
sunglasses
tie

VERBS
fit
match
suit
try on
wear

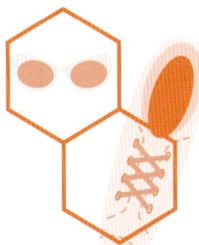

WORK WITH WORDS

TIP: Learn clothes words and accessories with the parts of the body where they are worn, eg *head / hat*.

TASK: Write clothes and accessories from the list for each of the following parts of the body: head, ears, eyes, neck, upper body, back, waist, lower body, full body, hands, wrist, feet.

Pages 104 and 105
FASHION

PARTS OF CLOTHES
button
collar
pocket
sleeve

MATERIALS
denim
leather
silk
wool

FIT AND LOOK
baggy
patterned
plain
tight

GO BEYOND
Write a description of three or four items in your wardrobe using some of the words in the lists.

Page 108
ADJECTIVES WITH -ABLE
affordable
breakable
downloadable
enjoyable
manageable
reasonable
recyclable
reliable
respectable
suitable
valuable
wearable

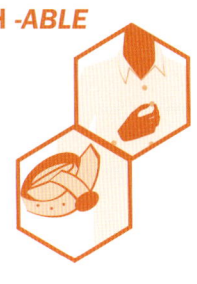

GO BEYOND
Make *-able* adjectives from the verbs below and then write a sentence for each adjective to show its meaning.
– accept
– avoid
– excuse

OTHER IMPORTANT WORDS AND PHRASES

allowance	eco-friendly	linen	outfit	stand out
barefoot	exploit	man-made	practical	status
be a hit	fair trade	match (v)	pyjamas	stylish
chic	footwear	matching (adj)	sacrifice	underwear
comfort	heel	nightwear	scholarship	vegan
cruel	label (n)	organic	sewing machine	

139

IRREGULAR VERBS

base form	past simple	past participle
be	was/were	been
become	became	become
break	broke	broken
bring	brought	brought
built	built	built
buy	bought	bought
can	could	been able to
catch	caught	caught
choose	chose	chosen
come	came	come
cost	cost	cost
do	did	done
drive	drove	driven
eat	ate	eaten
fall	fell	fallen
feel	felt	felt
find	found	found
fly	flew	flown
get	got	got
give	gave	given
go	went	gone
grow	grew	grown
have	had	had
hurt	hurt	hurt
keep	kept	kept
knit	knit/knitted	knit/knitted
know	knew	known
learn	learnt/learned	learnt/learned
leave	left	left
make	made	made
meet	met	met
must	had to	had to
pay	paid	paid
put	put	put
ride	rode	ridden
run	ran	run
say	said	said
see	saw	seen
sit	sat	sat
sleep	slept	slept
speak	spoke	spoken
spend	spent	spent
take	took	taken
teach	taught	taught
tell	told	told
think	thought	thought
understand	understood	understood
wake	woke	woken
wear	wore	worn
write	wrote	written

STUDENT A

UNIT 3 IN THE PICTURE
Page 29, Exercise 7

Music survey

1. Who is your favourite music artist or group?
2. Can you play any musical instruments? If so, which ones? If not, which ones would you like to learn?
3. Have you ever been to an opera or classical concert?
4. How do you usually listen to music – a) on the radio, b) online, c) on CD or d) on a music player?
5. In your opinion, which is more important in a song – a) the words or b) the music?

UNIT 6 GRAMMAR 2
Page 65, Exercise 5a

Centre FASHION SHOW

See the latest fashion for all the family

Today only at 16:30
At the main square, level 1

FREE

UNIT 5 LISTENING AND VOCABULARY
Page 54, Exercise 5

Read out each word to your partner. Your partner says the colour that he or she associates with the word.

tomato, sea, planet, car, fire, sky, ice-cream, grass, love, happiness

UNIT 7 SPEAKING
Page 79, Exercise 6

How to join the library if you are under 18
1. Fill in and return a membership form signed by a parent or guardian.
2. Bring a photo.

Borrowing from the library

Item	How long?	Charge	Charge if returned late
Books	4 weeks	Free	10c a day
Music CDs	4 weeks	€1	10c a day
DVDs and games	1 week	€2	€2

UNIT 10 GRAMMAR 1
Page 107, Exercise 5

1. My jeans have such small pockets …
2. My hair is so thick …
3. She has such long nails …
4. Her boyfriend is so good-looking …
5. He has such white teeth …

TIPS

UNIT 1 LANGUAGE & BEYOND
Page 12, Exercise 4

TIPS FOR ORGANISING AN EVENT

- Make sure all the people in the group give their ideas.
- Make decisions as a group. You can vote on things if people disagree.
- When planning and preparing the activity, give everyone a specific job to do.
- Make sure that everyone does their equal share of the work.

STUDENT B

UNIT 5 LISTENING AND VOCABULARY
Page 54, Exercise 5

Read out each word to your partner. Your partner says the colour that he or she associates with the word.

jeans football home chocolate sun space bus apple coffee anger

UNIT 6 GRAMMAR 2
Page 65, Exercise 5a

The Centre Cinema

All the latest films!
Tickets €10

Discount for pensioners, half price for under 10s

No children under five, no food, no drinks

UNIT 10 GRAMMAR 1
Page 107, Exercise 5

1 His feet are so big …
2 My parents wear such old-fashioned clothes …
3 She has such a lovely smile …
4 My pyjamas are so comfortable …
5 I feel so happy …

ANSWERS & SITUATIONS

UNIT 6 GRAMMAR 1
Page 63, Exercise 5

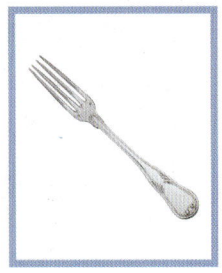

fork    headphones    key

sunglasses    pen 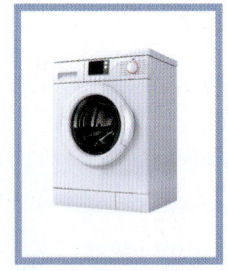   washing machine

UNIT 6 LANGUAGE & BEYOND
Page 66, Exercise 6

Situations
a You return a music player that doesn't work to the shop.
b A friend asks you to lie to his/her parents about sleeping at your house.
c A stranger sits much too close to you on the bus.
d Your grandmother asks you to turn your music down.

STEP-BY-STEP PROJECTS

Download more information from www.macmillanbeyond.com

HAVE AN AUCTION
- Find some interesting or unusual objects for your auction – *a souvenir, an old comic …*
- Make a catalogue with descriptions of the objects.
- Present your objects and bid for others.

Units 1 & 2

CREATE A FRAGRANCE
- Think of a concept for your fragrance – *Who's it for? What does it smell like?*
- Give your fragrance a name, and design a bottle and label.
- Create a print, audio or internet video ad for your fragrance.

Units 5 & 6

ORGANISE A MUSIC FESTIVAL
- Choose a location for your music festival – *a local park, a place in the country …*
- Make a plan of the festival area to show where things are – *stage, food and drink, toilets …*
- Choose the performers and make posters and tickets.

Units 3 & 4

MAKE A SOUNDSCAPE STORY
- Record several different sounds – *a door closing, a phone ringing …*
- Swap your recorded sounds with other students.
- Invent a story using the new sounds.

DESIGN A THEME SCHOOL
- Choose a type of school – *circus school, football school …*
- Draw a plan of the school and make a timetable for a typical school day.
- Make a poster to promote your school.

Units 9 & 10

Units 7 & 8

Macmillan Education
4 Crinan Street
London N1 9XW
A division of Macmillan Publishers Limited

Companies and representatives throughout the world

ISBN 978-0-230-45591-7

Text © Rob Metcalf, Robert Campbell and Rebecca Robb Benne, 2014

Design and illustration © Macmillan Publishers Limited 2014

The authors have asserted their rights to be identified as the authors of this work in accordance with the Copyright, Designs and Patents Act 1988.

First published 2014

All rights reserved; no part of this publication may be reproduced, stored in a retrieval system, transmitted in any form, or by any means, electronic, mechanical, photocopying, recording, or otherwise, without the prior written permission of the publishers.

Designed by emc design ltd.

Illustrated by Peter Cornwell pp65; Grant Cowan (Eye Candy Illustration) pp104-105 (main); Tom Croft pp85; Venitia Dean (Advocate Art) pp115 (main); Cyrus Deboo pp37, 50; John Dillow pp116, 117; Sally Elford pp6 (banner), 26-27 (banner), 28 (banner), 38 (banner), 50 (banner), 60 (banner), 69, 70-71 (banner), 72 (banner), 80, 82 (banner), 92-93 (banner), 94 (banner), 104 (banner), 114-115 (banner), 130-139 (icons); Bob Lea pp16-17 (main), 60-61 (main), 113; Chris Pavely pp24, 25, 34, 42, 43, 47, 52, 53, 76, 86, 89, 91, 107; Zara Picken pp16 (bottom left), 20, 108; Simon Williams pp118.

Cover design by emc design ltd
Cover illustration/photograph by Alamy/Losevsky Pavel, Alamy/Ian Nolan

Picture research by Susannah Jayes

The authors would like to thank all the team at Macmillan in the UK, Mexico, Poland, Spain and the rest of the world for everything they've done to make *Beyond* possible. Special thanks to our commissioning editor, managing editor and our publisher for their endless hard work and encouragement. We'd like to thank Studio 8 for their creative work on the drama group videos and EMC for coming up with the *Beyond* design concept. We'd also like to thank all the teachers and other individuals who have contributed to the course whose names appear on this page. Finally, we'd like thank our friends and families for all their support.

The authors and publishers would like to express thanks to all those who contributed to the development and formation of Beyond. In particular, we would like to thank the following teachers, contacts and reviewers: Cristina Moisén Antón, Argelia Solis Arriaga, Krzysztof Bartold, Paweł Bienert, Agnieszka Bojanowska, Samuel Gómez Borobia, Ma. Eugenia Fernández Castro, Jolanta Chojnacka, Elsa Georgina Cruz, Dominika Dąbrowska, Barbara Dawidowska, Galina Dragunova, Monika Drygiel-Kobylińska, Mauricio Duran, Natalia Evdokimenko, Maria Teresa Velázquez Evers, Marciana Loma-Osorio Fontecha, Monika Fromiczew-Droździńska, Patricia García, Axel Morales García, Miguel Angel Rodriguez García, Aleksandra Gilewska, Joanna Góra, Ewa Górka, Daphne Green, Agata Helwich, Bethsabe Ruiz Herrera, Robert Jadachowski, Patricia Guzmán Luis Juan, Anna Kacpura, Ruth Kanter, Regina Kaźmierczuk, Katarzyna Konisiewicz, Maria Koprowska, Bogusława Krajewska, Aldona Krasoń, Joanna Worobiec Kugaj, Joanna Kuligowska, Tadeusz Kur, Maria Kwiatkowska, Josefina Maitret, Javier Majul, Claire Manners, Laura Elena Medina, Carmen García Méndez, Iwona Mikucka, Talhia Miranda, Claudia Rangel Miranda, Armando Nieto, Joanna Nowak, Anna Nowakowska, Ewa Nowicka, Anastasia Parshikova, Paloma Carrasco Peñalba, Ma. Del Carmen Fernández Pérez, Joanna Płatos, Louise Emma Potter, Maria Teresa Portillo, Juan José Gómez Ramírez, Aida Rivera, Gabriela Rubio, Gabriela Bourge Ruiz, Irina Sakharova, Małgorzata Sałaj, Patricia Avila Sánchez, Jessica Galvan Sanchez, Miguel Angel Santiago, Karol Sęk, Barbara Sibilska, Tatiana Sinyavina, Agnieszka Śliwowska, Vlada Songailene, Ángela Siles Suárez, Beata Świątkowska, Ewelina Szmyd-Patuła, Agnieszka Szymaniak, Juliana Maria Franco Tavares, José Luis Vázquez, Irma Velazquez, Małgorzata Walczak, Dariusz Winiarek, Justyna Zdunek, Zofia Żdżarska, Dominika Zięba, Marzena Zieleniewska, Anna Zielińska-Miszczuk, Robert Zielonka.

The authors and publishers would also like to thank the following schools who allowed class observations – MEXICO: Centro de Formación Escolar Banting, Centro Escolar Las Águilas, Colegio América, Colegio Axayacatl, Colegio Donato Bramante, Colegio Edgar Morin, Colegio Francés Nueva Santa María, Colegio Gesi Secundaria, Colegio José Martí S. C., Colegio San Agustin, Colegio Sir Winston Leonard Spencer Churchill De México, Colegios La Salle Boulevares, Cristian Fernández de Merino, Erasmo De Rótterdam, Escuela De Ruán, Grupo Colegio Rosario Castellanos, Instituto Atenea, Instituto Crisol, Instituto Cultural Americano Mexicano, Instituto Manuel Acosta, Instituto Oriente Arboledas, Instituto Zaragoza, Liceo Americano Francés, Liceo Ibero Mexicano, Liceo Mexicano Japonés, Secundaria Simón Bolívar. SPAIN: IES Anselmo Lorenzo, IES Camilo José Cela, IES Complutense, IES Joaquín Turina, IES Laguna de Joatzell, IES Luis García Berlanga, IES Manuel de Falla, IES Máximo Trueba. POLAND: Gimnazjum nr 30, Gimnazjum nr 104 Warszawa Wawer, Gimnazjum nv120, Gimnazjum nr 141, Gimnazjum nr 145, Gimnazjum, ul. SZKOLNA 4, Publiczne Gimnazjum w Wiązownie, ZSP w Jazgarzewie. TURKEY: Ahmet Şimşek Koleji, Anabilim Koleji, Büyük Çamlıca Koleji, Doğa Koleji, Kirimli Fazilet Olcay Anatolian High School, Modafen Koleji, Sakıp Sabancı Anadolu

The authors and publishers would like to thank the following for permission to reproduce their photographs:
Alamy/AF archive p31(cr), Alamy/Agencja FREE p107(cl), Alamy/Amazon-Images p8(cmr), Alamy/Arcaid Images p102, Alamy/marc Arundale p143(tl), Alamy/Aruna Bhat p96(cr), Alamy/Thomas Boehm p96(tr), Alamy/John Bradshaw p14(b), Alamy/Kevin Britland p28(f/top), Alamy/BSIP SA p50(e), Alamy/J C Clamp p10(c), Alamy/ClassicStock p104(bcr), Alamy/Danita Delimont p96(cl), Alamy/Digifoto Gold pp63(5),142(bml), Alamy/Everett Collection Historica p73(7), Alamy/Fancy p110(t), Alamy/Findlay p28(d), Alamy/betty finney p97, Alamy/Peter Forsberg/Shopping p104(tmr), Alamy/fStop pp31(tl),105(cr), Alamy/GlowImages p88(tcr), Alamy/Jon Helgason p106(cr), Alamy/Jeremy Horner p94(6), Alamy/Image Source Plus p98(tcmrr), Alamy/david jack p112(cl), Alamy/Johner Images p32(cml), Alamy/Alexander Kaludov p55(tr), Alamy/Timothy Large - Life Style p22, Alamy/Betty LaRue p44, Alamy/Lebrecht Music and Arts Photo Library p105(tcml), Alamy/Mar Photographics p98(tr), Alamy/Jane McLoughlin p98(cmr), Alamy/moodboard p83(b), Alamy/Jeff Morgan 02 p28(c), Alamy/Vladimir Nenov p63(tl), Alamy/parkerphotography p105(tcl), Alamy/david pearson p94(3), Alamy/Chuck Pefley p84, Alamy/ONOKY - Photononstop p39(4), Alamy/Alexander Podshivalov p110(a), Alamy/Radius Images pp28(f/bottom),49, Alamy/Bjarki Reyr MR p64(f), Alamy/Christopher Scott p18(bcr), Alamy/Jan Sochor p143(bl), Alamy/Peter Steiner p105(tcmr), Alamy/Nik Taylor p20(tcr), Alamy/Art Directors & TRIP p88(tl), Alamy/John Warburton-Lee Photography p93, Alamy/whiteboxmedia limited p143(cr); Corbis pp9(tr),72-73(1), Corbis/peace!/amanaimages p78, Corbis/Bettmann p73(2), Corbis/Julian Calder p28(b), Corbis/Kevin Fleming p98(tmr), Corbis/Rick Gomez p87, Corbis/Hero Images p48(3), Corbis/E.O. Hoppe p72(3), Corbis/Rex Butcher/JAI p26, Corbis/Wolfgang Kaehler p96(cml), Corbis/Douglas Keister p143(br), Corbis/Frans Lemmens p143(cl), Corbis/John Lund p98(cr), Corbis/Lawrence Mann p9(cl), Corbis/Marianna Massey p114(cl), Alamy/Anthony Hatley p41, Corbis/Ocean p50(b), Corbis/Gabe Palmer p18(br), Corbis/Ed Quinn p94(2), Corbis/Radius Images p74(tr), Corbis/MARK BLINCH/Reuters p106(tcr), Corbis/Hugh Sitton p94(4),96(bcr), Corbis/Tom Brakefield-The Stock Conne/Science Fiction p116, Corbis/Rob Lewine/Tetra Images p48(1), Corbis/Bernd Vogel p98(tcmr), Corbis/Wavebreak Media Ltd p39(2); **Getty Images** pp10(a,d),29,73(6), 74(cr),82(e),112(cr), Getty Images/AFP pp28(e),82(f),94(5), Getty Images/Alija p62(tr), Getty Images/arabianEye p32(cr), Getty Images/Doug Armand p21, Getty Images/Keith Brofsky p20(tr), Getty Images/Peter Cade p92, Getty Images/Christian Science Monitor pp94-95(1), Getty Images/Creative Crop p110(c), Getty Images/Le Club Symphonie/Michael Crockett p106(cmr), Getty Images/CSA Plastock p14(a), Getty Images/Patrick Dieudonne p58, Getty Images/Dorling Kindersley p110(b), Getty Images/Echo p99, Getty Images/elkor p48(4), Getty Images/Mitchell Funk pp50-51(a), Getty Images/Gamma-Rapho via Getty Images p36, Getty Images/Glow Images, Inc p64(i), Getty Images/Phillip Graybill p98(bcr), Getty Images/PhotoAlto/James Hardy p71, Getty Images/Adam Hester p48(2), Getty Images/Cultura/Nancy Honey p88(tcl), Getty Images/Nancy Honey p88(tr), Getty Images/Garry Hunter p104(tr), Getty Images/ImagesBazaar pp82-83(a), Getty Images/Image Source p40, Getty Images/Juanmonino p39(5), Getty Images/Vicky Kasala Productions p106(cml), Getty Images/Renee Keith p107(tl), Getty Images/Keystone p73(5), Getty Images/KidStock pp12,18(cr), Getty Images/Ron Levine p38(7), Getty Images/Liza McCorkle p106(cl), Getty Images/Roy Ooms p39(6), Getty Images/Jose Luis Pelaez, Inc p32(cmr), Getty Images/PhotoGraphyKM p105(tml), Getty Images/Popperfoto p114(tl), Getty Images/Joseph O. Holmes/portfolio.streetnine.com p56, Getty Images/Hira Punjabi p64(a), Getty Images/Gabrielle Revere p106(cm), Getty Images/Andy Ryan p62(cr), Getty Images/Leigh Schindler p64(j), Getty Images/kristian sekulic p62(tmr), Getty Images/Paul Simcock p38(3), Getty Images/STOCK4B-RF p38(1),48(5), Getty Images/John Parrot/Stocktrek Images 114(tm), Getty Images/Superstock p73(4), Getty Images/Thinkstock Images p50(c), Getty Images/Michael Turek p33, Getty Images/Adrian Weinbrecht p32(cl), Getty Images/Steve West p50(d), Getty Images/WireImage p106(cr), Getty Images/yellowdog p81(tml); **Glow Images**/Mike Kemp p51(cl); **Mary Evans Picture Library** pp75,81(tl); **Masterfile** p11; **PHOTOALTO** p64(h); **Photoshot**/Xinhua p8(tr); **Punchstock**/Photographer's Choice p118; **Reuters Picture Library**/Carlos Garcia Rawlins p30; **Rex Features**/Associated Newspapers p73(8); **Alison Smith** p51(bcr); **Superstock**/ABK/BSIP/BSIP p55(tl), Superstock/Image Source p82(c); **Thinkstock**/Creatas Images p64(l), Thinkstock/Hemera pp14(c),63(tcmll),Thinkstock/Istockphoto pp10(b),19,54,63(3,4,6),51(cr),64(b,c,e,g,k),105(tmr),109,142(bl,bcm,bm), Thinkstock/Jupiterimages pp39(8),63(2),77,142(bcmll), Thinkstock/Ryan McVay pp63(1),142(bcl), Thinkstock/Photodisc pp6-7(1), Thinkstock/Martin Poole p64(d).

Commissioned photographs by Studio8 ltd, www.studio-8.com, 01865 842525.
pp 13, 23, 35, 45, 57, 61, 65, 66, 67, 79, 82(d), 89(mr), 101, 111

Page 7 stills: ITN Source

The authors and publishers are grateful for permission to reprint the following copyright material:
Material from article 'World's youngest conductor? Boy, 14, to direct Venezuelan orchestra' by Virginia Lopez, first published in The Guardian 20.05.12, reprinted with permission of the publisher;
Adapted material from Hans Rosling's PowerPoint Presentation 'The magic washing machine', reprinted with approval;
Material used from article 'The Manchester Color Wheel: development of a novel way of identifying color choice and its validation in healthy, anxious and depressed individuals' by Helen Carruthers, Julie Morris , Nicholas Tarrier and Peter Whorwell, published by BioMed Central 09.02.10.

These materials may contain links for third party websites. We have no control over, and are not responsible for, the contents of such third party websites. Please use care when accessing them.

Although we have tried to trace and contact copyright holders before publication, in some cases this has not been possible. If contacted we will be pleased to rectify any errors or omissions at the earliest opportunity.

Printed and bound in Thailand

2019 2018 2017 2016
13 12 11 10 9 8